MARK BATE

JAN PETERSON

MARK BATE

Nanaimo's First Mayor

Jan Peterson

VICTORIA | VANCOUVER | CALGARY

Heritage House Publishing Company Ltd.
heritagehouse.ca

CATALOGUING INFORMATION AVAILABLE FROM LIBRARY AND ARCHIVES CANADA
978-1-77203-182-9 (pbk)
978-1-77203-183-6 (epub)
978-1-77203-184-3 (epdf)

Edited by Lenore Hietkamp
Proofread by Rhonda Bailey
Cover design by Jacqui Thomas
Interior design by Peter Kohut
Cover image: *First Mayor of Nanaimo*, by George Henry Southwell,
courtesy of the City of Nanaimo
Illustration for chapter openings: Victoria, 1889,
from *Illustrated British Columbia*, 1889, plate 180

The interior of this book was produced on 100% post-consumer recycled
paper, processed chlorine free, and printed with vegetable-based inks.

We acknowledge the financial support of the Government of Canada through the Canada
Book Fund (CBF) and the Canada Council for the Arts, and the Province of British Columbia
through the British Columbia Arts Council and the Book Publishing Tax Credit.

21 20 19 18 17   1 2 3 4 5

PRINTED IN CANADA

INTRODUCTION

Mark Bate could not have envisioned the long and fulfilling life he would have when he immigrated to Nanaimo from Dudley in the Black Country in England. He came at the invitation of his uncle George Robinson, then manager of the Hudson's Bay Company's Nanaimo Coal Company. Coming to the far-off British Colony of Vancouver's Island with his aunt Maria, sister Elizabeth and cousin Cornelius Bryant was an opportunity to begin a new career. His uncle had promised him a job as a clerk with the coal company, a very different position from his job as a mine labourer in Dudley.

When he arrived in 1857 the coal mining industry was still in its infancy and Nanaimo a settlement with a collection of wooden houses along the waterfront, plus the Bastion, a fortress-like structure built by the HBC to instill fear into marauding First Nations from other parts of the Island. The local Snuneymuxw people were friendly and helpful to the newcomers, trading goods and services while working alongside the British miners. Bate found much to learn and explore in Nanaimo, and he was captivated by the countryside. Nevertheless, he felt the isolation of having mountains on one side, the Gulf of Georgia on the other, and no roads north or south, the only avenue for travel or communication by water.

When the HBC sold its interest in coal mining to the London-based Vancouver Coal Mining and Land Company, Bate moved up the employment ladder to accountant and eventually to manager of the Vancouver Coal Company, as it was known locally. Also moving up a ladder in the same company, beginning as a miner, Robert Dunsmuir discovered his own seam of coal in the Wellington area that, when developed, gave stiff competition to the Vancouver Coal Company mines. Dunsmuir was an astute businessman who could take immediate advantage of opportunities, while Bate had to wait for confirmation from his London office. Adding to

Bate's frustration, his mine superintendent, John Bryden, married Dunsmuir's daughter, a union that challenged Bryden's loyalties. But despite Bate's differences with Dunsmuir, the pair worked amicably on committees for improving the community.

Following Nanaimo's incorporation in 1874, Bate threw his hat into the electoral process when he learned that Dunsmuir's son-in-law James Harvey was running for mayor. Bate won, becoming the city's first mayor. With the Municipal Act as a guide, he ably moved the city through its fledgling years, juggling his duties as mine manager, mayor, and justice of the peace (see Appendix 2 for the years he was mayor). His wisdom and energy earned the respect of city residents.

In Bate's private life, he married Sarah Cartwright in 1859, a union that produced five sons and five daughters (see Appendix 1 for the Bate lineage). He was a man of many talents; he had a life-long love of music, wrote prolifically about early life in Nanaimo, and was part owner of two early newspapers and president of the Nanaimo Literary Institute. He was a founding member of Ashlar Lodge No. 3, and a member of many societies, such as the Odd Fellows and the Order of Foresters. He proudly boasted of having received every Governor General who had visited British Columbia since Confederation. There is much to learn about Nanaimo's first mayor.

1

A LIFE OF
PUBLIC SERVICE

ON DECEMBER 11, 1925, FIFTY years after Mark Bate was first elected mayor of Nanaimo, Mayor Victor B. Harrison presented the City of Nanaimo with a fine oil portrait entitled *The First Mayor of Nanaimo*, by George Henry Southwell. The painting was commissioned by the Native Sons of British Columbia, Post No. 3, as a gift to the city during the Diamond Jubilee celebrations of the municipality in 1924, to be hung in city hall as an "incentive for the youth of the community."

Bate had not seen the finished portrait until that evening and was moved by the thoughtfulness and generosity of the gesture. He looked at the painting and said,

I can now see myself as others see me. But what a difference, what a contrast between that face and the features of the first mayor when elected in 1875 . . . The first 25 years of incorporation mayor and councillors of Nanaimo were not paid for their services, yet all took pains—took the fullest interest in the work of serving their fellow citizens, each as an "Here in the strife." I know I gave my best service when in office—always endeavoured to do my duty effectively. The whole of us strived to deserve well of the ratepayers. To feel that you are doing all that is expected of you in a public capacity is very gratifying, a pleasure is given to the individual, in such a circumstance, which cannot be paid for in gold.[1]

It is clear from Bate's public service, both in his long service as mayor and through his many years as manager for the first coal mine company in Nanaimo, that acquiring "gold" was never his goal. He arrived in 1857 and very soon established strong roots, becoming well known among miners and administration alike and building a family whose descendants spread throughout Vancouver Island and beyond.

Bate could never resist reminiscing about those early days of Nanaimo, and audiences appreciated his perspective, given his long and accomplished life. He reflected on "Black Diamond City," as the town was sometimes called, when the first *Princess Royal* pioneers arrived 71 years earlier. His stories set the scene of a booming town with an abundance of food and a ready supply of coal and wood, where forests were alive with game and the waters teemed with fish. Despite the primitive living conditions and the lack of communication with the outside world, "they had food in plenty—fresh fat salmon and venison always." Those stories have proved invaluable in building a picture of the early pioneer days of Nanaimo.

2

A HUMBLE
BEGINNING

A LARGE AND LOVING FAMILY SURROUNDED Mark Bate in his childhood, including uncles and aunts from both sides of the family, as well as numerous cousins. They lived in the historic town of Dudley in the West Midlands, England, located six miles south of Wolverhampton and eight miles northwest of Birmingham. It is the largest town in the Black Country. The three counties of Worcestershire, Staffordshire, and Warwickshire border the town. Dudley had once been a Saxon village, complete with castle. Village life changed dramatically when the lord of the manor started a market sometime during the Middle Ages. People came from all over the West Midlands to buy, sell, or trade. By 1850 the region, once predominantly green and rural, had become the most populated and economically prosperous part of the Midlands, tied economically to coal mining, iron foundries, steel mills, and the glass industry.

The Black Country is an area roughly ten by twelve miles,

with Wolverhampton and Walsall in the north, Stourbridge and Halesowen in the south, and Dudley in the centre. Between 1801 and 1861 the town's population rose from 10,000 to 45,000, and the number of houses from 1,900 to 9,700.[1] Situated on a hill, it was a difficult place to base any kind of heavy industry. In bad weather, roads were almost impossible to navigate for heavy wagons. The many mines in the area operated mostly in the lower lying land to the north and west. Adding to the difficult conditions was the lack of a decent water supply, which was not solved until the turn of the century.[2]

DUDLEY, ENGLAND, 1837

Dudley was like many of the other small towns in the area, which identified with what was produced in their area. Brierley Hill grew from iron and steel products and glass, and Holly Hall and Woodside, usually mentioned together as a combined community, became known for the Woodside Colliery and Woodside Iron Works, founded in 1840 a quarter of a mile away from Woodside on land leased by Lord Dudley. The two separate villages of Holly Hall and Woodside were linked by High Street, but as the population grew and houses were built in the space between, the boundaries became blurred. The blast furnaces and a foundry of the iron works were conveniently adjacent to the Dudley and Stourbridge Canals, providing good access to local markets. When the railway arrived in 1850 it provided another avenue of transportation for goods and services. The company employed almost one thousand men, and was recognized internationally for its fabrication of heavy bridge girders, boilers, railway materials, and docks, and gained a reputation for quality and its ability to complete orders on time. Factory work provided good, stable, full-time employment to a large segment of the population.

The name of "Black Country" was coined because the area produced a high amount of air pollution. Black soot from heavy industry covered everything in the region. Charles Dickens describes the area well in *The Pickwick Papers*, published in 1837, the year Mark Bate was born. The narrator describes the route through the Black Country to Birmingham:

> The straggling cottages by the road-side, the dingy hue of every object visible, the murky atmosphere, the paths of cinders and brick-dust, the deep-red glow of furnace fires in the distance, the volumes of dense smoke issuing heavily forth from high toppling chimneys blackening and obscuring everything around; the glare of distant lights, the ponderous wagons which toiled along the road, laden with clashing rods of iron, or piled with heavy goods-all betokened their rapid approach to the great working town of Birmingham . . . The streets were thronged with working people. The hum of labour resounded from every house; lights gleamed from the long casement windows in the attic storeys, and the whirl of wheels and noise of machinery shook the trembling walls . . . The din of hammers, the rushing of steam, and the dead heavy clanking of engines, was the harsh music which arose from every quarter.[3]

THE BATES OF DUDLEY

Not much is known about the early life of Mark Bate or his family other than the information from birth, marriage, and death registrations. These documents did not become compulsory in England until July 1, 1837. Parish records therefore provide the only link to paternal grandparents George Bate and Sarah Silvers, who were married in 1804 at Wombourne, near Wolverhampton. The Bate name is quite common in this part of the Midlands. George and Sarah had ten children who survived into adulthood: Ann, Sarah, Mary, Joseph, Hannah, Thomas, Eleanor, Harriott, George, and Eliza. Large families were common, partly because infant mortality was high. People had many children and accepted that not all of them would survive.

Mark's grandfather George was a farmer and a shopkeeper in Woodside.[4] Their daughter Eleanor lived nearby with her husband, Joseph Silvers.[5] It is unknown if Sarah Silvers and Joseph Silvers were related, but the Silvers name is also common in Dudley. It was Joseph who registered the deaths of the grandparents and who also witnessed the marriages of their children.

Mark's father, Thomas Bate, was baptized on February 24, 1805, in the parish church of St. Mary's, Kingswinford, about five miles from Dudley. At the age of 20 he was a skilled glasscutter, an artisan, a role much coveted in the area. On November 1, 1824, he married Elizabeth Robinson in the same church where he was baptized.

Elizabeth was born on November 16, 1805, the eldest daughter of Joseph Robinson and Esther Shakespeare. There were eleven children in her family but only eight lived to maturity[6]: Elizabeth, Sarah, Joseph, John, Lucy, Maria, George, and Edwin. Esther's father was a prominent member of the Methodist Church in Dudley where he helped build Woodside Chapel and established a Sunday school there. The church history dates from 1812 when the first chapel was built on Hall Street. Their daughter Maria was the first child baptized there in 1816.[7]

Elizabeth Robinson's sister Sarah married Thomas Bryant, a marriage that produced two children, Cornelius, in 1838, and Thomas, in 1851, both close cousins of Mark. Elizabeth's sister Maria and brother George would play a large role in Mark's life.

During Thomas Bate's working life, five glassmakers lived in Dudley. The area was famous for its production of predominantly flint glass, which had a low glass content but as a finished product commanded a high value. It is unknown which company Thomas worked for. However, the Dudley Flint Glass Works owned by Messrs. Hawkes & Co. closed down in June 1842 when the partnership was dissolved and Hawkes retired. The company had specialized in enameled ornamental ware and in coloured glass.

The closure of the glass works coincided with Thomas's change of job in 1843.

This was a difficult time in Dudley. The miners were striking over a reduction in hours and pay due to a slump in iron production, and the local militia was called in to restore order among the general unrest in the area. Upon the closure of the Flint Glass Works, Thomas Shorthouse, clerk to the Guardians of Dudley Union, spoke about the high unemployment in the area:

> Also a great many glass-makers, who used to be getting £3 to £4 a week, are now breaking stones and scraping the streets . . . The great distress amongst the glass-makers results from the termination of Mr. Hawk's [sic] works, some of the largest in the kingdom for flint-glass, which are being pulled down.[8]

As a skilled glasscutter, Thomas would have made a good wage if he had worked for Hawkes. This would have been a trying time for the Bate family, with Thomas losing a good paying job as a glasscutter and having to work in the mining industry for lower wages.

FAMILY TRAVAILS

Mark Bate was the youngest son in a family of seven children; two siblings died, both named Ezra. It was quite common then when childhood diseases took their toll to give a later child the same name as the one who died in infancy. The name Ezra seems to have been an unfortunate one for the young family. His brothers and sisters were born in different communities: Ann, the eldest child, was born in Sedgeley, Staffordshire, Joseph was born in Dudley, and Sarah was born in West Bromwich, Staffordshire. Mark was born in Birmingham and was baptized February 12, 1837, in the parish church of St. Thomas, in Dudley.[9] Locals called this historic church the "Top Church" because of its location at the top of High Street. The church dates from 1182, and was rebuilt in 1818.

Parish records give other baptism dates for his brother and two sisters. Ann was baptized May 15, 1825, Joseph on July 5, 1829, and Sarah on December 22, 1833. The birth dates of two sisters are known—Elizabeth was born January 4, 1840, and Lucy on January 13, 1843. In 1841, according to the England census of that year, the family—parents Thomas and Elizabeth, and their children, Ann, sixteen, Joseph, twelve, Mark, four, and Elizabeth, one—was living in Holly Hall and Woodside. For some unknown reason, Mark's eight-year-old sister Sarah lived nearby with their grandmother Esther Robinson and her cousins George, who at age 19 worked as a bookkeeper, and Maria.

Thomas's occupation is somewhat unclear. On all the baptism records except Lucy's, he is listed as a glasscutter, which is also his occupation in the 1841 census. By 1843, according to Lucy's baptismal record, he had changed his occupation to "writing clerk, Cochrane & Bramah, Woodside Iron Works & Colliery." In 1845, at the time of his death, one newspaper report said that Thomas "kept machine for Messrs's Cochrane & Bramah at the Woodside Colliery near town."[10] This was a term used for someone who looked after the steam engines, which powered machinery used to lift coal or men up the shaft. The accident report was the first verification, other than on Lucy's birth certificate, that Thomas worked in the colliery. His death certificate, however, simply gives his occupation as "agent."[11]

This was a working-class community, judging by the occupations of the Bate family neighbours listed in the census: miner, collier, nailor, labourer, rope maker, boot maker, iron roller, furnace keeper, blacksmith, and stone miner. Many of these occupations were linked to the Woodside Iron Works and the coal and iron ore mines in the area. At least one member of every household worked, suggesting that one income provided a comfortable living and families were not destitute.

A few doors away from the Bate family, their neighbour's children, Joseph and Simeon Russon, aged ten and eight years, worked as iron rollers. At that time, no law restricted children working from an early age. Opinions differed about children working in a mine for 12 hours a day. Some believed it would affect their health, while others thought the children looked remarkably well "when cleaned on Sundays."[12] In 1844 a new law came into effect that prevented all children aged eight and under from working.

THE DEATH OF A FATHER

The year Mark Bate was born, 1837, was the beginning of the Victorian era: On June 20, Victoria became Queen of England. This heralded an era of technological progress, especially in steam power for boats, ships, railways, and factories, all requiring coal. The South Staffordshire coal seam that divided the counties of Staffordshire and Worcestershire was 30 feet (9 metres) thick, the thickest seam in all of Great Britain. It provided the fuel to accommodate heavy industry in the area.

The Bate family home would have been like many others in the Dudley area. Built of brick, these 'one up, one down' terrace-style homes had dirt floors that had to be swept daily. Some homes had two rooms upstairs. Families shared the washhouse and sculleries. These were called "brewhouses," and were generally outside building. Those who lived in Dudley baked their own bread in a shared oven, and the ovens in many parts of the town were external to the houses, built like furnaces; one oven would be common to all the houses in a court. Many people also kept pigs, which, as William Lee reported to the Board of Health in 1852, was unhealthy, as was the lack of a proper water supply.[13]

The men and boys in the family worked ten or twelve hours a day or more, six days a week, while the wives and daughters stayed home, cleaning, washing, and cooking. Children were expected to help out at home with the daily chores. Sunday was the only day off, when families usually attended the church or chapel of their choice, and children attended Sunday school. The Bate, Robinson, and Bryant families attended the Methodist Church in Dudley. Most social events revolved around the family and church. The musical group at the church may have been where Mark Bate was introduced to music and learned to play the violin, a passion he enjoyed for the rest of his life.

As a benefit for those who worked in the mines, coal was delivered to their home. When the men left for work early in the morning the women's routine would be to "slop out" then prepare the bed. This was done should an accident happen at the mine. Any injured miners were taken home and laid on the made-up bed, as there was no hospital available. (It was not until 1867 that a hospital was built in the area.) To cover the cost of a doctor should someone be injured, the workers paid a little each week or month toward a "sick fund," or else they relied on charity. All after-care was carried out at home. When an accident happened at the mine, a whistle blew to alert the town, and women put on their shawls and went to the mine to find out if any of their loved ones had been hurt or killed. There were no pensions or injury payment; families relied on each other and on charitable handouts.[14]

The rapid growth of Dudley brought with it disease and a high death rate. What was shocking was the average age of death. Lee reported that in Dudley Parish the average age of those who died was sixteen years and seven months, and he concluded, "As far as the duration of life therefore is concerned Dudley is the most unhealthy place in the country."[15] It is hoped that the Bate family lived in more clean and comfortable living conditions than that described in Lee's report.

Opportunities for recreation included hiking and outdoor activities, with lovely areas to explore, such as the ruins of the old Dudley Castle on the hill, which was covered with beautiful trees. However, the general population of working-class Dudley was more inclined to enjoy a few drinks at the local tavern after a hard day's work. One event that was well attended by all in the Black Country was the Dudley Castle Fêtes held for three days every Whitsun (a Christian holiday celebrated the seventh Sunday after Easter).

The Bate family settled in Woodside in 1843 when Thomas began working at Bramah and Cochrane, Woodside Iron Works and Colliery, the mine that supplied the coal to fuel the furnaces and forges of the Woodside Ironworks. This same year Mark's eldest sister, Ann, married William Sharratt. The young couple moved to live in Droylsden, Ashton under Lyne, Lancashire, where they raised five children.

Mark was eight years old when, on May 6, 1845, his father, Thomas, died in a traffic accident. He was only 40 years old. The *Wolverhampton Chronicle* reported the accident the next day:

> Yesterday (Tuesday) afternoon, between three and four o'clock, a fatal accident occurred to Mr. Thomas Bate, machinist, of Holly Hall, near Dudley . . . Bate was driving a phaeton into town when the carriage was upset, owing to declivity in the road, and Mr. Bate was thrown with such violence on the ground that he died from injuries to the head and other parts in the course of less than half an hour. Mr. Bate, we regret to say, has left a widow and six children.

After their father's death, Joseph, who was sixteen, and eight-year-old Mark had to work; the family probably needed the income. In the next census of March 30, 1851, Elizabeth is a widow and head of the Bate family, still living in Woodside, Dudley. Those children still at home included Joseph, Sarah, Mark, Elizabeth, and Lucy. Mark and Joseph worked as "pit labourers" in the Woodside Colliery.[16] The brothers worked long hours, from six in the morning to six at night. About this time, Mark's sister Elizabeth began living with her aunt, Maria Robinson, who lived next door to the Bryants.

On October 13 of the same year, Joseph married Sarah Ann Beesley, in Tipton Parish Church, Dudley.[17] The young couple settled in Dudley, where Joseph was employed as a "stone miner," someone who mined iron ore for the Woodside Ironworks.[18] Ten years later, Sarah moved with their six children to Yorkshire, where other family members lived. Later in the year Joseph left for Vancouver Island. The couple appears to have separated, and in 1871, Sarah married John Wadington, in Bamsley, Yorkshire. She claimed she was a widow on the marriage certificate, but Joseph was still in North America and did not return until 1874; he apparently did not stay in touch with his family.

SCHOOL AND LOVE

The year 1851 was an important milestone in English history: it was the year the Great Exhibition opened in London. On May 1, over half a million people gathered in Hyde Park around the Crystal Palace, a vast structure of iron and glass. The building, Sir Joseph Paxton's engineering masterpiece, was revolutionary for the time. The ironwork for the Crystal Palace had been manufactured at the Woodside Ironworks in Dudley. In July, a special train of the South Staffordshire Railway Company carried 300 employees from the Woodside Ironworks to spend four days in London at the Great Exhibition, for which their employer contributed a "handsome sum."[19] It is unknown if anyone from the Bate family made the journey to London for the event.

There is no information about where the Bate children attended school. One summary of Mark Bate's life says that "he attended Dudley Grammar School in Worcestershire and other schools."[20] However, there is no record of him ever having attended Dudley Grammar School, which is a highly regarded selective school of higher education for boys aged 11 to 18 years. Founded in 1562, the school celebrated its 400th anniversary in 1962. The register dates from February 5, 1849,[21] when Mark would have been 12 years old. He allegedly left the Grammar School at the age of 16, but his name does not appear in the school records.

Mark must have received some form of education as he could read and write quite well, but when he was 14 he was already working as a pit labourer. According to Bentley's Directory there were a number of schools in the area associated with Sunday schools. These were attached to every place of worship, some with as many as 600 children enrolled. The Wesleyan Methodists had three chapels with Sunday schools, including one in Woodside. Before children began working in the mines they would have had some amount of schooling, but parents often had to weigh the value of education against additional weekly earnings. Mark may have attended the Wesleyan Day School at Brierley Hill where his cousins Cornelius and Thomas Bryant were educated.[22] His education would have consisted of the rudiments of language and numbers, training in the three R's, plus a considerable dose of moral instruction. While little is known about how much education he actually received, later in life he himself praised his early education: "If it had not been for my good schooling, I should never have stood in the position I do today."[23] He proved to be a skilled writer and administrator and would have been a credit to any educational institution.

He had a close relationship with his brother Joseph, his uncle George Robinson, and his cousin Cornelius Bryant. All three men worked in related jobs in the mining industry. When Cornelius was 13 he worked as a "machine boy" in the mines.

There were changes in the Bate household in 1853 when Mark's mother, Elizabeth, remarried; the groom was William Thomas, a labourer. Sadly, on May 25 of that year, his sister Sarah, aged 20, died. Her death certificate gives the cause of death as "fever" and her occupation as a "stay maker."[24] She was buried beside her father, Thomas, in St. Thomas's Churchyard, in Dudley.

About this time, Mark met a young girl from Dudley and fell in love. She was Sarah Ann Cartwright, born August 18, 1839, in Kingswinford, Staffordshire.[25] The 1851 census lists her mother,

Maria, 38, as a widow on parish relief, and born in Oldswinford. She had four children: Charles, fourteen, who worked as a labourer; Sarah Ann, eleven; William, eight; and Ellen, two.[26] Mark and Sarah probably had hopes and dreams like other young people, but their lives were about to change dramatically.

GEORGE ROBINSON EMIGRATES

Mark Bate's introduction to Vancouver Island came through the letters from his uncle, George Robinson, and from reading newspaper articles about the discovery of gold in Britain's new colony. It was his uncle who was eventually responsible for bringing him to Nanaimo. Robinson was known to have a restless and ambitious nature that made it difficult for him to stay in one place for any length of time. No one was surprised when he agreed to manage a coal mine for the Hudson's Bay Company (HBC) in the Colony of Vancouver Island, on the Pacific Coast of North America. The former manager, Boyd Gilmour, had fulfilled his contract and was returning to Scotland.

George Robinson was born on May 23, 1825; he was 19 when he married Ann Saunders on her twentieth birthday, October 27, 1844. She was the youngest daughter of the Saunders family in neighbouring Holly Hall, Worcestershire. At the time of their marriage George was employed as a machine clerk at Springs Mine, in Dudley.[27] His sister Maria and brother-in-law Thomas Bryant witnessed the wedding ceremony. The Robinsons had two children born in England: Amanda Theresa, born January 1849, and Victor Ernest, born in April 1853.

George's wanderlust probably played a large part in his family's decision. The HBC agent, James Conner, who travelled the country recruiting new immigrants, painted a rosy picture of life on Vancouver Island and tempted many Black Country miners with the prospect of clean air, pure water, and available land. On March 24, 1854, when he was 29 years old and working at the

Eardington Colliery, Bridgenorth, George signed a contract to work as "Manager of the Company Coal and Brick Works on Vancouver's Island."[28] Deciding to leave family, friends, and familiar surroundings and go halfway around the world to an unknown country and face an uncertain future would have been a difficult decision for the Robinson family.

After he signed the contract, Robinson was instructed to recruit another 20 miners, married or otherwise, to go with him. He sent out a town crier from Dudley to several of the surrounding villages, looking for miners interested in going with[29] at a wage of five shillings a day. This group of new HBC recruits, mostly from the Black Country, would be forever be called the "*Princess Royal* pioneers," named for the ship they travelled in to the new world. Entire families signed up. From Holly Hall came the Robinsons. Four of the families were from Bate's hometown of Dudley, the Harrisons, Inchers, Ganners, and Millers, while the Meakin, Webb, Dunn, and two Baker families came from Brierley Hill. The York, Jones, and the Gough families came from Wordsley. Bromley contributed the Malpass, R. Richardson, and the Bevilockway families, while the village of Persnett gave up the Bull, Turner, and Hawkes families. The Lowndes came from Kingswinford, the Thompsons were from Brockmoor, the J. Richardsons came from Common Side, and the Sage family was from Graveyard. The Biggs family was the only family who came from outside the Midlands area; they came from the farming area of Paulton, Somerset.[30]

George, Ann, and their children Amanda and Victor, along with an unnamed maid, joined the others on the train journey to London, where they boarded the SS *Princess Royal* on her maiden voyage to Fort Victoria on Vancouver Island.

Once Mark joined them in the new colony, he would come to know his fellow countrymen through their work and social life in Nanaimo.

3

JOURNEY TO
THE NEW WORLD

T HE COLONY OF VANCOUVER ISLAND was a world away
from the West Midlands of England. The island is about a
quarter the size of Great Britain and is situated between the Pacific
Ocean, to its west, and to its east, the mainland, then called New
Caledonia and not yet a colony. The island had been inhabited
by Indigenous people for thousands of years and lay undisturbed
until the HBC decided it needed to establish new headquarters
following the signing of the Oregon Treaty in 1846, which separated the United States from British interests in the north. The
dividing line was the 49th parallel, which put the HBC Pacific
headquarters at Fort Vancouver in United States territory. The
site chosen for the new headquarters was on the southern tip of
Vancouver Island; the company named it Fort Victoria and had
begun building a fort there in 1843. In 1849 James Douglas, a chief
factor with the company, was appointed governor *pro tempore* of
the new Colony of Vancouver Island, a position he was not happy

about, for he viewed it as a demotion after years of service with the company. He accepted the appointment on the understanding that the position was only temporary.

Queen Victoria signed a grant in 1849 giving the HBC the exclusive trading rights over Vancouver Island for ten years, for seven shillings a year, after which the Crown could repurchase it. The hope was that the new Colony of Vancouver Island would stop American expansionism. Later that year, the Crown appointed lawyer Richard Blanshard as governor, but with little support from Douglas or the Company men he lasted only a short time and returned to England; Douglas was subsequently appointed governor. He now controlled both the HBC's Western Division and the Colony of Vancouver Island.

COAL ON VANCOUVER ISLAND

When a coal deposit was found at Fort Rupert on northern Vancouver Island in 1849, Douglas recruited experienced miners from Ayrshire, Scotland, to operate and manage the HBC mine there. Skilled miners like John Muir and John McGregor were disappointed when they found there was no mine, only the promise of one. They had been hired on a basis that recognized the customary arrangement of fixed wages for fixed output for a five-year term, and were to be paid partly on a piece-rate basis. Without a productive mine there would be no coal bonus. They did not share the Company's optimism about the coalfield there and objected when asked to do labourers' work. They had left secure mining positions in developed communities to fulfill a dream of a better life in the new world, and that dream soon turned sour. Some deserted for California, where they could mine gold, not coal.

In 1852, after another coalfield was discovered in the central island area, the miners were transferred to the new location, which was named Colvilletown in honour of Andrew Colville, then governor of the HBC. The coal seam was found on the shore of Wentuhuysen Inlet, also known as "Nanymo Bay," a place the Snuneymuxw people called "Syn-ny-mo," which later was corrupted to form "Nanaimo." The first shipment of HBC coal was loaded in September 1852 aboard the *Cadboro*, destined for Fort Victoria. Regular shipments to Victoria followed, and also to San Francisco. The initial Scottish workforce, assisted by Snuneymuxw labourers, opened the first mines, built the cabins, store and a sawmill, and extracted salt from a spring found at Millstone River; these developments founded the new mining village. The HBC continued to recruit more miners in Britain, and it was for this new location the miners from the Black Country had signed their contract.

PRINCESS ROYAL PIONEERS

When George Robinson's Black Country recruits, "23 men and 23 women with a quantity of children," boarded the *Princess Royal* in London, on June 2, 1854, they were indentured to the HBC for a period of five years.[1] The ship carrying them to their new home was newly built of solid oak and designed to carry spars and furs on this its maiden voyage. It replaced the *Norman Morison* that had carried earlier recruits to Vancouver Island.

The ship sailed from London, England, on June 3, 1854, by way of Cape Horn and Honolulu, and arrived at Esquimalt Harbour, near Fort Victoria, on November 24 after a horrific voyage of almost six months. The Robinson family and their maid shared a cabin with Charles Clark, his wife, Eliza, and their baby. Clark had been hired to teach school at Craigflower Farm, near Fort Victoria. The Robinsons' accommodation was better than that of the Black Country miners and their families, who were crowded below in steerage.

This was a journey they would never forget. The passage was plagued by winter gales, seasickness, bad food, and a shortage of it, and even a mutiny. The ship's log recorded two births and ten deaths, with several burials at sea. The first child to die was Mrs.

Clark's baby, on July 1. Passengers experienced treacherous seas as the ship rounded Cape Horn. These were bone-weary travellers when the ship finally docked in Fort Victoria. Governor James Douglas welcomed the ship but did not go aboard to greet them personally. They had to wait another three days before being transferred to the *Beaver* and the *Recovery* that brought them to Nanaimo, on November 27, 1854.

The mining village had an excellent deep-sea harbour sheltered by two islands, Newcastle and Douglas, the latter renamed Protection Island. The harbour lacked a dock where ships could tie up, so Robinson and the miners' families came ashore in three small boats. They landed on the rocky point known today as Pioneer Point. On the shoreline on that cold November day, the HBC flag flew above the fort-like Bastion and a row of whitewashed log cabins. The new buildings rose against the backdrop of Wakesiah Mountain, later renamed Mt. Benson, and a dark green forest, thick with Douglas fir and cedar as far as the eye could see. Black Country pioneers would later recall this day when the sun broke through the dark clouds as they stepped ashore, signifying for them a new beginning.

The young HBC officer-in-charge, Joseph William McKay, welcomed them ashore. From the grassy slope, the 21 Scottish miners and their families who had arrived two years earlier observed their arrival. The Scots included John Muir, Robert Dunsmuir, John McGregor, and Adam Grant Horne, who were to play a major role in the history of the area. The Snuneymuxw, who had occupied the area for thousands of years, looked on, as more white people settled among them.

Those who arrived in Nanaimo that day passed on memories of their landing to future generations. John Thompson, 19, the first off the scow that ferried the passengers from the *Recovery*, rushed up the rock by the Bastion, urging others to follow.[2] Five-year-old Samuel Gough remembered he lost a shoe as he stepped ashore; he also recalled that the first house he stayed in had mats nailed over the cracks in the walls to keep out the wind. His mother, Elizabeth, cooked family meals over a central fireplace and baked her bread in a community Dutch oven, something the Black Country women were familiar with. Some nights young Samuel lay in bed listening to rats scampering across the rafters. He recalled that at first families were fearful of the First Nation people, believing them to be hostile, but they soon found them friendly and helpful.[3]

Although some small log cabins had been built for the new arrivals, they still had to share accommodations until more housing could be built. The Robinson family was housed in the manager's house on land that now forms part of St. Paul's Anglican Church. The small cabin had been enlarged in preparation for his arrival. Arrangements were made for the miners' children to attend a school that was being taught by Charles Bayley, while the men became acquainted with the mines and were given their work assignments.

The population of Nanaimo had suddenly grown to over 150, according to a census conducted by Governor James Douglas that year. Fort Victoria's population was 232. McKay, the man who had accomplished so much in the first two years of Nanaimo's history, was transferred to Fort Simpson when the war with Russia broke out in 1854. He had supervised the development of the mining village and the building of the first homes on Front Street; he started a small sawmill to cut lumber for the mines and the settlement; he began the manufacture of salt from the salt spring on Millstone River, and as company representative he kept Douglas abreast of the coal mining activity. At Fort Simpson, McKay's tact, courage, and outstanding ability were relied upon to prevent the Tsimpsean First Nation from falling under Russian influence. McKay's replacement in Nanaimo was Charles Edward Stuart, who had served on many of the HBC ships. His latest position had been on the *Recovery*,[4] the ship that had transported the English miners from Victoria to Nanaimo.

As the new manager of the HBC's Nanaimo Coal Company, Robinson signed his name as a witness to the treaty between Governor James Douglas and the Snuneymuxw, on December 23, 1854. Robinson had only been in Nanaimo for 26 days. Other signatories included Douglas's secretary, Richard Colledge, and Charles Edward Stuart, plus members of the Snuneymuxw First Nation. This treaty formalized the HBC's claim to the coal deposits. The Snuneymuxw agreed to surrender all land in a designated area "entirely and for ever." In payment for the land, the HBC gave "636 white blankets, 12 blue, and 20 inferior." This was probably the most important document Robinson was ever to sign, for it laid the foundation of the coal mining industry to follow, but it also excluded the Snuneymuxw from deriving any revenue from the coal. This treaty was one of 14 made by Douglas between 1850 and 1854 in the areas on Vancouver Island where Europeans wanted to settle.

On May 7, 1855, the HBC further secured its future in the coal industry by purchasing 6,193 acres of Crown land in the Nanaimo area for one pound sterling per acre. The purchase included Cameron, Newcastle, and Douglas (Protection) Islands. Another 1,074 acres were reserved, 724 for public use, 100 for roads, and 250 for "the future benefit of the Indians."[5]

Robinson and Stuart worked together to ensure enough coal was mined to fill orders. This was an odd dual management arrangement. Stuart was the manager of the HBC interests in Nanaimo, while Robinson was manager of the HBC's local coal company. Keeping a close eye on every aspect of their lives was Governor James Douglas in Victoria. The HBC received a purchase order from the navy for one thousand tons of coal, to be ready by July 1855, and in June Douglas came to Nanaimo to make sure the coal would be ready on time. By the end of that year, the mine was extracting 30 tons of coal daily. However, that level of production was difficult to maintain because of technical problems, such as flooding and mechanical breakdowns.[6]

Miners employed in 1854 earned £78 a year for digging 45 tons of coal per month. This amount provided little incentive to work, Robinson noted, and resulted in "idleness." He urged that the miners be paid by the ton instead of a yearly wage. He restructured the wage system in 1856 so that the HBC paid miners as much as four shillings and two pence per ton and gave them free housing, tools, and medical services.[7] Everyone welcomed these reforms. Miners were expected to work 310 days each year, performing whatever tasks were essential to the smooth running of the mines and accepting company store credits or HBC blankets instead of cash when necessary.

In 1856, back in London, the colonial office heard rumours of discontent about the possible withdrawal of the HBC trading rights to Vancouver Island. The HBC was then warned that its trade monopoly would likely not be renewed. Perhaps word of the gold discovery on the Thompson River awakened a renewed interest in New Caledonia. It was this find, which after investigation, led to the Fraser River gold rush. New Caledonia became a crown colony in 1858.

ROBINSON'S TRAGEDY

Meanwhile, Robinson's extended family back in Dudley waited anxiously to hear how he was faring on Vancouver Island. Mail took weeks, sometimes months, to arrive. According to family members, he wrote regularly and waxed lyrical on the beauty and virtues of Vancouver Island. Unfortunately, none of his letters from this period survive.

Stuart recorded in the Nanaimo HBC daybook that Robinson's wife, Ann, gave birth to a boy on September 1, 1855.[8] The news of her death arrived in England on January 3, 1856. Ann probably died from "childbirth fever," also known as puerperal sepsis, a leading cause of maternal death. The baby also died, on February 21.[9] Ann's grave was reopened and the child was buried with her under the huge maple trees in Nanaimo's Pioneer Cemetery at Wallace Street and Comox Road.

Grieving his double loss, Robinson asked his brother-in-law, Thomas Bryant, if he would arrange for a suitable tombstone to be sent to Nanaimo to commemorate Ann's life. Bryant agreed and stored the finished stone until it could be shipped to Nanaimo. Many years later, his son Thomas remembered the tombstone from the hallway of his home and then as a grown man seeing it again in the Nanaimo Cemetery.[10] He noted the gravestone was "rather unique" because "it records the death of the first known white lady to be buried in Nanaimo."[11] The tombstone to Ann and baby is still at the Pioneer Cemetery and is inscribed as follows:

> Beneath this ground consecrated only by the sacred deposit it contains is interr'd the mortal remains of Mrs. Ann Robinson wife of Mr. George Robinson, Mine Agent, who departed this life January 3, 1856 aged 31 years. Whose many virtues and moral conduct as wife, mother, and friend, had ensured her the respect of all who knew her, and by whom her death is most deeply lamented, and regretted. Also beneath rests the mortal remains of Joseph Oscar, infant son of the above who died February 21, 1856 aged 4 months.

Ann's death was a severe blow to Robinson and may have undermined his relationships with the men working under him. In one bitter exchange, he accused the oversman, John McGregor, of negligence, because he was absent one day from work and left early on two occasions. Their argument became heated. Robinson threatened to report him to Stuart. McGregor called him a liar and a hypocrite. The enraged Robinson grabbed a hammer left by the smithy and knocked McGregor down with a blow to his head. McGregor was able to walk to the surgery where Dr. Thomas bandaged his wound, which was not considered serious. Robinson, distressed by his own action, reported the incident and his behaviour and thought he would be disciplined. Instead, it was McGregor who was sent off to Victoria to cool off. McGregor never returned to Nanaimo until after the HBC had sold its holdings.

BATE DECIDES TO EMIGRATE

Some time later, Robinson wrote to his sister Maria asking her to come to Nanaimo to help look after his other two children, Amanda, aged seven, and Victor, three. He also offered assistance to his nephews Mark Bate and Cornelius Bryant in obtaining work with the Company. He recommended Mark for a clerical position, and Cornelius for the schoolteacher's post being vacated by Charles Bayley. This may have been where Mark's credentials for the job were exaggerated in order to secure a position with the company.

Robinson's letter likely prompted family discussions within the Robinson, Bate, and Bryant families. Maria, then aged 40, decided she would come to Vancouver Island to help her brother with his children. For the three teenagers, Mark Bate, 19, his cousin Cornelius Bryant, 18, and Mark's sister Elizabeth Bate, 16, the decision was easy: this was an adventure and an opportunity for a new life in the far away British colony. Bate later remarked that before he emigrated, he read about gold discovered in a tributary of the Fraser River and about gold dust being brought to Nanaimo. And Uncle George, in his letters home, predicted that New Caledonia would become a second California. English newspapers enthusiastically promoted the gold rush, which encouraged a few adventurers to seek their fortune in the colonies, and many had their sights on Vancouver Island, considered "the England of the Pacific," as one British publication called it in 1858.[12] The general atmosphere of excitement about the opportunities of the Pacific Northwest would have enhanced Mark Bate's anticipation about his move to Nanaimo. He and Bryant did not sign a contact with the HBC before leaving England; they felt confident their uncle George would speak on their behalf for employment.

4

BATE BEGINS
A NEW LIFE

ON AUGUST 19, 1856, ANOTHER voyage of the *Princess Royal* carried the excited young passengers and their aunt from London to Vancouver Island. Cornelius Bryant's journal describes their voyage, which contrasted greatly with the earlier horrific experience of their uncle George Robinson and other Black Country miners and their families. Cornelius wrote that his grandmother, Esther Robinson, and his mother, Sarah Bryant, travelled with them on the ship from the East India Docks in Blackwall, London, to Gravesend, where they said goodbye. Bate's mother, Elizabeth, did not accompany them to say farewell to her son and daughter. The women went ashore on a steam packet for their trip back to London.

ABOARD THE PRINCESS ROYAL

Mark and Cornelius shared quarters between decks, after cleaning up the debris left by the previous occupants, a crew officer and a storekeeper, while Elizabeth and Maria shared a cabin. On the first day out, Cornelius writes, "we regaled ourselves in aunt's cabin on roast beef and white biscuits." Then during the first week at sea, all were seasick.

On September 1, they received the first allotted weekly supply of provisions from the ship's stores:

Collectively we receive 12 lbs. of preserved meats and soups: 4 lbs. of preserved tripe in stone jars, not like the other preserved meats which we get in tins: 12 lbs. of flour. Good supply of beef mustard, salt, pepper, tea, coffee, scotch oatmeal, rice and split peas; 12 lbs. of preserved potatoes (we all dislike the taste of them). We give the preserved meats, potatoes and soups away to the crew generally. 4 pints of preserved milk in tins. Large jar of pickles and vinegar (fortnightly). 4 lbs. of white loaf sugar. 4 lbs. of raisins. Plenty of suet, butter, salt beef and pork (4 lbs.), sea biscuits (16 lbs). We do not eat any of them at all, they are too coarse for our palate, although they are of the best quality (generally), for those who like the usual sea bread. 2 lbs. of first rate cheese. 1 pint of that infernal and fiery mixture of grog—my aunt and Elizabeth have my share always, and also Mark's as well.[1]

They made cakes and puddings with flour, and ate with utensils the ship procured. They also received three gallons of water "for us 4 per diem. We take our water to the cook at the galley when wanted." The cousins took turns in the morning going to the forecastle for clean water; this was the space at the front end of the ship below the main deck. Water had to be collected before 7:00 a.m. Mealtimes were set at 8:00 a.m., noon, and 5:30 p.m.

Cornelius had taken a pledge of total abstinence from alcohol three years before, and so refused the "grog." He regularly attended Sunday services on board ship, indicating that he was already attracted to a religious ministry, no doubt influenced by his mother, Sarah, who was known to be a pious woman active in missionary work for the Wesleyan Methodists in Dudley.

Life on the ocean continued to amaze the young men. One evening a flying fish dropped on the deck. They caught it, and ate it the next morning. Another time the crew hooked a large blue shark. They hoisted it up on deck, but the crew had difficulty killing it and had to use iron crowbars. They were helped in the struggle when the shark fell from the upper to the lower deck and broke his tail. The crew cut the shark up in portions, and the next morning Cornelius and Mark had shark for breakfast.

By the end of October heavy winds and waves that "rolled mountains high" threatened to envelop the ship as they rounded the treacherous Cape Horn. The weather grew warmer as they made their way north. On December 13 all hands were mustered to learn "the gun, sword, and small arms exercise, in case of emergency with the Indians in the Straits of St. Juan de Fuca." On Christmas day 1856, the family dined with Captain John Trivett. A happy Cornelius wrote, "The warmest Christmas day I ever spent in all my life. Plenty of merriment today."

The first time they saw land was memorable. On Tuesday, January 13, 1857, the Oregon coast came into view. Cornelius described a dense forest of pine and evergreens and snow-capped peaks towering above the vast territory.

The young men were excited to be near their destination. As the ship reached Cape Flattery, through the fog they could see land. They were told it was Vancouver Island. Next day they entered the Juan de Fuca Strait.

LANDING IN FORT VICTORIA

On Saturday, January 17, they went ashore at Fort Victoria with Drs. George Johnstone and Alfred Benson; the latter was to replace Johnstone in Nanaimo as colliery surgeon. On Sunday, as the *Beaver* towed the ship into Victoria Harbour, the *Princess Royal* exchanged the customary gun salute from the Bastion in the fort. The next day Cornelius attended Sunday services conducted by the HBC chaplain and inspector of colonial schools, Reverend Edward Cridge.

Bate later recalled landing at Fort Victoria. The HBC chief traders and staff at the fort greeted Captain Trivett and the officers and passengers. Some of the passengers who had travelled with them left a lasting impression. He wrote:

> Naval Lieut. John Coles, who had been on the HMS *Thetis*, was returning to Victoria with the hope of marrying Miss Mary Langford, only to discover she had already married Capt. Herbert G. Lewis. Another passenger was John Kennedy, the son of Dr. John F. Kennedy, who was then a Member of the Legislative Assembly representing Nanaimo. Others were Henry Wain, his wife and child; James Marwick, his wife and two children; Mrs. Merryman, Peter Irvine, and Victoria constable John Hall. He had been to England for a wife and came back without one, as he said, because he could not get the girl he wanted to accompany him out here. She was willing to marry him if he would remain in England. This proposition he declined.[2]

Bate told an amusing story about Constable John Hall. The life of a policeman in early Victoria was not very demanding and allowed some degree of latitude in dealing with prisoners. One particular prisoner had some notoriety; he was Captain John Mills who brought the barque *Colinda* out from London with Scottish miners and their families destined for Nanaimo. When the passengers mutinied, the ship was forced to put into the South American port of Valparaiso, Chile:

> There he illegally disposed of some ships stores. He was tried and convicted of the offence at Victoria and given into the custody of

Hall and imprisonment in the Bastion. The prisoner was allowed out on parole on certain days, returning at a stated hour for incarceration. One day he was quite late, the Constable became impatient, and when the culprit turned up, told him, if he was late again he would "lock him out."[3]

The family stayed 12 days in Victoria, and during that time Bate met some of the HBC staff, including Governor James Douglas's private secretary, Richard Colledge, and HBC retiree John Work, whom he described as "covered with a heavy Inverness cape and carrying a skookum walking-stick. He was rather, though kindly, inquisitive—agreeable always." He also met others whose names are familiar from the early history of Fort Victoria, including Dr. William Fraser Tolmie, Dr. John Helmcken, Roderick Finlayson, and Reverend Edward Cridge. He had long talks with Joseph William McKay, the first HBC officer-in-charge in Nanaimo, who, having returned from Fort Simpson, now worked alongside William John Macdonald and Cornelius Thorne in the Company store in Fort Victoria. McKay told him the fabled story of "Coal Tyee," a Snuneymuxw chief, and his meeting with the Victoria blacksmith that led to the discovery of "black diamonds" in Nanaimo. He also had tea with Judge David Cameron, his wife, Cecilia, and daughter, Edith, at their home, "Belmont," in Esquimalt.

He also visited the Puget Sound Agricultural Company farms of Captain Edward Langford, Thomas Skinner, McAuly, and Kenneth MacKenzie at Craigflower Farm where schoolmaster Clarke taught—the same Clarke who had arrived with Bate's uncle in 1854. Bate wrote, "I saw the country around Victoria in all its pristine beauty and grandeur. The picnic-looking spaces between the oaks, here and there, struck me as charming spots, which I had not expected to see in this far off land."

While Bate socialized among the Victoria elite, cousin Cornelius Bryant was busy securing his future employment.

Governor James Douglas interviewed him regarding his qualifications for the position of schoolmaster at Nanaimo, which was then vacant. Robinson had recommended him for the job. He was sent to Reverend Cridge for examination and afterwards was given a letter to return to Douglas regarding his abilities. Bryant wrote in his diary, "His Excellency congratulated me on my success and on the favourable opinion Mr. Cridge entertained of me in his note, and enquired as to the welfare of me and my relatives during the voyage."[4]

FIRST IMPRESSIONS OF NANAIMO

With Bate and Bryant's employment firmly secured, the family began the journey to Nanaimo. On Sunday, February 1, 1857, at 5:00 p.m. the *Beaver*, after dropping the *Recovery* in mid harbour, slowly and cautiously made her way to an anchorage near the entrance to Commercial Inlet. Bate recalled that memorable day of their arrival: "The whole inhabitants nearly were described on the hillside, curious maybe to get a look at the new arrivals. Once ashore, the heartiness of welcome from all was something never to be forgotten."[5] The new arrivals received a warm welcome from the early Scottish pioneers and the Black Country families—and their uncle, George Robinson.

Bate was to look back at that day and observe the reaction of the young man he was: "How did Nanaimo look at first sight to a stranger youth, who, full of ambition, aspiration, and determination, had come to make a start in life?" He described his new home that had changed only slightly since Robinson's arrival three years before:

> Rounding Light House Point, now known as Jack's Point, a glimpse was obtained of the clean, whitewashed row of houses standing on a rising eminence a little way from the water front, the grassy slope between the buildings and the harbour, looking

as fresh as spring, the towering peak of Wakesiah mountain under a heavy cloud, and the intervening tall timber, formed a somber looking background, giving the place just then a rather weird aspect.

As he turned to the east, he faced the coastal mountains "with their lofty crests, capped with a winter's snow. The sight was enrapturing, and for a minute or two the eyes were strained viewing the most beautiful of the grandest scenery imaginable."[6]

Despite the scenery, Bate soon learned, the Black Country pioneers who had come before him spoke of the isolation of the location and the lack of comfort that they struggled to remedy. They had shared tiny log cabins so roughly constructed that the wind whistled through the cracks. The interior furnishings consisted of benches and bunk-like beds; the rugs and mats were made partly with dog hair, sheared annually from the longhaired white dogs kept by the Snuneymuxw. The dog hair was woven with other hair to produce blankets, floor mats, and clothing.

By the time Bate and his fellow travellers arrived in 1857, they found

a brightness and warmth in every home. When visitors dropped in they would spread out the snowy tablecloth and bring out the best of everything the larder could afford. They found a dense wilderness, but were equal to the situation. They set to work with courage and cheerfulness; steadfastly held, as some of them said, a hungry hope for the good time coming. "Hope is the sweetest friend that ever kept a distressed soul company."[7]

The small HBC mining community consisted of approximately 45 buildings, constructed with one exception of hewn and round logs. The exception was the Stone House, built by stonemason William Isbister. The Bastion was the most formidable looking structure in sight. Two three pounder cannonades were its armament, used to salute His Excellency, the governor, whenever he arrives, and they served doubtless, to over-awe the Indians, whose tribal differences often led to war—war of the guerilla type.

Scattered around the village was evidence of commerce. There was a small HBC sawmill that cut lumber for the mines, a company store, Hirst's warehouse, two carpenter shops, a blacksmith shop, and a stable, plus the Snuneymuxw villages. A row of log cabins was located along the hillside with a grassy slope leading down to the harbour.

EXPLORING THE AREA

Robinson welcomed his sister Maria and the excited young relatives. After their long sea journey they were happy to finally reach their destination. Bate and Bryant were initially housed in their uncle's attic. Later they occupied the other end of the Robinson "duplex." Elizabeth and Maria immediately took over the task of caring for Robinson's children, Amanda and Victor. No doubt there was a happy family reunion that evening in the Robinson household, with three years of news from home to catch up on.

Bate spent his first week in Nanaimo getting to know the community. He noted the population on February 1, 1857, exclusive of Snuneymuxw people: "Adults: 51 males, 20 females, 2 Kanakas, 5 Iriquois: Children: 26 boys, 28 girls—a total of 132."[8]

He was given an introductory tour of the HBC mining enterprise. The mines were located near the shoreline of the harbour to exploit the coal outcropping and the shallow seams. Those in operation when Bate arrived were the Park Head Level-Free Mine, on the west side of Victoria Road, and the Dunsmuir Level-Free Mine at the foot of Nicol Street. They were called "level-free" mines because they sloped at an angle, allowing the mine to free itself of water by gravity. Below it to the south was the Dunsmuir Mine, developed by Robert Dunsmuir, a licensed free miner, who was able to mine the coal and sell it back to the HBC. Dunsmuir had been in Nanaimo since the first miners arrived from Fort Rupert in 1852. There was also a small mine on the north end of Newcastle Island, a small island of approximately 750 acres on the north side of Nanaimo's harbour.

Bate also visited the Snuneymuxw villages along the Nanaimo River, and at Millstone River, Departure Bay, and Nanaimo Harbour. He saw an abandoned village at Departure Bay where several totem poles stood at odd angles. The Snuneymuxw had left the site after being raided by Haidas, who killed over 400 of their people. Survivors returned only to bury the dead.[9]

This was his first experience with the First Nations of Vancouver Island. He wrote that after the advent of the whites, the Snuneymuxw began to scatter huts about the settlement and

> gradually gathered here and there on the waterfront and began to do business by way of trade in deer, salmon, herring, clams, ducks, etc. Very small value in powder, shot, tobacco, beads, ship biscuits and a handshake was acceptable to the Natives in those days for their fish and game.

They were highly mobile, and during the spring and summer months they crossed the Strait of Georgia to fish the Fraser River and travelled as far north as Qualicum River.

When Bate first saw the town, it was surrounded by forest, with rough and narrow pathways and cleared land in front of every home. He wrote that it was unsafe to travel at night without a lantern for fear of running into some obstruction or a raised stump. There was no road, nor the need for one, for there were no wagons, only horses. Trees were everywhere; when a tree was felled, a team of oxen yoked together could haul logs from the forest along greased skid roads to the company sawmill on Millstone River. A ravine almost encircled the town like a moat around some ancient fortress, which was actually the rocky peninsula where most of the town was located. It could not be crossed except over logs or fallen trees. To reach the mines, workers and visitors alike had to use a narrow trail on the hillside, which in wet weather was not easily mounted. The year after Bate arrived a wooden bridge was built over the ravine.

Transporting coal to the ships was labour intensive. Bate described the primitive mining operation. The Snuneymuxw were the "pushers" in the mine, and a stiff-kneed horse did the hauling. The bodies of the "skiveys," or baskets, by which the coal was conveyed along the main road, were made of cedar twigs, which, after being heated, were easily bent between the pine stubs, driven into auger holes made in the frames, and bolted on the wheel axels. The coal trucks were hauled over a wooden track by oxen. All the coal was tipped into a heap. Snuneymuwx labourers carried the coal to their canoes then transported it to ships anchored in the harbour, and shovelled it by hand onto the ship.

> In this work of conveyance, the Indian women as well as the men were engaged—the former as a rule, earning the most wages, or goods. Payment was made at the Hudson's Bay Company's store, in blankets, beads, shirts, and other articles.[10]

This simple method of loading coal continued for some time. Bate came to know the Snuneymuxw as industrious people who were "steadily occupied. Some have knowledge of agriculture, and are inclined to lead a pastoral life, while others worked about the mines."

BRYANT THE SCHOOLTEACHER

Cousin Cornelius Bryant soon discovered the drawbacks of his first teaching job. He began teaching the miners' children on February 12,

1857. He received a small salary from the HBC and was expected to gain the rest of his living by collecting fees from his pupil's parents. The list of pupils was almost a reflection of the passenger list of the *Princess Royal* in 1854: Bull, Biggs, Richardson, Turner, Meakin, Bevilockway, Miller, Sage, Ganner, Gough, and Malpass, provided most of the 32 pupils—22 boys and 10 girls. Bryant taught reading writing, grammar, arithmetic, geography, history, and scripture. Knowing Bryant's stern and upright character, no doubt the lessons were forcefully applied. He obviously had set standards, for he sent five-year-old Maria Biggs home because he felt she was too young. John William Meakin recalled being a little in awe of the six-foot, red-haired, red-bearded teacher. Amanda Meakin remembered her classmates were Emily Bate, Eliza Ganner, and Alice Beacham.[11]

An inadequate school building made teaching difficult. Later in the summer Bryant moved into a small log cabin previously occupied by his predecessor, Charles Alfred Bayley. In addition to his teaching duties, he completed the monthly pay accounts for the Nanaimo Coal Company, for which he was paid £6 a year.

Bryant noted in his journal he had been awarded a civic appointment, which gave him distinction but no pay: "Dec. 12, 1859: Received from His Excellency Governor Douglas the appointment of Postmaster at this place."[12] Unhappy about the lack of pay, he began lobbying the government. Finally, in July 1863 he learned he would receive a salary of £200 a year. Teaching school and acting as postmaster, however, were not complementary careers. People looking for mail or collecting the newspapers that were months out of date often interrupted his school lessons. Mail was delivered to Nanaimo by whichever boat happened to be stopping in the harbour.

Reverend Edward Cridge kept a close eye on his new teacher. He inspected the progress of the schooling when he visited in 1861, and reported, "Mr. Bryant continues to display the same assiduity in the discharge of his duties as heretofore."[13] On another visit,

Cridge accompanied HBC Chief Factor Alexander Grant Dallas and Governor Douglas. After preaching a sermon to the community on Sunday, May 10, he and Douglas again inspected the school and privately examined the pupils before leaving for Victoria.[14]

Bryant was disappointed that the village had neither a church nor any organized religion to fill his spiritual needs, so he took matters into his own hands, and eight days after his arrival in Nanaimo, he read publicly from a prayer book, trying to fill the void. After one service in November 1858, he noted, "one adult only at Prayers today." The following February, Reverend Arthur Browning, a Methodist minister, took charge and Bryant happily recorded that he preached "to a large company, the school being full."[15] About this time Bryant and several miners were received into the Wesleyan Methodist Church.

LIFE AND WORK IN A NEW LAND

On February 20, 1857, Bate began his new life as a clerk in the office of the Nanaimo Coal Company. Considering his previous work as a labourer in the Dudley mines, this office job would have felt like a step up—the beginning of a career. His first job was copying David Cameron's books for transmission to the London office. Cameron, the brother-in-law of Governor Douglas, had been hired as bookkeeper, or clerk, for the Nanaimo Coal Company, at £150 per year plus board. He never actually lived in Nanaimo, but had company books forwarded to him in Victoria. Cameron and Bate, in their earlier meeting in Victoria, would have discussed his position and what was expected of him.

Before long, Bate felt the isolation of living in Nanaimo. Weeks passed before he got news from home, news that "was the sweetener of a lonely existence. Postage of a half ounce letter to the Old Country was 30 cents, and yet how gladly was an opportunity embraced to send a letter off, and with what ecstasy a letter or newspaper was received."[16] He noted that the *Beaver* came along about every six months, the *Otter* more frequently, and an express canoe occasionally.

The cultural shock of living far from a developed town, so different from living in Dudley, would have been profound. Back home, he could easily make a trek to Birmingham or Wolverhampton and find a diversion from work in the bright lights of a city replete with theatre and music. Replying to a letter from his friend, Thomas Hughes of Brierley Hill, he wrote,

> I read it [the letter] over and over, your account of our doings in the distant past bring to my mind many, very many, pleasant reminiscences of earlier days and I felt a thrill of pleasure in returning my thoughts to the scenes and haunts of our childhood. I should still feel a glow of affection for the trees, the books, and the hills where in boyhood we wandered and whiled away many an innocent hour.[17]

In Nanaimo, however, the closest centre of social life was Victoria, considered by some as "something of a summertime resort for Nanaimo area miners."[18] Nevertheless, the countryside around 19th-century Nanaimo was beautiful. Bate enjoyed the outdoors and probably the clean air of Vancouver Island. He waxed eloquently about a walk along Millstream (Millstone) River, which gave him a feeling of "silent solitude." He liked to explore an area then write about it; often his words painted a picture no camera of the future could ever capture:

> The lonely magnificence of the scenery in the Millstream valley, its mossy glades, rivulets and water falls, who could fail to admire them? And then, when the banks were robed with maples in full leaf, and dogwood in all its floral beauty, what lovely spots were found for the good old-fashioned picnic, which the early residents well knew how to arrange and enjoy. A canoe trip to Nanaimo River, across the harbour outside Douglas and Newcastle Islands,

to Departure Bay, scrutinizing en route the rifts, caves and caverns in the cliffs, the strange romantic grandeur and remarkable appearance of the water-worn rocks, which looked like works of art produced by the chisel.

Sitting down at the site of an old Indian village, gazing across the Straits of Georgia, and around the Bay, resting in a mute incommunicable luxury of thought, one could drink in a Panorama of the fairest, the most enchanting pictures of Nature's painting—pictures in which this whole Nanaimo region abounds. There are several totem poles, rather elaborately carved, standing at this deserted village, which had belonged to a branch of the S'nenymos tribe that had quit the place many years before. On Jesse Island, under a bluff on the northern side there was an ancient Indian necropolis. Dozens of boxes were piled, one above another, moldering with age, containing the remains of Natives, there deposited.[19]

Bate climbed Mt. Benson and declared the view was one on which "many an artist eye would rest with wonder and delight. On a clear morning a view of the sunrise is unsurpassed in its gorgeous splendour by anything on the Pacific Coast." The naval officer Captain George Henry Richards and the officers of the survey ship HMS *Plumper*, who spent a week on top of the mountain making astronomical observations in the summer of 1859, agreed with his opinion. They placed a large Union Jack on the peak, which could be plainly seen from Nanaimo. The flag remained there until destroyed in a windstorm.

BATE AND HORNE MARRIAGES

No letters confirm how much Bate missed his girlfriend, Sarah Ann Cartwright, and it is unknown when he got the letter informing him he was a father, or even if he was shocked at the news. Their daughter, Emily, was born on February 8, 1857, her birth registered in Dudley. Bate had only been in Nanaimo a week when she was born. Did he know Sarah Ann was pregnant when he left? Perhaps he did not know, or he might have postponed his travel plans. Any discussion on the subject of unplanned pregnancy with young unmarried couples in those days was not as open as today. No doubt he would have been overjoyed but anxious about this new life coming into his care. He requested of the HBC free passage for Sarah and baby Emily to join him in Nanaimo.

The following year, Sarah and Emily made the long journey to Vancouver Island on another voyage of the *Princess Royal*. They arrived at Fort Victoria on February 2, 1859.[20] Bate would have given them a warm and loving welcome, and held his daughter for the first time, no doubt happy to have Sarah back in his life. His aunt Maria and his sister Elizabeth would also have welcomed the new baby into the family.

Sarah arrived just in time for the first Bate wedding in Nanaimo. Mark's sister Elizabeth had fallen in love with a strapping young Scot from the Orkney Islands of Scotland, Adam Grant Horne, aged 28. Horne had been indentured to the HBC since 1851. He was first assigned to Fort Rupert, where coal mining first began on the Island. In 1853 he was transferred to Nanaimo where the next coal field was being developed, and was placed in charge of the HBC store, selling goods and products and trading with the Snuneymuxw for salmon, venison, and furs. He became a local celebrity following his successful exploratory expedition across Vancouver Island in 1856, from Qualicum to Alberni. Other trips followed, which solid-ified contact between the HBC and the Tseshaht and Hupacasaht First Nations in the Alberni Valley. Adam and Elizabeth made an imposing couple. Elizabeth was petite, reaching only to the height of Adam's shoulders, with dark hair, while Adam was a handsome man with dark red hair, and about six feet and three inches tall.

The Horne wedding was held at noon, February 22, 1859, in the schoolroom in Nanaimo. The happy celebration brought the

Bate, Robinson, and Bryant families together, perhaps for the last time. Reverend Richard Dowson, a fellow of Saint Mary's College, Windermere, England, and a travelling missionary, conducted the Church of England ceremony. Dowson and his wife Hannah had travelled with Sarah and Emily on the voyage to Fort Victoria.[21] Those witnessing the ceremony were Mark and Sarah, George Robinson and his new bride, Caroline, who had come up from San Francisco for the event, Captain Charles Edward Stuart, the HBC officer-in-charge, Cornelius Bryant, and Company surgeon Dr. Alfred Robson Benson. There is no hint of romance in Horne's stark observation in his diary: "At 12 a.m. I was married by the Rev. Dossen [sic] at Nanaimo in the schoolroom to E. Bate."[22]

The young couple began married life in a house at the corner of Commercial and Bastion Streets. Their first child was Adam Henry, born on December 9, 1859; Ann Elizabeth arrived on January 23, 1862. Both children were born in Nanaimo before the Horne family was transferred to Fort Simpson.

Mark and Sarah, who were married in 1859, may have married at the same time as Mark's sister, though the actual date is unknown. Sarah's recent arrival in Nanaimo with Emily may have prompted them to legitimize their union, and Elizabeth and Adam's wedding would have given them the perfect opportunity. Aunt Maria was not present for the weddings; perhaps she was looking after baby Emily and the Robinson children, Amanda and Victor.

ROBINSON RETURNS TO ENGLAND

In the fall of 1858, meanwhile, Robinson went to San Francisco, looking for new markets in California for Nanaimo coal. While there he attended a ball given by the French Consul, Monsieur Gautier. There he met Madame Gautier's English secretary, Caroline Dakens. Two weeks later they married.[23] As they were both still under contract to their employers, Robinson returned to Nanaimo and completed his five-year contract, while Caroline stayed behind to fulfill her commitment to the Gautiers. Was it love at first sight, or had they known each other before? Perhaps she was the unnamed maid who accompanied his family on the *Princess Royal* voyage four years before. Whatever the situation, their sudden marriage left many questions.

Robinson's decision to return home to England with his children in the fall of 1859, after he completed his HBC contract, may have been influenced by Caroline's desire also to return home. Another factor may have been that the HBC's ten-year trading agreement with the Crown was about to expire, leaving the future of the coal industry in Nanaimo in doubt. Bryant wrote in his diary that his uncle and cousins left for England on November 21, via Victoria, San Francisco, Panama, and New York. He made no mention of Aunt Maria, but it appeared she also returned to England with them. The Robinson family settled at Eastbourne, Sussex, where Caroline, 42, gave birth to a daughter, Georgiana Caroline, on November 19, 1861.[24] After the arrival of Georgiana, the family moved to Kidderminster, where Robinson became manager of the Caldwell Brick Works, and where Amanda, ten, and Victor, six, attended school.

Robinson left his name on the mining industry of Vancouver Island. His stay was not always a happy one. He and his family would return to the Colony of Vancouver Island, but not to Nanaimo.

5

NEW
MANAGEMENT

WHEN THE FRASER RIVER GOLD rush began in 1858 in New Caledonia, an area without governance and sprinkled with HBC forts throughout, Great Britain began to sit up and take notice of its far-flung colony on the Pacific Coast. Thousands of gold seekers flooded Fort Victoria, transforming the small settlement into a bustling town. Every ship that arrived carried more men hoping to improve their lives with gold.

FROM NANAIMO TO THE GOLDFIELDS

Bate found this an exciting time in Nanaimo:

> We were suddenly enlivened after what seemed the quietude of years. Ocean steamships *Commodore* afterward called *Brother Jonathan*, river steamer *Surprise* and *Seabird* three or four times a week, with hundreds, yea thousands, of eager gold seekers on the way to the Fraser River. This was the period of the Fraser gold

excitement with all its attendant effects, when hardy pioneers of California and an impetuous host from other countries made a rush from the placer diggings of New Caledonia. A brisk and profitable business was done by one or two Nanaimo gentlemen in trading every canoe available from the Indians, and selling them to miners who were anxious to explore the rivers and creeks, tributary to the Fraser.[1]

The excitement reached Nanaimo, and it was not long before some of the miners declared their intention of going to the diggings and asked for an advance on their wages. Richard Richardson, 48, a *Princess Royal* pioneer from Dudley, left to make his fortune. When he returned, he told his friends he would soon be off to the Old Country. Bate noted, "He walked around for a few days with affected dignity, dressed quite stylishly, and assumed the airs that some persons do when suddenly becoming rich."[2] It turned out his riches came from the sale of the equipment he had taken to the goldfield.

Bate could not resist experiencing the goldfields personally, so in July 1858 he boarded the *Surprise* for the journey to Fort Hope. There he and the engineer from the ship rode horseback to Hills Bar, between Hope and Yale, where he saw miners panning for gold. They concluded the prospects did not look very encouraging,[3] though the agricultural market was expanding rapidly to meet the needs of the miners who were arriving daily.[4] However, for Bate, coal offered more potential there than agriculture but that required more capital outlay than the HBC was prepared to spend.

CHANGES TO THE HBC AND
ISLAND GOVERNANCE

The British government became alarmed by the influx of Americans, and not wanting to see New Caledonia fall into the hands of the United States the way Oregon had, quickly established the new Colony of British Columbia, distinct from the Colony of Vancouver

Island. On November 19, 1858, the new colony was proclaimed. Douglas was offered the position of governor at an annual salary of £1,800, while remaining governor of the Colony of Vancouver Island. By supplementing his income from government revenues, he managed to secure £3,000 per year.[5]

When the HBC's charter of Vancouver Island expired the following spring, on May 30, 1859, its exclusive trade monopoly was not renewed. As governor of both colonies, Douglas had to divest himself of all interests in the Company. Until this time, he had served two masters, as head of the HBC Western Department and governor of Vancouver Island. His successor, Alexander Grant Dallas, his son-in-law, was placed in charge of the Company's Western Department, and under his leadership the company retrenched and began divesting itself of its coal, transport, agricultural, and industrial operations, keeping only its wholesale and retail business, the beginning of what is known today as "The Hudson's Bay." Dallas never shared Douglas's support of the coal industry on Vancouver Island, but he did initiate a new style of management in Nanaimo: that of having only one general manager.

Captain Charles Stuart had represented the HBC and the Colony of Vancouver Island in Nanaimo and it was he who administered law and order as justice of the peace. One of Dallas's first actions as the new head of the Western Department was to fire Stuart for drunkenness, and then to recommend Charles Samuel Nicol as the new general manager in Nanaimo. Nicol was an engineer and a land surveyor, with no mining experience. Whatever Dallas's knowledge of Stuart's conduct that caused his termination, it differed from that of Bate and the residents of Nanaimo, who all thought highly of him.

Although Bate had been in the colony only a few years, he had come to know Stuart. He described him as "a gentleman of much energy of character, though suave in his manner. He stood high in the estimation of the Hudson's Bay Company, and had been many years in their service in command of the vessels first engaged in trading on the northern coast. He was a warm, opened handed friend. Many of the inhabitants of Nanaimo of his time have reason to bless his memory. He was one of those good-natured, noble souls."[6] Stuart died in 1863 on board his sloop, *Random*. He was buried in the old Pioneer Cemetery in Nanaimo. Every December 25, for a number of years, his friends in Nanaimo held a memorial service for the old master.[7]

In 1860, the colonial government next appointed Captain William Hales Franklyn as its representative in Nanaimo, as stipendiary magistrate and government agent. He was born in Kent, England, and became a captain in the British navy. Without any credentials for the job, Franklyn had only been in the colony a year when he received the appointment. Prior to this, he had been captain of a Pacific and Orient steamer and lost his job for throwing a passenger in irons. According to Dr. John Sebastian Helmcken, Franklyn earned the nickname the "British Lion" because "he was all British—bristled with it all over."[8]

In the early days of the colony, magistrates issued liquor licences and fined people who broke the law. They were a power within the community before city councils were elected to govern. Although the position was unpaid in the beginning, the Legislative Assembly in Victoria eventually assigned Franklyn a yearly fee of £150, which many felt was far too much for what he did. He did not endear himself to the residents of the coal mining village, for he was unwilling to live in town, preferring Cob Tree Farm in the Cedar area south of the town. When his journey back and forth by canoe each day became too tiresome, he finally moved into town, and in 1862 he built a two-storey brick mansion at the corner of Franklyn and Dunsmuir Streets, adjacent to the present-day city hall. From this fashionable home, he entertained visiting government and naval personnel.

Initially, an old store built by Adam Grant Horne in 1863 served as a courthouse.[9] Then in 1865, a two-storey wooden building on Front Street was purchased and renovated for multiple uses: courthouse, post office, harbour master's office, government agency, and police quarters.[10] The strange-looking old structure, sitting on stilts with a flight of stairs up to its entrance, looked unlike any official judicial building, but it served many functions. Chief Justice Matthew Baillie Begbie was a regular visitor to the Nanaimo courthouse. Franklyn and Nicol were the new faces of authority in Nanaimo: Franklyn represented the colonial government, and Nicol the HBC's Nanaimo Coal Company.

THE MINE UNDER NEW MANAGEMENT

Charles Nicol was born March 31, 1830, in London. His parents died when he was a child, so his uncle raised him. The family lived in Suffolk. Little is known about his older sisters, Harriet, Euphemia, and Emma. He and his brother, James, joined the British army in 1847. Charles served as ensign in the 68th Light Infantry, and he and James fought in the Crimea war from 1854 to 1855. On their return to England, Charles was appointed inspector of county jails in Suffolk.

Nicol arrived in British Columbia during the Fraser River gold rush. On March 1, 1859, Douglas appointed him high sheriff and justice of the peace for the Colony of British Columbia. He reported to the commander of the Royal Engineers' detachment for duties related to law enforcement, but he was soon assigned to do building inspections, townsite surveys, road maintenance, and land leases.[11] He resigned this position and arrived in Nanaimo in 1860 as the new general manager of the Nanaimo Coal Mines.

As a newcomer to Nanaimo, Nicol welcomed the experience of people who had knowledge of the town and the coal operation. His office staff included Mark Bate, copying clerk; James Farquhar, accountant and bookkeeper; Adam Grant Horne, clerk and storekeeper; and Dr. Alfred Benson, colliery surgeon. This small complement of people managed the HBC's Nanaimo Coal Company.

HBC records in 1861 show Bate made a reasonable wage, over £100 a year: for "copying in office 7 months" he received 69 pounds 15 shillings, another 10 pounds for "keeping time of men," and an additional 21 pounds 17 shillings 10 pence.[12] This was a modest wage compared to Nicol, who made £900 annually, or James Farquhar, the bookkeeper, who was paid £225, or the surgeon, Alfred Robson Benson, whose salary was £250. Benson had worked with the HBC since the first settlers arrived but not always in Nanaimo. In 1860 he married Ellen Phillips. Their marriage was short-lived, for she died in 1863. A stained-glass window was placed in St. Paul's Church as a memorial to her.[13]

FORMATION OF THE VANCOUVER
COAL MINING AND LAND COMPANY

Back in London, Nicol's brother, James, approached a group of investors about buying the HBC's Nanaimo Coal Company. He formed the pioneering British firm, the Vancouver Coal Mining and Land Company (VCML, referred to in Nanaimo as the Vancouver Coal Company), on August 1, 1862, expressly to purchase the coal holdings in Nanaimo. With this purchase the Vancouver Coal Company became the biggest mining concern anywhere in Canada during the latter part of the 19th century. The first chairman was Thomas Chandler Haliburton, a politician, judge, and author from Nova Scotia who had recently retired to England. He is better known as a literary figure and satirist, and creator of the famous comic character Sam Slick. The board of directors included Agnes Strickland, an English author and historian, and solicitor John R. Galsworthy, grandfather of the playwright.[14] Alexander Grant Dallas, governor of the HBC, also became a director in the new company that was buying the coal operation from his employer.

The company managed to raise £100,000, of which £40,000 was used to purchase the HBC property. In November 1862, James Nicol secured a contract transferring

all HBC lands in the Nanaimo District including Newcastle, Cameron and Douglas (Protection) Islands. Involved were 6,193 acres, the amount of land purchased by James Douglas for the Nanaimo Coal Company from the Crown on May 7, 1855 at a price of £6,193. For his service, he was paid £1,000 cash and 400 shares valued at £10 each.[15]

The real estate deal included all the mines, machinery, buildings, barges, horses, cattle, rights, easements, privileges, and title. The HBC store and trade goods were held back and stored in the HBC warehouse until sold to Thomas Cunningham and Company, and £6,000 was written off for what the Vancouver Coal Company called "HBC rubbish."

Although the HBC's general manager, Charles Nicol, was in a conflict of interest position while his brother James negotiated the sale, he suffered no consequences and continued in his position. The transition from one coal master to another was an easy one; the miners probably noticed no changes in their workplace. Looking to the future, however, with the harbour under new ownership, the Vancouver Coal Company had an advantage over any future speculator wanting to open coal mines behind the HBC land, for they would have to negotiate passage for their product across the Vancouver Coal Company land to reach tidewater, as was later the case with the Harewood Mine.

Most of the office staff for the new company was recruited from the Nanaimo Coal Company. Nicol divided management responsibilities: Bate became chief clerk, reporting directly to him, and Robert Dunsmuir was appointed mine superintendent, overseeing the miners and labourers. A small fleet of company coal ships, transferred at the time of the land purchase, made up a third arm of management. Carefully observing the Nanaimo operation from the London office were the Vancouver Coal Company board secretary Samuel Robins and managing director John Wild. Bate developed a close working relationship with both men.

In all his writings about his early life in Nanaimo, Bate made no mention of his clerical work for the mining company. He was a manager in waiting—learning all he could from Nicol about the mine operation. The small office staff performed a variety of jobs, including inventories, payrolls, purchasing, record keeping, and correspondence. Bate called Nanaimo the Newcastle of the Pacific Coast, or the Pay Sheet city, "because of the big payrolls dealt with by the owners of our precious Black Diamonds."[16] Here coal was king. All of this would eventually become his responsibility, but throughout the 1860s, Nicol closely supervised his office staff.

The coal company did not expect any difficulty maintaining production at the current level, but over the preceding years, no efforts had been made to upgrade the coal operation. Little attention had been given to purchasing new machinery, building coal sheds, or providing any sort of loading equipment. The HBC had seemed more interested in extracting the most easily accessible coal for the lowest possible cost.[17] While Nicol had wide-ranging powers and responsibilities—he controlled miners' contracts and decided the price for coal, and he dealt directly with business and government leaders—he still lacked the authority to make any financial decisions. This slowed the growth of the coal operation.

NEW OPPORTUNITIES FOR BRYANT

The sale of the HBC affected schoolmaster Bryant. Dallas informed him on November 21, 1859, that the company would no longer pay his salary and that he must ask Governor Douglas how he would be paid; in addition he must give up the house he occupied. But he was not left homeless; he was given two rooms at the end of a larger house where his uncle George Robinson had lived. Another room in the same building was set aside for the school. His connection with the HBC was not completely severed, as he continued copying and making out the accounts for the miners' wages each month for James Farquhar, the accountant, for which he received six pounds a year.[18]

The spiritual needs of Bryant and the mining village were served when the first church was built. Dallas deeded land behind the present-day Globe Hotel to the Methodist Church in June 1860. The church was named the Ebenezer Wesleyan Methodist Church, after its first resident minister, Reverend Ebenezer Robson. Local volunteers built the church using California redwood. The church had four gables; the north and south wings formed transepts, and was furnished with rich stained-glass windows and four ornate bronze chandeliers. The dedication service was held on November 27, 1860.[19]

The HBC also donated land just off Dallas Square for the first Anglican church. Nicol laid the foundation stone for the church and a rectory on Christmas day, 1861; however, the transfer of land became complicated by the sale of the mining operation to the Vancouver Coal Company. The deed was not transferred to the bishop until after the church was completed in 1862. Until this time, Reverend Good held Anglican services in the schoolroom. The first service in St. Paul's Anglican Church was held June 8, 1862, and the deed finally conveyed in July 1864. The consecration service was held August 27, 1865.[20] Just two weeks before, the Roman Catholics had also dedicated their own small wooden chapel and named it St. Peter's. With three denominations for residents to worship, this would have pleased Bryant and no doubt Bate.

Bryant's financial outlook must have improved sufficiently for him to consider marriage to Elizabeth A. Murdow, a young woman from Brantford, in Canada West. Reverend John Hall married them on March 15, 1864, in Victoria.[21] Hall was the first Presbyterian clergyman to arrive in the colony, in 1861. Bryant and Elizabeth's first son, Wesley Robinson Bryant, was born in Nanaimo on December 12, 1864. They had two more children, Maria Jane, in 1866, and Theodore, in 1871.[22] All the children were baptized in the Wesleyan Methodist Church in Nanaimo. The Bryant family home was at the corner of Franklyn and Wallace Streets.[23]

Under pressure from his many activities, Bryant informed the colonial secretary on October 17, 1864, that he could no longer fill duties as both schoolteacher and postmaster; he resigned as postmaster on December 29, 1864, but continued teaching. It was not until May the following year that his replacement James Trevor arrived to take over the position of postmaster, and he was hired at a rate of $485 per year for each position—clerk to the stipendiary magistrate and postmaster. When Bryant learned Trevor would be paid for duties Bryant had done for free for five years, he wrote to the colonial secretary suggesting he be paid the same rate; in this he was successful. Nevertheless, education was not a high priority in the young colony. The *Colonist* reported on December 6, 1867, that the teacher in Nanaimo had received neither pay nor allowance for rent, fuel, and other expenses. For the year of 1867, he had received not "one cent of remuneration . . . and although this is the most inclement season of the year not a pound weight of fuel is provided beyond what the teacher finds himself!" Bryant continued to work with both the miners and the Snuneymuxw and in 1867 was appointed "exhorter" (a religious speaker) to the Nanaimo Wesleyan Mission. The following year he became a licensed "local preacher" on the Nanaimo circuit. Two years later he gave up teaching completely and dedicated the rest of his life to the Methodist church. Upon resigning as schoolmaster in 1870, he received a complimentary letter from his cousin Mark Bate, then chairman of the school board, accepting his resignation with regret:

> The local board take this opportunity of recording and testifying to the faithful, assiduous and efficient manner in which you have discharged your arduous duties during the thirteen and a half years you have held the position.[24]

Bryant's first posting as a preacher was to New Westminster, then back to Nanaimo, and his third posting was to Chilliwack. It was there that Amanda Robinson, who had lived with the Bryants since they were first married, met and married Cory Spencer Ryder. The cousins continued to keep in touch.

6

MORE FAMILY
ARRIVE

BATE AND SARAH SETTLED COMFORTABLY into married life. Their family grew with the arrival of their first son, Mark Jr., on May 17, 1860. Reverend Robson baptized him and Emily on November 11; these may have been the first baptisms in the new Wesleyan Methodist Church. Another daughter, Sarah Ann (Sally), was born July 16, 1861, and a son, Thomas Ezra (Tom), on March 31, 1863; they were also baptized in the same church. With four small children, this was a busy time for the young family.

MORE IMMIGRANTS

Meanwhile, on February 2, 1862, more members of Bate's family arrived, again on the *Princess Royal*.[1] They included his aunt, Maria Robinson, returning to the colony; his youngest sister, Lucy; his older brother, Joseph; and his wife's brother, William Cartwright. On February 5, 1862, the *British Colonist* recorded the arrival of the ship:

The Hudson Bay Company's ship *Princess Royal* (arrived) in the Outer harbour yesterday morning from London, England, with several passengers and a large cargo of assorted merchandise . . . the cargo of the *Princess Royal* is the most valueable [sic] ever brought to the Colony. Passengers were Miss Robinson, Miss Bate, William Cartwright, Joseph Bate, William Biggs, Robert Bacham, Alice Hannah Bacham, Mrs. Rowling and Master Rowlings. Lost overboard. Shortly after rounding Cape Horn, in a gale the *Princess Royal* lost her Second Mate and an able Seaman. They were engaged in taking in the jib when the vessel pitched forward heavily and when she recovered the men had disappeared.

Upon arriving in Victoria, Joseph, Lucy, and William travelled to Nanaimo to meet their relatives. Aunt Marie decided to stay in Victoria.

William was reunited with his sister Sarah. He stayed on in Nanaimo working in the mines. On December 14, 1869, he married Mary Finlay at the home of Noah Shakespeare in James Bay, Victoria.[2] Mary, 15, was the daughter of Christopher Finlay who was recruited by the HBC in the Orkney Islands for the coal mine at Fort Rupert. Her father was a well-known personality in Nanaimo. Bate knew him to be proficient in mathematics, and he served as assistant in the HBC store and office. Some children also remember him as a stern headmaster when he temporarily filled the position as the community waited for another teacher to arrive.

Two years later the Cartwrights had their first child, a girl they named Mathilda (Tillie). About this time they decided that farming in the southern part of the island would be more to their liking. In October 1872, they moved from Nanaimo to a farm in Sooke, where they raised ten children. Bate bought Cartwright's property in Nanaimo to enable the couple to buy the farm in Sooke.[3]

LUCY BATE AND PETER SABISTON

Bate's sister Lucy was only in Nanaimo a year when she married Peter Sabiston on April 19, 1863. He was another HBC recruit from the Orkney Islands, who came with his brothers, John and James, in 1851. He had originally been posted to Fort Simpson, but he was not a happy man; either he did not like work or did not like working for the Company. While in Fort Simpson, he entered into a union with a First Nations woman, who bore two of his children, one in 1853 and another in 1857. A year later, he left the northern community to join his brothers in Nanaimo, abandoning his children and their mother.[4]

Peter was a restless young man, though he seemed to settle down after he met Lucy. In the next year of their marriage, he purchased 88 acres of farmland in the Mountain District. Later he became a construction contractor and built several houses in Nanaimo, including St. Andrew's Presbyterian Church; he also constructed some bridges and a railway trestle in the area. Later he settled into the hotel business, operating at various times the Royal, the Miners, and the Commercial hotels.

Lucy and Peter had no children of their own, but they adopted a six-year-old orphan, Aggie Powley, who was said to be a beautiful little girl. They raised her with as much affection as if she had been born to them. In 1881 Peter and Lucy went on a three-month visit to San Francisco, then travelled to the Orkney Islands, possibly to visit his ailing father.

On September 28, 1892, the *British Colonist* reported that Peter Sabiston "of the Commercial Hotel, is lying dangerously ill of pneumonia." He died two days later. Lucy remained in Nanaimo, where she was loved and respected. Her adopted daughter, Aggie, married an American and returned with him to the United States.[5] Lucy died on November 10, 1927, at the age of 84, having lived in Nanaimo for 65 years. Lucy willed her house at 163 Wallace Street to Isabel Muir, known as Bella, in recognition of her long years of help and companionship. Isabel was to cement her ties to the Bate family by marrying Herbert Brown, grandson of Adam Grant Horne and Mark's sister Elizabeth.

OTHER RELATIVES

As for other members of Mark's family who arrived on the *Princess Royal* in 1892, Mark's brother Joseph is a bit of a mystery. Little is known about his stay in the area, though his name appears in the early records of the Nanaimo Literary Institute. His aunt, Maria Robinson, pursued a career as a dressmaker in Victoria. She married John Spence on February 17, 1863, in the Victoria Wesleyan Methodist Church, a year after her arrival back on the island. Maria may have known Spence previously from the ships he served on that periodically docked in Nanaimo. He and Captain John Sabiston were reported to be one of the crew that rigged up the scaffold at Gallows Point for the hanging of two young First Nation men found guilty of murdering a young shepherd at Christmas Hill sheep station near Victoria in 1852.[6] Spence was 65 years old and had signed on with the HBC in Stromness, Orkney Islands; he worked for over 44 years as a ship's carpenter on the *Prince Rupert* out of York Factory, the *Cadboro* and *Vancouver* in the Columbia district, and the *Beaver* in the Western district. Spence began buying property in Victoria in 1854,[7] and retired there in 1861.[8] He and Maria only had a few years together before he died in Victoria on September 29, 1865, at their home on Superior Street. He was buried in the naval corner of Quadra Cemetery.[9] Four years later Maria married an American miner named Harvey (Henry) Snow on January 2, 1869, at the Metropolitan United Church, in Victoria.

Mark's uncle, George Robinson, also returned to Vancouver Island with his wife, Caroline, and their three children, Amanda, Victor, and Georgiana, but this time Robinson settled in Victoria, a city greatly changed since he first saw it in 1854. The precise date of his arrival back on the island is not known, but Amanda told relatives that when she was 14, she went to live with Elizabeth and Cornelius Bryant, in Nanaimo; her 15th birthday was January 23, 1864. Robinson bought three lots fronting Frederick Street within the city but across the harbour in an area known as Victoria West. There he built a small house he named Woodbine Cottage. Caroline was 47 at the birth of her first child here, Fanny Augusta, in 1866, and three years later gave birth to George Thomas, in 1869. These could not have been easy births for her considering her age.

Nanaimo's former mine manager now turned his talent to photography, then in its infancy. He rented premises on the east side of Government Street to conduct his fledgling business, George Robinson's Photographic Studio. When he worked in Nanaimo he had purchased one of the early cameras and taken early photographs in Nanaimo, but he did it quietly for "he did not think his employees would think it very proper for him to be using such fanciful equipment."[10] Since returning to Victoria he hoped to turn his hobby into a business. Amanda Theresa Gough, who later married George Norris, publisher of the *Nanaimo Free Press*, remembered trips taken to Victoria with her family. In 1867 they had individual portraits taken at George Robinson's Photographic Studio.[11] Unfortunately, this was not a profitable venture, and by 1871, Robinson was in Olympia, Washington, exploring another career, this time as a dentist. The following year, he and Carolina returned to Dudley, England, with their children, Georgiana, Fanny, and George Thomas. There he became manager of Blowers Green Colliery.

Robinson's two children from his previous marriage, Amanda and Victor, remained in British Columbia. Amanda married Cory Ryder, of Chilliwack, in 1872. They were the first couple married in the Sumas Church in that community. The young man had just arrived the year before from Kingston, Ontario. The couple had two children, Herbert and Edith. Amanda died in Chilliwack in 1928. Victor married Charlotte Aslett of Victoria, on November 9, 1875.

They had three children, Edgar, Florence, and George. Victor died suddenly in Victoria in 1884.

COMMUNITY LIFE

Mark Bate settled into married life, and like other pioneers, wanted to improve his family's quality of life and that of his community. From the knowledge his employers and government officials had of him and his background, Bate fit the mould of the sort of upper class British male they would welcome into their inner circle. However, research has shown he was from a working-class family and had worked in the mines from an early age; it appears that few people outside his family knew of his past. By good fortune, or thanks to his uncle George Robinson, he had landed a job in HBC administration and moved up the ladder of influence in the community and in the colony.

Most of his friends and working associates were white British men; family, church, school, community and music, occupied his leisure time. Nicol in particular set an example for Bate, by his management of the mines and his involvement in the community. The mine manager was in a position of authority and was expected to provide leadership in the community and to participate in social events. Bate joined Nicol in establishing the Nanaimo Literary Institute in 1862. In early records, Nicol is president, Reverend John Booth Good is vice-president, and Bate is one of the founding members.

Literary institutes, or mechanics institutes, as they were sometimes called, were a product of industrial England where workers looked for self-improvement through education. The institute provided evening lectures, lending libraries, and periodical reading rooms. In Bate's hometown of Dudley, a publication of the Mechanics Institute wrote that it was important for every man to "get intelligence instead of alcohol . . . get knowledge and getting knowledge you get power."[12] In 1857 the *Dudley Weekly*

Times noted that "the town's institute in its first decade, had been enjoyed almost exclusively by the middle classes." Bate's knowledge of the institute in Dudley may have influenced his participation in the group in Nanaimo.

Despite the name, those who developed such institutes in Canada were not working-class men, but rather businessmen, doctors, managers, and clergymen. Few miners joined the group in Nanaimo. This was an all male club; although not explicitly stated, women were likely not allowed to be members. The original membership was a "who's who" of Nanaimo: Bate and his brother Joseph, Robert Dunsmuir, James McGrath, Nicholas J. Jones, Gideon West, John Sabiston, Cornelius Bryant, Edward Wilson, Thomas Cunningham, David Gordon, and George Poole. The institute had three vice-presidents, Reverend E. White, John Christy, and Reverend John Booth Good. The librarian, Robert Fulton, and his assistant, Samuel Gough, supervised a collection of books and magazines; their choice of publications reflected the membership and their interests.

The society met in the schoolroom of St. Paul's Anglican Church. Bate described the schoolroom as a "handsome, tastefully designed structure, much used in the Sixties and Seventies for concerts, lectures, and literary entertainments generally."[13] As vice-president of the institute, Reverend Good held veto power and kept rigid control over who could join, excluding men he considered to be living "in states of fornication, habitual drunkenness, or other gross immoralities."[14]

After Nicol left Nanaimo the onus fell on Bate to keep the group viable. He was frustrated with the slow pace of development and argued for change. He protested barring men with social issues, arguing instead that the institute should hope for the possibility of their rehabilitation. He was determined to entice new members, noting the "cheerless existence" of the group. He suggested that no name be left untried "that would render the Institution popular and secure for it official support."[15] The membership voted to change the constitution, which took away Reverend Good's veto power. He retaliated by banning the group from using the church hall, though he eventually came to accept the new constitution.

Tired of holding meetings in rented facilities, the society decided to build its own hall. The Vancouver Coal Company granted a piece of land on the southwest corner of Bastion and Skinner Streets, but since members were not considered a corporate body, they could not hold land. Adding the names of the colonial secretary, treasurer, and chief justice to the Board of Trustees and naming Arthur Edward Kennedy, Governor of Vancouver Island, as their patron, resolved the situation. The contract to build was awarded to David Gordon and Jacob Blessing. Governor Kennedy laid the cornerstone on November 14, 1864. His appearance in the town was cause for a big celebration. The *British Colonist* reported, "A monster bonfire made up of material which had formerly composed one or two of the old style houses was lighted ... The progress of improvements is fast clearing away the relics of olden times."[16] The governor and his wife and daughters were paraded to the building site, where he laid the cornerstone. A guard of honour, composed of four First Nation constables in uniform, added to the formality of the occasion.

Fundraising began in earnest as the building took shape. The two-storey building had a reading room upstairs and a meeting room downstairs, with a hall large enough to hold 250 people. When completed, Gordon and Blessing, the contractors, were congratulated on their fine workmanship. This was the newest and grandest building in Nanaimo at that time. Here members could meet, talk, and read, and perhaps feel connected to the world they left behind in Britain. Initially, completing the inside of the building was on hold due to the lack of funds, but that did not prevent the hall from being used for local and visiting performers. The first Nanaimo concert held in the hall was a big success. The program, the *British Colonist* reported, consisted of songs and instrumental pieces: "The opportunity of spending such a pleasant and social evening in a place so remote as Nanaimo, is indeed a treat rarely afforded lovers of music."[17] A song was composed for the occasion:

> Where is Columbia after all! Or yet Vancouver Island!
> Were it not for Nanaimo's wealth, her precious gem—black diamond;
> The only place for immigrants, and all dead broken miners,
> A country soon would be "gone in" were it not for Nanaimo.

NANAIMO IN THE MID 1860S

Nanaimo had grown in the few shorts years since Bate arrived. St. Paul's Anglican Church undertook a census in 1863, which recorded the nationality of those living in the community. There were "233 English, 95 Scots, 11 Irish, 17 Welsh, 4 Americans, 15 Canadians, 4 Spanish, 4 Kanakas, 11 Dutch. Of these 6 were coloured, 95 married, 118 single men, 6 spinsters, 25 co-habitating, 22 half-breeds, and 156 children."[18] The number of children was quite large in proportion to the total population.

John Meakin became the Nanaimo correspondent for the Victoria *British Colonist* newspaper in 1862.[19] On January 31, 1863, in one of his first articles about Nanaimo, he also quoted the church census, which counted the white population as 403, with 49 women, 198 men, and 156 children. The boys attended Bryant's school, "non-sectarian and well adapted to the present wants of the place." A girls' school, Meakin added, "conducted by the Misses Joyce, in the new St. Paul's school room, under the auspices of the Church of England, is also non-sectarian, the dogmas of the English Church not being taught, except at the wish of parents. Its attendance is, however only 17, including several Indian girls; but it is hoped an improvement will take place in that respect."[20] This is the first indication that any First Nations children attended the day school. A missionary teacher, Thomas Crosby, arrived that year and took over the education of the Snuneymuxw children on the reserve.

Meakin noted that more homes had been built during the

previous six years, their construction greatly improved from the first log cabins. Nicol and Franklyn occupied the two finest homes. A variety of stores had sprung up, such as William Copperman's general trading store, Alexander Mayers' "Red House" dry goods store, and the new store Adam Grant Horne had just built, plus two bakeries and two butcher's shops. The one store where almost everything could be purchased was the Vancouver Coal Company store. The first road in town was blazed in 1858 and cleared of stumps, though it terminated at a large swamp. Within the next two years, however, other roads were made and bridges crossed the rivers, allowing the free movement of people and oxen pulling wagons. Little opportunity existed for organized sports or for social interaction, although the town had two churches, which offered some solace. Only two societies had been formed so far, the Nanaimo Literary Institute, and the Total Abstinence Society, formed by Bryant in his battle against the evil grog. One of the town's leading citizens, Robert Dunsmuir, who was known to enjoy a drink or two with fellow miners after work, was a member.

What Nanaimo wanted most, to relieve its isolation, was a road to Victoria. A trip to Victoria took several days by steamer. The wagon trail that wound its way to Victoria could not be relied upon as it was often blocked by fallen trees and was at the mercy of winter weather. Farmers used the road to drive their stock to market in Victoria. Another trail led north to Comox. But who in Victoria was listening to the small coal-mining town recently purchased by the Vancouver Coal Mining and Land Company in London, England?

AGITATING FOR TOWN IMPROVEMENTS

Until the mid 1860s, political affairs were of little interest in the village of Nanaimo, but if the town wanted anything to change, its concerns had to be voiced. And so began, in 1863, a period of campaigning, mostly in the *British Colonist*:

Surely if we are a part of the Colony we can claim a part of services of its representatives. We want a Port of Entry, a Small Debts Court, and Mail Communication established. When these are furnished, we shall stop political agitation. Nanaimo should be made a Port of Entry; shipping is increasing and it would help "our promising town" and not injure Victoria.[21]

The agitation must have worked, for a year later the Vancouver Coal Company boasted, "Nanaimo is a port of entry; the harbour has been carefully buoyed, and is available at all tides; and a commodious wharf is nearly completed, giving greater facilities for the loading of ships of deep draught." Improvements to its mail service would have to wait a few years. Sometimes mail took weeks to come from Victoria by boat, and people suggested, not for the first time, that if it came by road, it would be safer, cheaper, and faster.

Nanaimo found an ally in Amor De Cosmos, the editor of the *British Colonist*, who expressed outrage at the treatment the town received from government. De Cosmos was one of the more colourful characters in early British Columbia history. Born William Alexander Smith in Nova Scotia, he arrived in Victoria with the gold prospectors from California. After changing his name, he began his own newspaper to fight perceived corruption, encroachment of American interests, and the excesses of the HBC, taking particular aim at Governor James Douglas and his patronage appointments. Within a few years he sold his interest in the newspaper to David William Higgins and in 1863 became a member of the Legislative Assembly of Vancouver Island. It was in this capacity that he made a trip from Victoria to Nanaimo and Comox in 1865. He wanted to "acquaint himself with the state of the road, the nature and appearance of the country through which it passes, and to gather any and all information he could."[22]

At his stop in Nanaimo, a public dinner was given in his honour in the Institute Hall, to which 40 guests were invited. By all accounts, he delivered his usual colourful speech, attacking the policies of the House of Assembly and supporting more representation from outlying districts. The event attracted many of the leaders in the community. There were many speeches and toasts, by Bate, Dunsmuir, and others. After all the toasts it is reasonable to assume everyone was feeling very good for there were more songs, speeches and more volunteer toasts. "The party, after spending a very agreeable evening, broke up at an advanced hour."[23] De Cosmos continued on his journey up island to Comox, no doubt buoyed by the favourable response he had received in Nanaimo.

Any angst about the lack of progress on an improved road connection to Victoria may have been directed toward the local representative in the House of Assembly of Vancouver Island, David Babington Ring, who was elected in 1861, pledging to work toward a road to Victoria. His lack of success in this did not endear him to his constituents in Nanaimo.

Miners in Nanaimo were more concerned about earning a living and feeding their families than they were about politics, and the political will to build that road would have had to come from their midst. The very nature of the early settlers in Vancouver Island's two major towns differed. Nanaimo was mainly a community of labourers, miners from Britain, while in Victoria, from an early stage the HBC had attracted a middle class elite. Opportunities for professional or business enterprise in the early days of Nanaimo were limited. But it was the mining community that had the biggest payroll—"Pay Sheet City," as Bate often called it, which kept the early colony afloat; clearly Nanaimo wanted a share of the wealth. Some historians have suggested if the road to Victoria had been constructed at that time, it is unlikely Dunsmuir would have received the Esquimalt and Nanaimo Land Grant.

7

CHANGING
TIMES

AFTER COMMITTING HIS FIRST MARRIAGE to the history
books, Charles Nicol entered into a second marriage, with
Maria Aspinwall on September 2, 1861, in Victoria. The couple
would have seven children, four born in Nanaimo.[1]

A RAILWAY AND A LOCOMOTIVE

As his family settled into life in Nanaimo, Nicol began upgrading
and modernizing the Vancouver Coal Company operation. The
first railroad, a horse-drawn affair running on wooden rails covered by metal straps, was replaced by steel rails, a locomotive,
and new pumping machinery. The director's fourth report, dated
November 29, 1864, mentions that "2 iron barges, fails, one more
(6 hp) locomotive, and ironwork for 40 additional waggons" had
been supplied at Nicol's request.[2] The locomotive was named the
Pioneer and came complete with its own engineer, Harry Cooper,
and fireman, Thomas E. Peck, the first two railway men west of

Canada West (soon to be called Ontario). Nicol improved the coal wharf. The locomotive proved its worth and decreased the cost of handling the coal. It could pull 12 wagons at a time over an elevated bridge onto the new wharves, which allowed several ships to be loaded at a time. The London directors were so pleased they added new rails and more equipment, and in 1866 a second locomotive arrived from England. It was given the name *Euclawtaw*, after a First Nation group from Campbell River.

Before these improvements, shipping delays had been a reality. The old wharf had extended less than 200 feet from shore, which meant that only one ship (or two sloops) could be loaded at a time. No chutes or ramps existed, and all coal had to be shovelled into the holds of ships by dockside labour. After the introduction of the new railway system, however, each car passed over the scales on the wharf then was tipped into a chute, shooting the coal into the hold of the waiting ship. Another problem that had caused delays was the way in which vessels approached and left the dock, especially at low tide; ship captains invariably had to call for a tow, a task usually performed with rowboats manned by labourers. By 1863 Nanaimo showed a glimmer of the future success it would enjoy from the coal industry. Records show that 353 ships plus 71 Royal Navy steamers loaded over 8,700 tons of coal here during that period. The next year, over 15,500 tons were shipped, a big improvement over the previous six months.[3]

Even at this early date, coal from Nanaimo attracted attention around the world, particularly Russia. In 1864, the Russian steamship *Prince Constantine* took 350 tons to Sitka as a trial shipment. This was followed by news that a large Russian ship was being refitted for the purpose of proceeding to Nanaimo for a cargo of coal.

Nicol began reshaping the harbour. With permission from Governor Douglas he began filling the space between the mine and a small wharf leading shoreward from Cameron Island. On

April 14, 1864 he constructed a new wharf, 200 by 500 feet, along the southwestern shore. Since a considerable amount of ballast was needed as underfill, Nicol proposed driving parallel lines of "iron and coppered" piles joined by "grid iron" to prevent the landfill from slipping into and contaminating the harbour.[4] He also received permission to build a 250-foot wharf on Vancouver Coal Company property at Pimbury Point, in Departure Bay.

BRYDEN SENT TO DEVELOP MINES

Management got a boost to its team in 1863 when the directors in the London office hired John Bryden, aged 30, to work as a "coal viewer" for £300 a year. The company hoped he would provide Nicol with the expertise needed to develop the mines. Bryden was born in Dalzellyie, Ayrshire, Scotland. In 1862 he earned a second-class certificate in mining and metallurgy from the Society for the Encouragement of Arts, Manufactures, and Commerce, after attending night classes at the Andersonian Institution in Glasgow.[5] In Nanaimo, he began to work under Robert Dunsmuir, the superintendent of mine operations. This was the beginning of a long association between the two men, and the start of a difficult relationship with Mark Bate. This triumvirate held the power of the coal industry in the Nanaimo area for two decades.

With competent staff taking care of company business, Nicol began taking an interest in community life. In 1864, he was appointed justice of the peace for Nanaimo, an unpaid position. The following year he was appointed to the Vancouver Island Legislative Council, a duty that required him to spend considerable time in Victoria.

TOWN LOTS

The Vancouver Coal Company's long-range plan involved not only the coal operation but also investments in its land holdings and other commercial opportunities as they arose. In 1863, it set apart

500 acres for a town site. Two plans were designed for the town site, one by Robert Homfray and one by Andrew Hood, showing streets, residential lots, squares, and park-like areas. Hood's plan was accepted as the official map of the town and was duly deposited in the Land Registry Office in Victoria.[6]

The streets were named after Vancouver Coal Company's directors, HBC employees, royalty, local dignitaries, and political appointees. The unique design showed streets radiating westward from the harbour in a fan-like manner, rather than the usual square grid of most towns. The company wanted to first test the value of its land in Nanaimo, so they displayed the plan in Victoria in May 1864.[7] One hundred lots were sold by auction, then another public sale was held in Nanaimo for its employees. The proceeds from the sales were credited to the £14,000 mortgage held by the HBC. The sales clearly demonstrated that the Vancouver Coal Company's real estate alone, without its coal, would eventually help balance the purchase price.

At the sale in Nanaimo, conducted by Magistrate William Hales Franklyn, Bate paid $80 for a lot at Wesley and Franklyn Streets.[8] Nicol bought farmland, lots 2, 3, and 4, located at Pine and Comox Streets, valued at $100, $80, and $70. His 160-acre farm had 32 acres under cultivation, and employed three labourers and several casual workers to grow vegetables, potatoes, and barley and take care of the livestock.[9] John Meakin was one of the first miners to buy a lot—lot 16, on Esplanade—for which he paid $100. This lot later became part of Sam Robin's gardens. Meakin built another home at Prideaux and Albert Streets. Nicolas Jones paid $50 for lot 8 on Comox Road, and William Copperman bought two properties, lot 5 at Albert and Selby for $175, and lot 15 on Albert Street for $62.50.[10]

The Vancouver Coal Company noted that the sale of the town lots was another "proof of the confidence entertained in the future prospect of this Colony."[11] The sale netted the Vancouver Coal

Company $21,076. The second sale in Nanaimo gave miners the opportunity to own their own property. Come election time, Bate, Nicol, and Meakin, and other local property owners would have a vote in the future of their community.

There is little doubt that the people of Nanaimo felt neglected by the authorities in Victoria. In 1865, just before the union of the two colonies, revenue from Nanaimo was estimated at $12,000, of which $7,472 remained after all expenses were met.[12] The colonies were on the verge of bankruptcy. British Columbia's debt was just over a million dollars, and Vancouver Island's stood at $293,698.[13] In May, the Bank of British Columbia refused loans to the government in New Westminister, and the Bank of British North America cut off credit for the government in Victoria. The union of the two colonies seemed in the best interests of both. While the two had a war of words over union, the people of Nanaimo were focused inward—on the possibility of incorporation.

NEWSPAPERS

Bate and a group of his friends and associates began publishing the town's first community newspaper, the *Nanaimo Gazette*, in 1865. Joseph McClure was the first managing editor. The board of directors of the Nanaimo Publishing Company Ltd. included Bate, Charles Nicol, H.W. Alexander, Thomas Cunningham, and Charles Alport, as secretary.[14] Although the first editorial of the fledgling newspaper promised to be independent, it clearly voiced the views held by the management of the Vancouver Coal Company. When Bate was interviewed by a news reporter later in life, he recalled,

> I was in the newspaper business with three of my friends, and we established the "Nanaimo Gazette" located on Bastion Street. The old building had been erected in 1852 and was the home of Jesse Sage where he and his family lived until moving into a much larger

house. The paper unfortunately lasted for about six months before it folded, and the four of us lost money in the venture. The Sage home was used as a Recreation Centre, chess and reading room before we moved in.[15]

Bate loved to write and would have relished the experience of supervising the editorial department and voicing opinions about local and provincial affairs. The *Gazette* took aim at the colonial government. It complained about the lack of funds for local improvements, and spoke out against the main issue of the day— Nanaimo incorporation. Not everyone agreed with the editorials, which were seen by some influenced by ties with the Vancouver Coal Company, and demanded the paper sever its connections. This would have been difficult to do, considering advertising in the small community would never keep up with the costs of running the newspaper. The *British Colonist* weighed in, suggesting perhaps the paper was "too honest for the upper ten of the busy hamlet!" The *Gazette* editor, Joseph McClure, was under economic pressure and in June 1866 the newspaper was sold. It emerged later as the *Nanaimo Tribune* when Bate joined McClure as part owner. However, like its predecessor, it lasted only a year. Nanaimo did not yet have the population to make a newspaper viable.

THE QUESTION OF INCORPORATION

Should Nanaimo incorporate and become a municipality? New Westminster had incorporated in 1860, and Victoria in 1862. The *British Colonist* of September 6, 1865, posed the question in an editorial:

There is no earthly reason why every community on the island possessing a few hundred people should not govern itself. We feel certain Nanaimo would be none the worse for having municipal privileges and the present magistracy represented by a Mayor

Chairman of Town Council. A saving of some money and of considerable discontent would be the result.

A property holder in Nanaimo who responded suggested the editorial expressed the sentiments of the majority of property holders in
town. The response revealed the discontent with the local state of
affairs, including the condition of the streets and the incompetence
of the government's representative:

> There is no earthly use in breaking one's neck on a dark night
> by tumbling over obstructions in our so-called streets, and one
> portion of our town divided from the other by a ravine, impassable
> at high tides. We want our taxes appropriated to better advantage
> than paying large salaries to useless officials and their satellites
> who are only dead weight on the prosperity of the town.[16]

Now that the question of incorporation had been thrown open
for public discussion, the community was divided on the issue.
Those in favour hoped for a better form of government. Two fac-
tions were opposed. One was the management of the Vancouver
Coal Company, which did not want to relinquish control of the
settlement. The other faction feared incorporation would end
up curtailing some of the less than legal activities they currently
enjoyed with impunity.

In February of 1866, John Bryden chaired one of the largest
public meetings ever held in Nanaimo. Those who attended
favoured incorporation, as did Bryden. A petition was considered
unnecessary and a resolution was approved. Nanaimo's representative in the Legislative Assembly, Thomas Cunningham, then
presented a Bill of Incorporation, which would levy property taxes
on local homeowners. On March 29, the Vancouver Island House of
Assembly passed a bill for the incorporation of Nanaimo, which was
then sent to the Legislative Council, where it passed first reading.[17]

Some who opposed the proposal held an irreverent funeral for the bill, which a letter writer decried:

> One reverend gentleman employed the occasion [of the public meeting] to give a severe rebuke to those who came to oppose the object of the meeting—and who had been engaged on Saturday night last, in a mock procession to inter the Incorporation Bill. Those parties attending this procession, and composed almost entirely of the lawless and disorderly portion of our community who supply the poor natives with the cup of death and destruction concluded their diabolical mummery with the most impious desecration of the funeral ritual of the Church of England rehearsing that solemn service with wanton buffoonery.[18]

The legislature received a second petition claiming the previous one was false and had contained names of people in the United States and England. The government struck a committee to investigate allegations brought against the opponents. While it decided the charges were unfounded, it also decided that no adequate case had been made for incorporation and that the central government could continue to deal with the town's requirements. The bill's second reading was postponed, tabled for future consideration.[19] The incorporation movement was defeated.

Bate opposed incorporation from the beginning, and used his voice in the *Nanaimo Gazette* to make his point. On May 19, 1866, he presented the history of the question, noting that if the Legislative Council wanted to throw out the bill they would have found a way to do it. His editorial stated the Vancouver Coal Company opposed incorporation and that municipal institutions "could not be granted until the value of the property owned by the petitioners was greater than that owned by the Company," suggesting that had incorporation been realized in 1864 when town lots were put on the market, the results of the auction might have been different.

Nicol, who had originally helped draft the bill for incorporation, had changed his mind, believing it important to wait until the two colonies, Vancouver Island and the mainland area of British Columbia, were united. Since he represented the company, he held the largest vote. The company was in no hurry to relinquish its control of the town; it had only recently allowed private property ownership. For the time being, the issue of Nanaimo's incorporation was set aside.

CHANGES TO THE VANCOUVER COAL COMPANY

When Justice Haliburton died in 1865, the board of the Vancouver Coal Company changed. Charles W.W. Fitzwilliam, another MP, became chairman, and John Galsworthy his right-hand man. A new course would be set: no more lavish expenditures, only "judicious expenditure in the right direction."[20] The London office did not like what was happening to the bottom line of its coal operation in Nanaimo, and in 1866 hired former sawmill owner Captain Edward Stamp to investigate and forward his recommendations to the London office. A year later, John Wild, a company shareholder and later manager, was also sent to Nanaimo to investigate the "present condition and management" of the property.[21] Nicol was subsequently discharged. In November 1867, Fitzwilliam, as the board chairman, stated that Charles Nicol had retired from the company with £300 as compensation for loss of salary. He said, "The directors wished it to be distinctly understood that Nicol's services had been dispensed solely with the view to economy."[22] According to Galsworthy, Nicol owed his position to a former director (his brother James), "who had a good deal to do with the affairs of the Company and not to its advantage. That man's nominee had remained as financial agent (for the Vancouver Coal Company) at a salary of one thousand pounds a year. Financial agent, being another term for getting rid of money, that gentleman's services were dispensed with."[23]

By this time, Nicol had already left for San Francisco, where he remained until 1869, to head the British Columbia coal industry's first foreign sales office. He then travelled to Europe and worked in a variety of managerial positions in Portugal and Spain. He returned to London in May 1890 to live with family near Plymouth. After he unsuccessfully attempted to establish a coffee plantation in Nicaragua, he returned to California and spent his remaining years there with his son and daughter. He died in Mill Valley in October 1909 at the age of 79.

In the short time the family lived in Nanaimo, the Nicol family had earned the community's respect. Bate continued to keep in touch with Nicol.

8

BATE APPOINTED
MANAGER

IN 1867, AFTER BATE HAD been in the colony for ten years, he succeeded Nicol as manager of the Vancouver Coal Company. James Clarke Lawrence, Lord Mayor of the City of London, signed the official document appointing "Mark Bate of Nanaimo, in Vancouver Island, to conduct the commercial and financial affairs of the Vancouver Coal Mining and Land Company Limited." Samuel Robins and John Wild witnessed the document.[1]

COMPANY HIERARCHY AND COMPETITION

Bate now had to deal with the company hierarchy. He would come to know and respect the company agent, John Rosenfield (Rosy), of San Francisco, a shipping and commission merchant who had been responsible for much of the coal sales since 1863,[2] and Captain John Bermingham of San Francisco, who owned and operated the SS *Prince Albert*, running between San Francisco and Victoria.[3] There was yet another person in the mix: Samuel M. Robins, the secretary and principal administrative officer, located in the company's London headquarters. He was a man who could influence the minds of the directors about the colliery operation. Bryden took over as the superintendent of mine operations after Dunsmuir left the company in 1864.

The discovery of coal by Dr. Alfred Benson near Chase River, south of Nanaimo, in 1863, brought a new coal company into the industry. Benson applied to lease 3,000 acres but was informed he had first to form a company. But the lease terms were vague and he felt discouraged, until he found a partner with money to spend. He was the rich and eccentric Horace Douglas Lascelles, seventh son of the Earl of Harewood and heir to his family's Yorkshire estate, a commander of the Royal Navy's gunboat *Forward*, stationed at Esquimalt. Benson told him of his find and offered him a partnership. With the initial start-up money secured, the Harewood Coal Company was formed. The partners decided to buy the land outright, and Benson applied for 9,000 acres of land, south and west of the Vancouver Coal Company claim. They paid a dollar an acre, but the mineral rights were only good for 18 months; after that time, if the government was not satisfied, others could claim the rights to the coal. This land grant southwest of the city became known as the Harewood Estate. They decided to look for new investors.

Benson persuaded his friend Dunsmuir to leave his job with the Vancouver Coal Company to help them develop the new mine, in return for a share in the profits. He joined them in 1864 and within weeks found the outcrop of a workable seam. For a time it seemed like they had everything—the land, the money, and Dunsmuir's coal mining experience. The Harewood Coal Company then applied to the provincial government to build a railway to Departure Bay. The charter they received stated the line must be constructed by April 1866. The Vancouver Coal Company opposed the application because it granted Harewood a monopoly that included the "whole of the deepest and best water frontage at Departure Bay," frontage that had previously been granted to it. However, since it had not developed the land, the government felt justified in re-granting it to Harewood.[4]

Bate, writing in the *Gazette*, argued that the harbour in Nanaimo would be the better choice for a terminus. He suggested that "should Nanaimo, instead of Departure Bay become the terminus of the Harewood Railway, the benefits attendant upon a concentration of population and of wealth will be ours. Should the opposite course be decided upon the new settlement will be a great loser in many respects." He continued to suggest that churchgoers would find the distance to Nanaimo too great and schools would be difficult to reach. And there would be the expense and difficulty of crossing the "Big Swamp":

> Now is the time to make every effort in our power to induce the Harewood Company to abandon their purpose of carrying their railway to Departure Bay; and bring it into town, and use the Nanaimo Harbour as their shipping point. Could this be accomplished, the fact of Nanaimo becoming a town of some importance would almost be ensured.[5]

After a year, the Harewood Coal Company was deeply in debt. Dunsmuir quit and returned to the Vancouver Coal Company after reporting to Benson and Lascelles that their venture would never be a success unless they could build a railway to get the coal to the harbour at Departure Bay. To build it to the Nanaimo Harbour, the Vancouver Coal Company would have had to allow an easement through its land to the sea. When the railway was not built in the specified time, the Harewood Coal Company was granted an extension, but the line was never built.

Dunsmuir had learned a few lessons from this experience and no doubt took this knowledge into his next venture. Lascelles quit and then joined J.J. Southgate in real estate. When he died in 1869, the estate passed to his sister. Harewood was then leased to Captain Thomas A. Bulkley.

BATE AND COAL POLITICS

On February 18, 1873, Bate received a letter from the Vancouver Coal Company managing director, John Wild. His letter shows the warm association between the two men:

My dear Mr. Bate:

I reached England again after an absence at the Cape of Good Hope of nearly two years at the end of last month. I arrived alone only just in time to find my home desolate & myself a widower. I had hurried from my duties at the mines hearing of my wife's illness but by no means prepared for such catastrophe. The first intelligence I received was the sad event I now inform you of. I should certainly not have been here but for the summons I received unfortunately the medical men differed as to the care in treatment & I was told with the good intention of my friends not to become unnecessarily alarmed.

My present knowledge of the concern under your care is of course limited for I only attended the first board meeting a few days ago, but I was gratified at hearing back excellent accounts of the general position & working of the affairs out in the Pacific. I am pleased beyond measure at the assurances of all my colleagues of their complete satisfaction with your management & exertion. I consider that I have personally to thank you & I hasten to do so reserving all comments on events that have transpired until I become better posted up in them. I have the interests of the company very warmly at heart. Several of my family are shareholders . . .

I hope you have had your health amidst all your labours & anxiety & that you have been able to bring up your family in the way you would like. I beg to be remembered most kindly to

Mr. Alport whose clear elegant handwriting I admire . . . Mr. Nicol I understand has an appointment in Spain, but I have not yet seen any of his family. I will write again soon.

—John Wild[6]

Wild also wrote that he thought South Africa was unlikely to become a customer for coal and that "one day ship loads of 'Douglas Pines' would be better than anything presently being procured from the Baltic." This was a commodity that Nanaimo would in later years capitalize on, after the coal mines closed.

Bate kept a close eye on mining opportunities across Vancouver Island. On August 24, 1873, he reported to Wild:

There is great excitement among us just now about the discovery of whole mountains, the reports say, of iron ore on an Island near Comox. Some of the government officials are staking off claims, and a day or two ago the Lieut. Governor and four or five other gentlemen went to the island.[7]

The lieutenant governor at this time was Joseph William Trutch.

This was the beginning of the infamous Texada Island incident. It resulted in an inquiry that lasted months. A commission was established to look into suspicions that members of the government had attempted to acquire possession of all or part of Texada Island. The owner of the *British Colonist*, David William Higgins, may have added fuel to the scandal with his regular innuendo in the paper against his former colleague, Amor De Cosmos, and George A. Walkem, then premier of British Columbia, who both testified they were innocent.

Bate's interest may have been sparked by what he was hearing from London. He wrote to Higgins looking for information about the claims: "I hear from London that Mr. Sproat, the agent general of British Columbia is offering for sale Texada Iron Ore claims. Do

you know on whose account? I should like to ascertain."[8] Gilbert
Malcolm Sproat, the province's agent general in London, later told
the inquiry that he talked Texada Island up in London because it
was his job to promote BC.[9] On October 8, 1874, the commission
announced that it found no evidence of wrongdoing.

Bate wrote to Premier Walkem after hearing of his visit to
London and meeting with "our folks": "They would be glad to hear
your explanation of the Texada business, as far as I was mentioned
in connection with it, and I am obliged for your good words."[10]
Whatever knowledge Bate may have had about the incident, he never
disclosed. Some believed the commission was just a whitewash.

The ownership of the Harewood Mine continued to occupy
Bate's attention. He learned of Captain Thomas A. Bulkley's lease
of the Harewood Estate on April 8, 1874. In his monthly report to
Wild he mentioned he had heard that W.C. Ward had a share in
the concern, "which seems quite probable from his reference to
Mr. Bulkley in one or two letters he has written to me." Ward, the
manager of the Bank of British Columbia, had told Bate that when
Bulkley left for England, he had inquired if Wild was still in London.

Bate cautioned Wild about some question "affecting our mutual
interest" that Bulkley wanted to talk over: "I thought it might be well
to keep on terms with him as friendly as possible . . . and see how
Harewood will pan out, as the Gold diggers say."[11] Bulkley was invited
to call at the company office at No. 2 St. Mildred's Court, London.

Bulkley had to find a way to get the coal from the Harewood
Mine to tidewater. After a railway was ruled out, the decision
was made to build an innovative aerial tramway to carry the coal.
Bate was concerned about the encroachment on Vancouver Coal
Company lands from the route such a tramway might take. Initially,
he understood that Bulkley had planned to run a line from the mine
to the beach at the site of Bolton's marine ways at the mouth of
Millstone River. Bolton held three lots in Block 51 belonging to
the Bank of British Columbia, in the location of the present-day

Maffeo Sutton Park. Bate anticipated the discussion Bulkley might have with Wild and gave Wild some advice: "It maybe prudent to have in mind the probable relations the new firm may bear to us after a time, that is, the prospect of amalgamation, in some way, if Harewood should turn out well."[12]

Bulkley had contracted to tunnel in to see how much coal was present. A month later, he confided in Bermingham that the tunnel had turned out badly and said he had been "sadly beside the mark in his calculation of the output of coal. He had expected four tons for every yard of tunnel, but the contractors were already in one hundred and forty yards and had only turned out twelve tons of coal." The news about the mine did not get any better.

Unfortunately for Bulkley, the Harewood Mine turned out very badly indeed. He visited the mine where at first glance his men had met a face of coal four feet thick; he was "so elated that he treated them with a barrel of beer."[13] However, the day he left for Victoria the coal cut out, and none had been found since. Months later the mine was still at a standstill and the miners idle, although Bulkley still expected to get them working to prove, or cut through, the stone barrier. By September he began looking for another seam.

THE TRAMWAY

Writing in December to the land agent, H.F. Heisterman, in Victoria, Bate advised that the proposed Harewood aerial tramway would actually end at Nanaimo Harbour, not Departure Bay, as was first speculated: "We have had numerous enquiries about lots, in conveyance. The road it is thought will go between Dunsmuir's house and Victoria Crescent."[14] He told the land agent that the value of the land to Bulkley would have to be settled by arbitration, which he also told his directors. Bate intended to nominate Heisterman as the arbitrator, but the board named another person.

In April 1875 Wild approved the right-of-way through Vancouver Coal Company land. Bulkley had to pay more that he had calculated, but he seemed confident about the success of the tramway. Two months later, however, he had not paid a single installment on the land granted to him for the right-of-way. Bate complained, "We need the money badly just now. While shipments are small we have several extra demands coming upon us . . . duty on the Boring machine, municipal taxes, and government road tax still due."[15]

Bulkley's aerial tramway from the Harewood Estate and Mine is still remembered today, perhaps because of the method of getting the coal to the wharf at Cameron Island three miles (4.8 km) away. Four-legged tripods up to 50 feet (15.2 m) in height supported a cable powered by a donkey engine at the mine. Buckets of 200-pound (90 kg) capacity loaded with coal were attached to the cable that shuttled them to the waterfront for shipment, across Vancouver Coal Company land via Albert Street to Cameron Island. Despite the money invested, the tramway was plagued with equipment breakdowns.

The Harewood Mine would never be a paying proposition. Coal was only mined between 1876 and 1877 and sold locally. Bulkley abandoned the lease around 1878. The Bank of British Columbia sold the Harewood Estate and Mine to the Vancouver Coal Company on April 22, 1884. As Bate had earlier predicted, the two companies amalgamated. The tripods remained in place for another 12 years before the coal company had them removed.

THE DIAMOND BORING MACHINE

The much-anticipated diamond boring machine—the machine Bate mentioned in his complaint about the lack of payment from Bulkley—arrived in Nanaimo from England on October 13, 1875, after a six-month journey around Cape Horn, brought by John McKay, the engineer in charge. The machine, valued at $10,000, could sink a borehole in a coal seam in a few minutes. The machine was put on display on Esplanade for everyone to see.

After a few years Bate became a little exasperated with McKay.

"With no Diamond Boring going on Mr. McKay is next to a nuisance. Since the last bore was stopped, nearly a month and a half ago, he has been lounging. I hardly know what we can do with him."[16] The machine was apparently not difficult to handle, as others had run it at various times without McKay's expertise. Despite Bate's frustration with the operator of the machine, it proved a valuable asset to the company.

DUNSMUIR IN NANAIMO

Early buildings in Nanaimo were modest log cabins built by the first miners. Dunsmuir had occupied one on Front Street since his arrival in 1852. But with a growing family, he built a new home in 1858, a rustic log construction much grander than any of the miner's cottages, on the hillside at the corner of Albert and Wallace Streets. He named it Ardoon after a Scottish mansion in Dalmellington. The house was destroyed by fire in 1872 and rebuilt the following year even grander than the previous one, still with the same name. The new two-storey building had a deep verandah and delicate gingerbread clinging to its steeply pitched eaves. The house had a commanding view of the harbour and was surrounded by trees and shrubs, well tended by a Swedish gardener. Dunsmuir moved in with his wife, Joan, and five children. Their first two daughters, Elizabeth and Agnes, were born in Scotland; James was born in 1851 at Fort Vancouver, in Oregon Territory; and Alexander in 1853 and Marion in 1855, both in Nanaimo. His family was to grow by five more girls.

Bate and Dunsmuir had several things in common. They both had large families, they had worked in the mines back in their home countries, and they came to Nanaimo after an uncle signed with the HBC. Dunsmuir came with his uncle Boyd Gilmour, who had been hired in Scotland as a mine manager, and Bate came at the urging of his uncle George Robinson, the man hired to replace Gilmour. Bate's and Dunsmuir's paths crossed many times, through both their work in the mines and their involvement in the community.

9

A RENAISSANCE MAN

THE YEAR 1867, WHEN BATE became the manager of the Vancouver Coal Mine, was a pivotal year in the history of the province. The two colonies of Vancouver Island and British Columbia amalgamated on November 19, 1866, to alleviate financial difficulties, resulting in the unified Colony of British Columbia, with Frederick Seymour as premier. After a dustup between the two capital cities of New Westminster and Victoria for prominence, Victoria became the new colony's capital. About the same time, Ontario, Quebec, Nova Scotia, and New Brunswick joined together to form the Dominion of Canada. The British North America Act, as the Constitution Act was originally called, created the Government of Canada and was signed by Queen Victoria on March 29, 1867, and proclaimed on July 1. John A. Macdonald was the first prime minister. The question of joining the new dominion soon came to the west coast. British Columbia joined Confederation four years later, in 1871, but two other choices had been considered: remaining a British colony or annexation to the United States. It was clear where Nanaimo stood on the issue; it supported annexation with the United States because of the town's close connection with the United States as a trading partner. The Nanaimo *Tribune*, a reincarnation of the *Gazette*, saw the British connection as a "fast sinking ship," whereas the United States was a "gallant new craft, good and strong, close alongside, inviting us to safety and success."[1] For Victoria the choice was simpler, with its historic ties to the Crown and the benefits it could reap from Confederation.

BATE ON HALIBURTON STREET

After Bate was appointed manager, the family moved into the manager's house on Haliburton Street, previously occupied by Nicol. Nicknamed the "boarding house," it had originally been built for that function, but no one had managed to make a success of it. The Vancouver Coal Company converted it into offices and a residence for the manager.

Bate now had six children, ranging in age from one to nine years; the two latest had been born in the years prior to their move: George Arthur, born April 18, 1865, and Lucia (Lucy) on November 18, 1866. Their new home was a large building, over 80 feet long.[2] They lived at one end, and the other end housed the company offices. Bate described how warm the place was; every wall of the part where they lived, "between the inside plastering and weather-boarding, was filled to the eves with sawdust to keep away the rats. The warmth of the rooms in winter was thus ensured."[3] Next door were the three Richardson cabins, one occupied by Richard and Elizabeth Richardson, former residents of Dudley. Opposite the boarding house were the homes of Sam Fiddick, Ambrose Fletcher, Robert Dunblane, and James Miller, whose orchard tempted many young people in the neighbourhood.

Haliburton Street was one of the main streets in town, straight as an arrow and perfect for horse racing, a regular community event. Many of the miners relished gambling, and races of any kind were the focus of attention at most summer events. Prize money in the hundreds of dollars drew competitors and punters from as far afield as Portland, Oregon.[4] Judging took place on the convenient balcony of George Baker's Dew Drop Inn that overlooked the finish line. While the town may have been isolated, its distance from the larger centre of Victoria seemed to foster a greater community spirit, particularly evident during sporting events such as horse racing, soccer, and cricket.

When the summer weather came along, opportunities for work stoppages abounded, such as on May 24, the queen's birthday, which certainly held more significance for the British settlers than Dominion Day, which also marked the anniversary of British Columbia's entry into Confederation: in some minds that was a forced marriage of convenience. Residents also had no trouble joining their American friends in celebrating July 4, Independence Day; ties to the United States were strong. Miners claimed unofficial holidays as well, such as "Saint Mondays," also called "Blue Mondays," the first Monday after being paid. The miners of British Columbia continued this tradition that had apparently begun in the Black Country of England, where many miners, including Bate, hailed from.[5] Festivals and holidays were also an excuse to drink, one of the most popular social activities in early Nanaimo. Payday was incomplete without a visit to one of the saloons.

On the family front, Bate kept in close touch with his sister Elizabeth and her husband, Adam Grant Horne, who lived in Fort Simpson from 1864 to 1867, after Adam rejoined the HBC. Elizabeth gave birth to Lucy and Sarah, the first white children born at Fort Simpson. Lucy died in childhood. The family moved to Comox, then largely undeveloped, where the HBC operated a trading store. Four more children were born, Herbert, Tom, Emily, and David. David died at age six. Another child, also named Lucy, was born in 1875 in Nanaimo, but died at age five. The oldest son, Adam Henry, often visited his Uncle Mark and Aunt Sarah on holidays, and formed a close friendship with his cousins. Although the Horne family lived many miles north of Nanaimo, the family connection remained strong.

LABOUR ISSUES

Nanaimo was in the unique position of having the only mining operation on Vancouver Island engaged in the export of coal. The Vancouver Coal Company's coal and its facilities for shipping it became well known and appreciated. The directors in London and their shareholders congratulated themselves on the progress being made with their fledgling company. Nicol had done a good job of improving working conditions, and with the addition of the locomotives, the cost of loading and shipping was reduced. A railway line extended from the Park Head Slope to the coal jetty at the foot of Wharf Street. Despite all these improvements the shareholders in London were still not satisfied with the financial returns of the coal operation.

As the industry grew, so too did the need for skilled and unskilled labour. The government hoped that reports of poverty in Nanaimo would not get out to the rest of the world and drive potential settlers away. Workers received monthly regular wages, and promptly, but it was a long time from one month to the next. Additional miners were also hired for a dollar a day when the mines needed more workers, a decision approved by John Wild, managing director of the Vancouver Coal Company in London. The average wage was $2.33 for a ten-hour day based on a six-day week. A skilled worker could earn $3.50 per day, though the rate also fluctuated based on the quality of the seam they were working on. When the seam began to dwindle, as it often did in the changeable geology of the Nanaimo area, the mine would pay daily rates instead of piecemeal, in an effort to keep the men happy.[6] Miners unwilling to take a cut in pay when piecemeal rates dropped were denied access to the best spots in the mines.[7] Some workers could not keep up with living costs. Merchants had to offer credit, or no business could be done. Some workers who came to Nanaimo had no intention of settling. The steady supply of ships in the harbour delivered a number of unscrupulous itinerant workers who came and went.

The first record of Chinese living in Nanaimo was in 1867 when in May the *Daily British Colonist* in Victoria reported, "Considerable excitement, we hear, exists at Nanaimo on consequence of the introduction of Chinese borers. The colliers threaten with violence the first Chinaman who forgets his Celestial origin so far as to descend to the 'bottom pit' of a coal mine."[8] In 1869 the province's Ministry of Mines recorded 36 Chinese workers in Nanaimo.[9] Bryden kept a close eye on them and soon found out the newcomers learned quickly and worked hard. However, the community viewed them with suspicion, as they spoke a different language and wore different clothes, and miners viewed them as a threat to their jobs, causing discontent throughout the industry. When the mines began sending Chinese labourers underground, they were replacing local teenaged boys who were contributing to their family income.

COAL SHIPS

A few of the ships that docked in the harbour to load coal on a regular basis were the *Arkwright*, the *Emma*, the *Maude*, the *Otter*, the *Prince Alfred*, and the *Panther*. The last two ships met an untimely end. On January 21, 1874, Bate had a full load of coal—1,750 tons—ready for the *Panther*. There was about two feet of snow on the ground and it was bitterly cold. By the time the coal had been loaded and the ship was about to leave for San Francisco, the wind had picked up and was "a perfect hurricane. Trees were toppled over by the dozen, and I thought the House was going down. I never remember anything like it," Bate recalled. The *Panther*, being towed by the steamship *Goliah*, got caught in the winds in Trincomali Channel between Galiano Island and Saltspring Island. In zero visibility and blinding snow, the *Goliah* had to cut itself free to save herself. When they were able to look for the *Panther*, there was no sign of the ship, and *Goliah's* captain reported the loss of the *Panther* and its crew. Meanwhile, the *Panther* blew across Trincomali Channel, and was wrecked off Wallace Island.[10] According to Bate, attempts were made to float her, but she was abandoned as a total wreck.[11]

Some parts of the ship were salvaged. Later in November Bate complained about the cable, riggings, and other items from the *Panther* cluttering up the company's wharf. He said the pier was completely "encumbered up with the articles," and demanded they be removed immediately. He had been assured that arrangements would be made to send them by the first San Francisco–bound ship. Within a month they were removed off the wharf.[12]

The same year, another cargo/passenger steamer of concern to Bate, which regularly called into Nanaimo, also foundered. The *Prince Alfred* struck Duxbury Reef, about a mile (2 km) west of Bolinas in Marin County on California's north central coast, in foggy weather and became waterlogged. All the crew and passengers landed safely. The steamer had been on its way from Victoria to San Francisco, loaded with coal, wood, charcoal, hides, and gold (valued at $24,127).[13] The wreck could not be saved and the ship sank. The last time the ship was in Nanaimo was in June 1874, when it loaded coal from the Fitzwilliam Mine on Newcastle Island. Bate expressed his concern to Captain Bermingham in San Francisco about the "disaster of the *Prince Alfred*." Rosenfeld had told Bate the steamer was only partially insured. Bate expressed his concern for Bermingham,"whether you are a great loser by the wreck or not . . . I trust some good friend will have a boat at your service to carry out the mail contract."[14]

Bate was a renaissance man. His passion for reading, writing, and music lasted throughout his lifetime. In 1864 he organized the Nanaimo Philharmonic Orchestra Society with a few miners who had musical talent and instruments. The musicians included himself and Thomas McLean on violin, Thomas Hindle on cornet, Joseph Lawlese on flute, the local blacksmith, John Holden, on violincello, and Thomas Parker on piano. The orchestra gave its first concert in the Institute Hall in December 1865. The community welcomed this sextet of amateur musicians during community events. Over time others joined the group and strengthened its musical repertoire.

In the summer of 1872, Bate formed the Junior Brass Band, supported by St. Paul's rector, Reverend James Raynard, the mine surgeon Dr. Wm. MacNaughton-Jones, and John Holden. Bate was able to purchase instruments from Messrs Boosey and Sons for $300. The band first performed at Queen Victoria's birthday celebrations, on May 24, 1873. The president was Reverend Raynard, "a high class musician" who had been choirmaster of Yorkminster Cathedral, in England. He left to take a position as rector of Saanich, but planned to return periodically. Unfortunately, his health failed and after a brief illness he died. Bate took over as president and conductor of the band. He managed to keep the band alive with his sons Mark, Jr., and Thomas, and other players such as Joseph Randle, the brothers John and Thomas Morgan, and David Nebb. The bandstand erected in Dallas Square was well used for evening concerts in the summertime.

Bate was pleased with the group, as is evident in a letter he wrote in 1873 to his friend, David Pearce, in Brierley Hill, England:

"I am still in the music line—as fond of it as ever. We have a fine band here of 24 performers beside drums (4) and cymbals. I play a cornet that is in the band. I stick to the violin too, and a few of us spend two or three evenings a week playing to amuse ourselves."[15]

Occasionally when the *Arkwright* was in the harbour loading coal, its skipper, Captain Harris, joined the group. Bate missed him after he relinquished his command of the ship. The new captain was "not very fond of music, and no musician in any sense of the word," wrote Bate to Captain Harris.

> You, no doubt, like myself will have your fill of singing and playing at home among the little ones, and you will have opportunities of listening to a class of music superior to anything we can look at here. I must confess I should dearly like to be in a place where I could sit and listen two or three nights a week to first class vocalists and instrumentalists, but that time I imagine is not near at hand so I content myself with such "treats" as we get up among ourselves.[16]

The brass band became the Silver Cornet Band in 1889, and continues to perform today as the Nanaimo Concert Band.

COMMUNITY GROUPS

Bate's love of music extended into his association with Freemasonry. He described it as "an efficient and powerful factor in the development of intellectual faculties, steering the mind with useful and valuable knowledge."[17] The Nanaimo Masons formed in 1865 with Bate, Franklyn, a few other local men, and several naval officers. Meetings were first held in a house on Cavan Street rented for $25 a month. The group petitioned the Grand Lodge of England for a warrant for a new lodge to be established in Nanaimo, but that warrant got lost with the sinking of the San Francisco mail steamer *Brother Jonathan*, which wrecked on an uncharted rock off the coast of Crescent City, California, on July 30, 1865. The ship carried 244 passengers and crew with a large shipment of gold. Only 19 people survived the wreck. A duplicate document was duly sent and the Nanaimo Lodge inauguration took place on May 14, 1867. Bate and Franklyn were charter members of Lodge No. 1909.

Bate described the opening of the lodge:

> The ceremonial connected with the opening of the lodge was
> grand. The spectacle of Grand Lodge Officers in dazzling splendour
> of their Regalia, then now, with showy silk banner, in procession
> from the lodge room to St. Paul's Church was witnessed with
> admiration by nearly the whole population of the place—then a
> mere mining hamlet.[18]

The Caledonia Lodge formed about the same time but according
to the Scottish style of Masonry rather than the English style. For
the first two years the master was S.D. Levi, followed by William
Stewart then John Renwick. It was not until 1873 that the two
lodges began to talk about a possible amalgamation. The idea took
root and resulted in the formation of the Ashar Lodge. Money was
raised to construct a building, and each lodge pledged $162.50 to
buy the site on Commercial Street on land once owned by Joseph
Webb. The foundation stone was laid on October 15, 1873, and
the lodge building opened the following year. The building that
occupies that site now was constructed in 1923. Some alterations
to the building have been made over the years. The Ashlar Lodge
remains today part of Nanaimo's built heritage.

Bate was instrumental in getting a new organ for the lodge.
Using his connections with the coal company, he asked company
agent Captain John Bermingham, in San Francisco, if he would
purchase a "Mason & Hamelin [sic] Harmonium for the Masonic
Lodge here, of which I am organist."[19] He wanted the best instrument he could get for $85.00. No harmoniums were available in
Nanaimo, and he hoped Bermingham could get a good price. He
suggested Bermingham might ship the instrument on the *Shooting
Star* when it next came to Nanaimo.

The harmonium duly arrived in Nanaimo: "The instrument
is safely at hand, and will, I doubt not, give every satisfaction. I

am sure the members will gladly make up the $8.50 because the instrument will be superior to anything we expected to get for $93.50."[20] He thanked Bermingham for not charging for freight.

Bate was also active in six "friendly societies" or benevolent associations such as the Ancient Order of Foresters (AOF), the Ancient Order of United Workman, the Independent Order of Odd Fellows (IOOF), the American Legion of Honour, the United Ancient Arch of the Druids, and American Legion of Honor. The Nanaimo *Free Press*, (April 16) listed 16 such organizations in town in 1889. These friendly societies, formed to be of mutual benefit to members, originated in Great Britain, for the most part, and the early miners brought them to Nanaimo. The Ancient Order of United Workmen and the American Legion of Honor were founded in the United States. These societies provided an outlet for social activities such as picnics, sports competitions, concerts, and dances. They also existed largely to mitigate the financial trauma of suddenly losing a breadwinner. These were the days before unemployment insurance, pension plans, or welfare, when people banded together to help each other.

The AOF in Nanaimo was instituted June 30, 1875, under the name of Court Nanaimo Foresters' Home, No. 5886. Many prominent men in Nanaimo's history served as officers and "passed through the Chairs," among them Bate, James Knight, Joseph Randle, Lawrence Manson, and Ralph Smith. The first Foresters' Hall, built on Commercial Street, was destroyed by fire and replaced by another. The AOF played an important role in providing insurance against industrial accidents:

Premiums in the late 1880s ran from $10 for twenty-year-old subscribers to a maximum of $45 for 40-year-olds. When a member of the local lodge suffered burns from an explosion in one of the mines in 1885, the AOF agreed to pick up his nursing bill: twenty-one days of attention and support cost the order

$52.50, the equivalent of at least half a month's wages. A single fatality two years later cost the AOF $1,000 in benefits paid to a miner's widow.[21]

Widowhood was a common occurrence, as was being left an orphan.

The Ancient Order of United Workmen, Nanaimo Lodge, was instituted on March 19, 1881 with 34 charter members, including Bate. The Nanaimo Lodge and Perseverance Lodges were amalgamated on August 1, 1890, into Nanaimo Lodge No. 53.

The IOOF Black Diamond Lodge No. 5 was instituted April 7, 1874, the year the city incorporated. The lodge first met in a two-storey building at the corner of Bastion and Commercial Streets, where the Royal Bank now stands. After meeting there for a few years, the lodge purchased the Odd Fellows Block in March 1878 and built another two-storey building, which later became the Fletcher Music store. The IOOF was founded to give aid, assistance, and comfort to its members and their families. They also did charitable and volunteer work.

Bate valued his association with the benevolent societies and enjoyed the friendship and social interaction of their membership.

10

TENSIONS
RISE

OPINIONS VARY AS TO THE effectiveness of Bate's management style. From the beginning of his association with Bryden, the two did not agree on how to manage the workforce.

MANAGEMENT STYLES

Bryden was admired by those who worked under him. The company in London hired a mining engineer, Edward Gawler Prior, and sent him out to work with Bryden, the mine supervisor. After Bryden's death in 1915, Prior conveyed his esteem of the man, based on his memory of when they first met:

> Standing well over six feet tall, straight as an arrow, with magnificent chest and shoulders, hair and closely cropped beard as black as a raven, and with eyes of piercing brightness but kindly withal, I thought here indeed is, and he was, a born leader of strong men. For five years and more I was with him every day underground in the

mines and around the works, and the longer I knew him the more I came to see what a splendid character he was. Utterly fearless where duty called, he never asked a man to go where he would not himself lead, and no one who has not lived underground in a colliery can have any conception of the daily risks to life and limb that such a life entails. He was an efficient, just and kind manager and held the respect and esteem of every man working under him.[1]

Bate and Bryden came to know and respect Prior, who was to become premier of the province. Prior was born in Yorkshire, England and was educated at Leeds Grammar School. He articled with an engineering firm in Wakefield, where he qualified as a mining engineer. Bate hoped Prior brought a few years' experience in mine work, though Bate did not know the length of Prior's contract, and he mused, "He will, no doubt, be found very useful, and of no small service in keeping surveys up to the mark." After only a month on the job, he thought Prior was "an exceedingly useful man here." Bryden helped Prior become familiar with the mining operation. The young man seemed willing and anxious to do anything in his power, but Bate concluded after a year that he lacked experience and understanding.[2]

Bryden was also described as a hard-liner who treated the men firmly. He would dismiss anyone who complained about wages or working conditions, and he did not like making concessions, believing they led to greater demands.[3] Bate, however, refuted his decisions and argued with him openly, which undermined Bryden's authority as mine supervisor.

SUSPICIONS

The tension between Bate and Bryden increased following Bryden's marriage to Robert Dunsmuir's daughter Elizabeth on August 27, 1866.[4] While the two men's relationship was first strained over the running of the mine, Bate became suspicious about his mine superintendent's decisions and his close association with the Dunsmuir family after Dunsmuir became a competitor in the mining industry. Bryden in turn became frustrated by Bate's increasing interest in civic affairs.

Bate and Sarah added more children to their family, bringing the total to ten. Life could not have been easy for Sarah, caring for the children while her husband was busy with work and other commitments, but she had some help from a Chinese cook/domestic named Ling Ah.[5] Her domestic situation would have been slightly different from that of Joan Dunsmuir, who also had ten children, but in addition to a Chinese cook, she also had an English parlour maid and the Swedish gardener. There may well have been some personal rivalry between the two families, that, however innocent, would have contributed to the strained relations between Bate and Dunsmuir's new son-in-law.

DUNSMUIR'S COAL

While Bate and Bryden were busy managing the Vancouver Coal Company, Dunsmuir continued to explore the countryside around the company's land, looking for an elusive coal outcropping. Many stories abound about his discovery of coal in the Wellington area near Diver Lake. These tales have survived several generations. His find may, however, be less to do with happenstance and more to do with following a map.

In the early 1980s, a local man, Arthur Leynard, investigated the mystery of what led Dunsmuir to Diver Lake in the first place. He found an 1860 map of the area, published in Victoria by Rudolph d'Heureuse, a mining engineer and surveyor, showing the subdivisions in the districts of Cedar, Cranberry, and Mountain. The map indicated rocky ledges at the foot of Little Mountain, and written next to the rock ledge symbols was the comment, "Coal crops out in many places of this district." The location of these ledges was about two miles from the waterfront. The map would have been available to Dunsmuir. Leynard theorized, "If he followed the general line of the ledges to the northwest, parallel to and about two miles from the waterfront, he eventually would have reached the Diver Lake area. He would also have followed that alignment by the outcrop on the south bank of Chase River and by the early Harewood prospect."[6]

Through hard work and determination, Dunsmuir's long search finally paid off. In October 1869, he found the coal seam that was to make him rich. His friends William Isbister and James Hamilton helped uncover and prove the worthiness of the seam, but their names would be only a footnote in the history of the Wellington coal mine.

Dunsmuir was not a rich man at this time, and he lacked the capital to start a mine. He obtained his first financing at a high rate of interest from Captain Bermingham and John Rosenfeld, the two San Francisco businessmen he knew from his work with the Vancouver Coal Company. Bermingham was an American pioneer mariner and supervising inspector of steam vessels in Pacific waters, who began his career with the Pacific Mail Steamship Company as an engineer, the first company to buy coal from Fort Rupert. In 1867 he was superintendent of the Holiday line of ocean-going steamships.[7] Rosenfeld was not only the agent in San Francisco for the Vancouver Coal Company, as a wholesale coal dealer, but president of John Rosenfeld Sons Inc., shipping and commission merchants in San Francisco.[8]

By 1870 Dunsmuir had already spent $11,500 and was refused a land grant of one thousand acres until he could produce evidence of a financially sound company. Unknown to him, he was sitting on one of the largest coal deposits in the area and lacking funds to proceed must have been frustrating. He was reluctant to form a company or take in partners, but when Lieutenant Wadham N. Diggle was willing to invest $8,000, Dunsmuir made him a silent partner. Remembering how the Harewood Mine was financed, Dunsmuir also sought help from two other naval officers he knew, Rear Admiral

Arthur Farquhar and Captain F.W. Egerton. With the help of these three men, plus his two sons, Alex and James, Dunsmuir secured the Crown grant. Now that Dunsmuir, Diggle and Company, as the new enterprise was called, were in business, the Vancouver Coal Company had real competition in the coal market for the first time. One of the first things the new company did was to build a narrow-gauge railway to transport the coal from the Wellington Mine to Departure Bay for shipping. The company also built a new wharf to accommodate steamships from the Pacific Mail Steamship Company, who had signed the first contract for Dunsmuir's coal.[9] He also formed a partnership with Henry Berryman of San Francisco to distribute Dunsmuir coal from his sales office there, and to charter ships to run between Golden Gate and Departure Bay.

STRIKE OVER CUT IN PAY

Nanaimo would experience many bitter strikes, but one of the first was during Bate's early years as manager, in October 1870. The strike was precipitated by the decision to cut the price per ton paid to the miners by "one bit," or 12 and a half cents. The price for coal in San Francisco had dropped, and the company could pay its shareholders only 15 per cent, compared to the previous year's 20 per cent. To replenish reserves, the board voted to cut the miner's wages. On October 3, the miners went on strike, and two days later those who loaded coal at the wharves joined them. Even the Chinese and the Snuneymuxw, who received lower wages, walked off the job. Bate waited anxiously for instructions from London. However, the board decided to hold its ground, and with tons of coal sitting on the dock, they felt they could afford to be firm.

Things turned ugly when a crude homemade bomb was hurled through a window in engineer Andrew Hunter's home. He was a target because he had been ordered by Bryden to keep the steam engine going to pump water from the Douglas Pit. Fortunately, the bottle failed to explode when the neck broke off.[10] The strike dragged on for several months. More threats were made and the non-striking employees became fearful. The provincial government proclaimed that all persons found using threats or force would be punished promptly and severely. The warship HMS *Sparrowhawk* was dispatched and remained in the harbour for several weeks, to be relieved by the HMS *Boxer*. In an altercation just prior to Christmas, a miner was stabbed and another seriously injured. During the winter, after the stores cut off all credit, the strikers nearly starved. Some dug for clams and went fishing. It seemed the only people working were the 50 quarrymen working at the Newcastle Island quarry, who gave $91.50 to needy families.

One man, Charles Montgomery Tate, a former engineer and later a Wesleyan lay preacher, worked at the mine in charge of one of the pithead engines. He recalled the search for food during the strike:

> During the winter we organized a begging party to wait on the few settlers on the various islands between Nanaimo and Victoria. We hired an old Indian named Kwal-a-kup, with his large war canoe, and picked up potatoes, and other vegetables, besides an occasional sack of flour, some groceries, salt meat, and other edibles.[11]

With enough coal stored at the docks to satisfy the needs of visiting ships, the company simply waited out the strike. Six months later, the miners finally accepted the reduction in wages. By that time the stockpile of coal was reduced considerably.

BC JOINS CANADA

In 1871, the time had come to make a decision about joining Canada. H.L. Langevin, the federal minister of public works, prepared a report about the social and economic state of British Columbia. The First Nations population was noticeably absent from his study, which revealed that

Nanaimo had 395 white males, 206 white females, 44 coloured males, 48 coloured females, 35 Chinese males and 1 Chinese female. There were 39 employed in agriculture, 22 in trading and 161 in mining. During that year there were 20 births, 5 deaths and 4 marriages.[12]

Many colonists living on Vancouver Island wanted the responsible government enjoyed by the other Canadian provinces, but others wanted no part of it. The strongest lines of communication on the west coast, developed over the years, ran north and south, not east and west. Prime Minister John A. Macdonald held out the promise of a trans-Canada railway like a carrot on the stick. On April Fools Day, 1871, the House of Commons approved British Columbia's entry into Confederation. Five days later, the Senate authorized the union, and on May 16, Queen Victoria gave her consent. On July 20, 1871, British Columbia became part of the Dominion of Canada. Confederation celebrations were fixed for July 1.

The *Sessional Papers* of that year reveal that under the Constitution Act, 1871, of British Columbia, the electoral district of Nanaimo comprised "the tract of land included in a circle with a radius of 17 miles from the Bastion in the City of Nanaimo, . . . and is allotted One Member of Parliament for its representation."[13] The Scottish born Robert Wallace, a Conservative, was the first Member of Parliament for the Vancouver riding (Vancouver Island) during the final months of the first Canadian Parliament, from December 15, 1871, to July 8, 1872. He did not run for reelection to the House of Commons in 1872.[14] Wallace was a commission merchant in Victoria and had served as alderman from 1863 to 1864. He returned to Scotland in 1887.

The next representative for the Vancouver Island riding was the Irish born Sir Francis Hincks. Another Irishman, Arthur Bunster, owner of the Colonial Brewery in Victoria, followed him in 1874. He was reelected in 1878 but was defeated in the 1882 election by David William Gordon, who was born in Upper Canada and settled in Nanaimo as an architect and builder. He served the community until 1893.

11

FAMILY
LETTERS

BATE MAINTAINED CLOSE TIES WITH his family back home in England by writing letters. Some of the letters written when he was manager of the Vancouver Coal Company have survived. They disclose the difficulties he experienced and the decisions he made as manager. They also reveal what was happening in his family life and provide a greater understanding of the man and his insecurities. Elevated into the position as manager without any managerial or business experience, he did what he thought was best for the company. He became friends with management and business associates and shared with them events about his family.

BATE'S MOTHER

When Bate's mother, Elizabeth, was 68, in 1873, he learned from her recent letter she had been unwell but that her health was improving. He expressed concern for her wellbeing and sent a sovereign to help her financially, assistance he hoped to increase in the weeks to come:

I know my dear mother that it must be an uphill work to get along comfortably as things are now at home, and I pray that you may be blest with strength to bear any privations to which you may be subjected . . . It would grieve me sorely to know that you suffered from anything I can provide. Thank God I am in a position to take care of you as far as money can do it, but what I send you I certainly hope will be applied in a proper way. I mean to keep you comfortable at your house. Get all the clothing you need and all that is necessary to eat and drink. It does me good to hear from you that father-in-law is steady and I trust he will continue in that course. If we are spared we shall all see each other again before long.[1]

Then almost as an afterthought he added that he and Sarah had a new addition to their family, a daughter Elizabeth, named after her. She was born on February 18, 1873. Regarding his other children, "Emily, Mark and Sarah Ann are growing up fast. Thomas and George are also getting fine boys. Lucy is a little darling." The next month his sister Elizabeth and her husband, Adam Grant Horne, sent Bate's mother a bill of exchange for £5. Bate suggested to his mother that she reply immediately it was received and thank them for "their goodness." Bate also sent a photograph of Horne. Sending photographs back home was a common thread throughout his letters; it seemed important to him to share how his family was growing and how well everyone was faring.

Bate missed hearing news from his sister Ann and wondered why she had not written to him. She and husband, William Sharratt, had moved from Dudley and taken up residence in Droylsden, Ashton under Lyne, Lancashire. When he finally received a letter from her, he told his mother, "I can hardly tell you the good it has done me to get a few lines from her."[2] Ann had commented on a photograph their mother had shown her of Bate when the family lived at Holly Hall. The photograph resembled Mark Jr. at his father's age. Bate proudly replied that his son was growing very fast and was a robust boy who would be 13 years old on May 16.

In another letter to his mother he asked if there was any property near her that he could buy, "I mean a patch of ground with a cottage or small house upon it. I suppose you still live in the same place as you did when I left home?"[3] This was an odd comment, as if he did not know where she had been living all these years. He then asked if his mother had seen his uncle, George (Robinson), since he had returned to England the previous year.

Bate became concerned for his mother's welfare, for she still had not let him know if she had received the money. His letter conveys a touch of homesickness:

> Our little ones are frequently inquiring when we are going to take them to England to see their Grandma, and as comfortable and prosperous as my position is here, I feel like preparing to go home, if only just for the trip. Were it not for our large family, I do not think I should hesitate long to make a start. We could reach London in less than a month from the time of leaving Nanaimo.[4]

He continues with family news typical of his letters:

> Elizabeth and her husband and all their children were well when I heard from them about a week ago, and I am pleased to state they are prospering—doing better than for some time past. Their oldest boy, Adam Henry, has been staying with us for a week or two during the School Holidays, and our boys, of course, were glad of his company.

Bate's concern for his mother was deeply felt. With each letter received from home her condition appeared to be deteriorating. In March 1874 he confided in his cousin, Thomas Bryant, Cornelius's brother:

The life of my dear good mother for 20 years and upwards has been a most trying one. How much I long to see her I cannot begin to tell you, but as I am unable to leave here to visit England yet awhile I shall do everything possible to provide her a comfortable house, as far as the necessaries of life can do so. I sincerely trust that she does not want for anything. With advancing age my dear mother will not study appearances or dress very much and while I should greatly like her to always look respectable and be kept tidy, I am still more anxious that she should be warmly clothed and that her health should be considered—should have first attention.[5]

He understood it might be awkward for Bryant to check on his mother. He did not seem to have a high opinion of his stepfather, William Thomas. "I earnestly hope, however, that he has long ere this time given over his drinking fits and that he is living a better life than he did when I was at home. I am glad to say we are all quite well here." This was the first time Bate mentioned that his home life after his mother remarried had not been the happiest. A half a sovereign was enclosed for Thomas Bryant to spend on his mother.

Sarah Bryant, Bate's aunt, wrote with bad news of his mother's condition in March 1874, and it pained Bate to hear how she was declining. He replied: "I pray to God, she may be ushered into the Realms of Eternal Bliss. When I think about her hard life she endured within my recollection . . . my heart yearns to embrace her."[6] Aunt Sarah did not indicate what her medical condition was, but from Bate's reaction he did not expect to get another letter from his mother again. He learned later she had had another stroke, which had impaired her considerably, both physically and mentally.[7]

He reassured his aunt that he was doing well, earning £750 a year, with a good house and fuel grants. "I am by frugality and steadiness gradually saving a little money and endeavouring to lay a foundation for our children to build upon in the far off and unknown future." He wrote that he and Sarah had visited Aunt Maria in Victoria and expected her to spend a few weeks visiting them, and suggested it was time for Uncle Joseph to retire from business:

> I know full well the harassing character of most business exercise—of whatever class, and I can tell from some years' experience of the great anxiety of mind from one cause or other that attends the fastidious management of even small establishments. You can imagine what my responsibilities are when I mention that the Company whose office here I control pay away in wages $20,000 a month. Our workmen earn large wages. I believe there is not a better place in the world for a coal miner than Nanaimo.[8]

He was quite surprised when his cousin David Botham wrote in January 6, 1875, enclosing a short note from his mother. "I had supposed my good old mother would never pen a line to me again . . . what a thrill of pleasure I felt to see her familiar hand writing once more."

In one of his last letters to his mother he proudly told her about her grandchildren and the good life they enjoyed:

> Mark and Tommy are robust romping fellows, full of life and fun and having nothing to do but attend school and learn their lessons. They are growing very fast. Mark and Sarah Ann are at the head of the first class in their schools. If my mind does not change I shall give Mark about two years at college and Sallie 2 or 3 years at the college Emily went to. As far as education is concerned we mean for all the children, if we are spared, to have a good start in life. If it had not been for my good schooling, I should never have stood in the position I do today. We have [a] few thousand dollars on deposit at interest—four houses, 100 acres of good land and other

property—shares in business etc. so that you will see we have not squandered my earnings. We have not been sparing either. We have had everything we want, kept servants in the house, and spent hundreds of dollars in the various ways a person of any standing is called upon to [do].

A DAUGHTER ELOPES

In the spring of 1873, when Bate's daughter Emily was away from home furthering her education at Queen's College in Victoria, Charles (Charlie) Augustus Alport, a clerk who worked in Bate's office, approached him with a delicate question: Would he give consent for him to marry Emily? Alport had received a letter from his Uncle Percy in Beaufort, in South Africa, inviting him to move there and take up a business opportunity that might not happen again. His uncle was the brother-in-law of the prime minister of the Cape of Good Hope, "both wealthy and influential."[9] Bate was shocked and immediately moderated his consent by stating Emily was only 15 years old and "told him that neither Emily's Mamma nor myself were willing to part with her yet awhile."[10] Alport asked Bate to show the letter from Uncle Percy to his wife, Sarah, with the hope they would change their mind.

A week later Alport approached Bate again, wondering if he had reconsidered. Bate's answer was the same: He could not think to part with her for another year or two. Alport argued he was afraid his uncle would not keep the offer open. Bate said he would be sorry to lose him, but if he thought the position offered by his uncle would be better than anything he could ever expect to attain in Nanaimo, then he should go. As if leaving his opposition to the marriage open, he said that he and Sarah would have no objection, if they were so much attached to each other, to Emily meeting him in England in two years' time. Alport seemed pleased and asked, "You pledge yourself to that?"[11] Bate again told him if Emily wished to meet him, or go with him, she should do so when of age. Alport had not yet written to his uncle, and agreed to think about it.

But the young couple decided not to wait. Disobeying her father's wishes, Emily married Charlie Alport on July 10, 1873, in Victoria. The registration of their marriage shows he was 30 and she 16 years of age. Witnesses were Mary Clarke and Charles James Prevost of Victoria. Reverend Thos. Derrick, of Episcopalian faith, conducted the ceremony.[12]

Emily did not say goodbye to her parents before they left for England, where Alport's parents, Eleanor and Henry Rose Alport, lived. Bate, writing to Wild in October 1873, observed that Alport had made plans to take Emily to South Africa even before he asked for her parents' permission. He asked, "Can you imagine what pain his conduct has caused myself and Mrs. Bate—how deeply it hurt us to be so shamefully bereft of a child?" Bate said he had got over the loss, but Mrs. Bate had been in hysterics for nearly three weeks. He telegraphed Alport in San Francisco informing him of his mother-in-law's health, and begged him to come back. As if resigned to the loss of his daughter, Bate concluded, "He appears to have got away as quickly as the steamer could carry him."[13]

Despite his unhappiness at losing his daughter, Bate told Wild he had had "unbounded confidence in Mr. Alport," and that he could never have looked for "such perfidy" from him.

Had I anticipated his intentions I would not [have] allowed an elopement to take place . . . I see how Alport pressed the child and got her to commit herself, as he no doubt easily could do from his greater age and experience. For nearly four years till she was 15 and a half years old Emily has been away from home at Queens College, Victoria, and you will think it natural for me to desire a year or two of our dear child's company for our own comfort as well as for the good of her younger brothers and sisters. She has gone, however, and I have not the least doubt that her husband, who apart from this one rash and dishonorable act has always been an upright and worthy man.[14]

The departure of his clerk increased Bate's workload. He complained to Wild that he had been at his desk nearly all day and night, "even Sunday," so the official business of the company would not suffer. By the end of the month, a new clerk had been hired, a Mr. Loat, at $100 a month.[15] The new clerk got along well in the office, but Bate doubted he would last. He said he tried to make things as pleasant as he could and gave him lots of encouragement, but still, "Alport's equal would be hard to find. He always appeared to anticipate my wishes and was a most faithful worker."[16]

Emily's departure preoccupied his thoughts for weeks to come. He learned later that the first clergyman the couple had asked to marry them refused because of Emily's age. The second was not so concerned. Emily wrote a long letter to her parents after they arrived in England. Bate immediately telegraphed Alport, pleading with him to come back to Nanaimo, saying that he would welcome him back. It is doubtful Alport received this communication as they had already left London on October 24 for the Cape of Good Hope, South Africa.

Bate continued to rationalize his family situation. "If he had only brought Emily here to us if only to say goodbye, we might soon have forgiven his rashness and sent him on his way rejoicing." This might have spared them the pain and his wife's unhappiness. "We cannot do other wise than wish them much joy and prosperity, wherever they may go."[17]

The following day he wrote to his mother telling her of Emily's marriage. The language Bate used to describe his son-in-law reveals few of his anxieties about his daughter's marriage. Alport was a "noble fellow, a steady and worthy man" and had very wealthy friends in South Africa. "He has been a clerk in our office for some years so that I can bear testimony to his good character."[18]

He also notified his friend, David Pearce, from Dudley, of her marriage and acknowledged that he did not want her to marry so young. "If she had only waited two or three years longer!" Again he stressed that Alport was a fine, clever fellow and would make a good husband. He again mentioned that Alport's uncle in South Africa, who had sent for him, was wealthy. The uncle's wealth may have been reassuring to Bate and may have helped lessen his concern. Bate also realized that he did not like the prospect of becoming a grandfather at only 36, a subject he and Sarah had laughed about.[19]

Bate hoped that Wild would have seen Emily when she and Charlie were in London, as Alport had an appointment to meet the company secretary, Samuel Robins, but he did not take her along to the meeting. However, Wild did corroborate all that Alport had told Bate regarding his uncle's business position in South Africa. Wild had also lived in South Africa for a few years, and was able to set Bate straight about the climate. Bate had thought the area was deluged with rain in the cold season, and that in the hot months "scarcely a shower falls to refresh the earth."[20] Wild's opinion was that "the Cape was a better place to enjoy life than Vancouver, and that the climate at Beaufort is all that could be desired."

Alport hoped the family anger against him would subside and begged to be accepted into the family. He thought they would meet again before too many years, and that all his past misdeeds would be forgiven. This was more easily said than done, as the Bate family continued to grieve for Emily. Bate wrote to Wild:

> My earnest wish is that the future will bring them all the happiness they are no doubt looking forward to. They have full forgiveness from me not withstanding the great anguish Alport caused in my house by leaving and taking the child away, as he did. Mrs. Bate still grieves about her darling—cries almost every time the little ones talk about Emily and has made up her mind her daughter will never see her again. Of course, I try to make her believe other wise.[21]

The episode of Emily's elopement faded somewhat from Bate's letters. On a happier note he again wrote to his friend David recollecting their earlier days with friends from "the distant past" and the changes the country had undergone in the 17 years since Bate left the "shores of dear old England."

> About 2 months ago there arrived in this town (Nanaimo) an old Brierley Hill gentleman named Jeremiah Westwood who I think you know. He knows you very well . . . and being a musical man himself, he is acquainted with nearly all the "Fiddlers" etc. around the neighbourhood of Brierley Hill. I have had a long chat with him, and I assure you he gave me a very interesting account about many of my old associates. I am still in the music line—as fond of it as ever.[22]

A letter from another friend, Thomas Hughes, from Harts Hill, Brierley Hill, written on January 21, was hand delivered in Nanaimo on November 29, 1873. Why it took so long to arrive is not explained. Bate read it over and over, for it brought back many memories of his early years and "the scenes and haunts of our childhood . . . of the circumstances connected with our going to the Baptist Chapel to meet the girls." Hughes was the superintendent engineer with Messrs. Cochrane and Co. Bate compared his salary with that of his friend:

> Certainly 130 pounds per year appears a small salary for the important and probably laborious duties, which are imposed on you. As you suppose we pay a man occupying a similar position to yours a much larger salary. I am still in the office to which I was posted some 5 years ago, have a gross income of 750 pounds a year, a fine house, fuel, etc. furnished, grates, and of course am saving money. It costs me considerable, however, to get the children well

educated. 400 pounds has been spent on one girl (Emily), who I am proud to say is in every way an accomplished young lady, a good linguist, a good pianist and a beautiful singer. Our oldest boy now nearly 14 (Mark Jr.), I intend to make a coal and mining engineer because he is so far forward with his mathematical studies, and is fond of mechanical drawing. Our family largely outnumbers yours—we have five girls and four boys. Pretty good you will say for us young folk. My wife is not yet 35.[23]

Meanwhile, Bate's brother Joseph had not been heard from for some time. Bate confided to his sister Ann in February 7, 1874, that he had not heard from their brother since he stopped in New York on his way home. "It is a mystery to me what has become of him. He may turn up, as I sincerely hope he will one of these days. I would give anything almost to know where he is." Joseph came to Vancouver Island with Aunt Maria in 1862, and stayed in Nanaimo for a few years but had not been a presence in the Bate family for some time. Bate had made many inquiries about him but could find no trace of him beyond New York. Apparently a fellow traveller wrote to him advising that Joseph had left for England.

The same year, Bate praised his adopted country for the first time in his letters home, when inviting his sister Ann and her husband William to join him: "British Columbia is a glorious country. Would you like to come out and take up farming? I have lately bought 100 acres of splendid land for farming purposes, and if I am to make any use of it I shall have to have somebody to 'plough and to sow.'"[24] He told Ann that their sister Elizabeth had given birth to a daughter on February 8 in Comox, and the child's birthday coincided with Emily's: "We have a girl each born on the same day of the same month." Fittingly, Elizabeth and Adam named their child Emily Maude. He also let Ann know that they may be getting a visit from Aunt Maria, as she would be returning to England soon and might drop in on them for a visit.

Emily was never far from her father's thoughts. They wrote regularly, and Bate thought the couple "seemed comfortable and contented." In October 1874 he asked Wild if either he or Robins would accept a commission to buy a piano to be shipped to her. Alport's agent in London would arrange the shipment.

"If you can oblige me without any inconvenience to yourself, by ordering a good piano suitable for transportation to Beaufort. I shall be much pleased. I mean a good instrument as far as the machinery and material are concerned. A case richly embellished."[25]

Correspondence regarding the piano continued into the spring of the following year. Wild sent him a Collard and Collard illustrated book of pianos, including prices. Bate thought the prices were "frightfully high," and a cheaper one might be just as good for the Cape climate of Beaufort. However, after looking through the book, he and Sarah decided they would leave the selection up to him, and sent a draft of £80 to cover the costs. Emily's last letter had noted that Alport was ill. She thought the climate oppressed him: "It is probably also he is too much confined to his place of business, going out at sunrise and returning at sunset."[26] No one explained the nature of Alport's work. Bate learned in June the piano was shipped on May 25. "Emily will be delighted to get it, and seeing that Alport was so much in favour of a Collard & Collard I am rather pleased one of that make has been purchased."[27] Alport had recovered his health and was in good spirits.

The piano sent from England would be enjoyed for many years to come by Emily's ten children.[28] Alport had signed a four-year contract with his Uncle Percy that expired in 1878, but nothing more is known about the couple's remaining years at Beaufort.

12

LABOUR ISSUES AND
LAND TRANSACTIONS

BATE WAS CONSTANTLY UNDER PRESSURE to produce enough coal to fulfill shipping requirements. Flooding, fires, and breakdown of machinery were everyday headaches. Heavy rain during the winter months led to flooding in the mines. Occasionally, episodes of spontaneous combustion occurred in the coal's fine dross, or dust. If it was discovered early it was easily to put out, but a fire could spread rapidly and continue for a long time if not tended to immediately. The Park Head Mine fire of 1862 had begun that way and burned for years. Bate explained what happened:

> To keep themselves warm, the miners made a bit of a fire just at the Adit [entry to the mine] mouth, left it smoldering when quitting work for the day. A strong wind arose during the night, the fire spread rapidly, and the next morning the mine was in flames. Stoppings [barriers] were put in, and the airshafts closed, but the coal, dross [coal dust], etc. under a considerable area, burnt

for many years. The overlying strata were rent by the heat, and volumes of smoke and steam escaped through the openings where the rocks were parted.[1]

LABOUR PROBLEMS AGAIN

Bate also had to resolve labour problems, but he lacked the autonomy to make decisions on his own. He had to await instructions from Wild in London or Rosenfeld in San Francisco. This became especially difficult when the miners went on strike. Bate often had to play a waiting game; either the board did not trust him to make decisions, or it preferred to keep a tight reign on his administration.

In 1874, the miners went on strike because of problems with the colliery surgeon, Dr. William McNaughton-Jones. They suspended work abruptly and demanded the doctor's removal, taking the risk of leaving the district without a doctor. For eight days no coal was extracted. Neither Bate nor Bryden could have prevented the problem. Miners' sickness and accident funds hired and fired doctors by a majority vote. For a dollar a month, a doctor contracted with the miners to provide all the health care for them and their families. The company deducted this money from their pay. For a doctor to make a decent living he had to keep the majority of fund members happy to maintain his position, but for some reason, they became unhappy with Dr. McNaughton-Jones. Bate wanted to talk to the miners about engaging another doctor, but Bryden objected, saying he was not going to "knock under to the men—not going down on his knees to them."[2] The doctor had already let his patients know his connection with the company had ceased by posting a notice on his office door. Bate explained to Wild that 99 per cent of the men had signified a "want of confidence" in the doctor by presenting a petition to that effect. A week later, Bate called the situation "a most vexatious affair." There were a number of troublemakers he said he hoped to get rid of as soon as possible.

Dr. McNaughton-Jones left to take charge of the Royal Cariboo Hospital in Barkerville. He stayed there for two years before taking the position of medical superintendent of the New Westminster lunatic asylum.³ In 1878, Bate learned that the doctor had returned to Nanaimo to take a position with Dunsmuir, Diggle and Company. The city directory of 1882-83 confirmed that Dr. McNaughton-Jones was working as the company's colliery doctor in Wellington. He moved to Victoria in 1890 and became Dominion Health Officer and quarantine inspector in charge of William Head Station.⁴ Dr. Loftus R. McInnes, who had practiced in Toronto and New Westminster, replaced Dr. McNaughton-Jones at Bate's company in 1877; he was reported to have "great surgical skill and good common sense." After a couple of years, the miners thought otherwise about Dr. McInnes. He was accused of being unable to cope with his workload due to being "not young" and "of somewhat a corpulent nature and slightly short of wind."⁵

Bryden tended to deal with the miners and tradesmen firmly, especially those who complained about wages or working conditions. However, Bryden later admitted to Sam Robins that be believed the company could have take a stronger stand in the face of strike activity. He mentioned the issue with the doctor as typical of the divide between management and workers, because "they compelled us to discharge an efficient doctor, and accept one who was at the time a cripple, and when they had accomplished this, they boasted that they were masters of the field and could make their own terms with the company."⁶

Management also had to cope with the unofficial holidays—the "voluntary work stoppages." Bate was of course familiar with this custom of the British miners, but as a mine manager, he considered the "Saint Mondays" just another annoyance. Payday was usually on a Saturday and workers with spare change left in their pockets on Mondays often visited one of the saloons.⁷ By 1874 Nanaimo had eight outlets for liquor sales, and more watering holes sprang up north and south of Nanaimo—taverns, halfway houses, quarter-way houses—and within ten years the town added three breweries to the mix. There was no shortage of ways to obtain liquor. Bate always took a dim view of workers who drank on and off the job, and "habitual drinkers who lost time at work were dismissed."[8]

There always seemed to be a worker shortage and the need for a steady workforce of men with experience in the mines. Using Snuneymuxw and Chinese workers helped relieve the labour shortage; however, both these groups were in great demand at the fisheries on the Fraser River, where they received higher wages than they did working in the Nanaimo mines.[9] And the Chinese liked to leave in the spring to go prospecting for gold then return in the winter.

Another labour problem was added to Bate's concern when Dunsmuir began recruiting Nanaimo workers for his Wellington Mine. He soon learned that Dunsmuir had a knack of taking away his best men, whether they were miners, engineers, or road workers. "What seems very strange to me, the persons whom my colleagues crack up as smart useful hands, are the ones to go."

The BC Mining Report of 1874, signed by Bate, reported there were 284 men employed by the Vancouver Coal Mines company; of these, 204 were white, 61 Chinese, and 19 First Nations. The value of the plant, machinery, and railway was estimated at $93,657. Four mines were then in production: Douglas, Chase River, Newcastle, and Fitzwilliam. The Chinese were paid an average of $1.25 per day, First Nations labourers received a slightly higher wage of $1.50 per day, and white labour earned between $1.75 and $3.75. Miners earned up to $5.00 a day.

LAND TRANSACTIONS

As mine manager, Bate was often distracted by outside influences, many of them related to land transactions. Always on the look-out for good investments for the company, in 1874 he tried to secure what was known as the "Cornish Farm." Two Cornishmen named Thomas Nicholas and Sam Francis owned 600 acres in the Mountain District, south of the Dunsmuir mine at North Wellington only a short distance west of Diver Lake. Their farm, and others nearby, helped supply much of the produce for the town.

Bate wrote to Nicholas and Francis, asking them to allow his company to explore for coal on their property. For this the company would deposit $500, which would be forfeited to them if the arrangement did not work out, or they could accept a royalty payment on how much coal would be extracted. Even the road-building expense would be born by the company.[10] Bate speculated about the price they might want for the surface rights and for the mineral rights, but the men told him they would not sell. Afterwards he talked to Bryden about the land acquisition, concluding, "There can be nothing done with them." The next morning Dunsmuir visited the Cornishmen, and before long James Harvey, Dunsmuir's son-in-law, began pressuring them to sell. This looked to Bate as rather suspicious, and so he decided in the future to "keep his own council" and not tell Bryden about any other possible land purchases in the neighbourhood of the Wellington Mine.

The Cornishmen did not sell, and in 1876 discovered coal on their farm themselves, and proceeded to sink a shaft and mine the coal; this became known as the South Wellington Mine. Bate helped them construct the road and granted permission to cross the company's railroad grade for the three-mile-long roadway they built to the wharf, directly opposite the Fitzwilliam Mine on Newcastle Island, near Midden Bay.[11] They even purchased a locomotive, *Premier No. 1*, from San Francisco. Despite all the help from Bate and the Vancouver Coal Company, however, in 1878 Nicholas announced they were broke.

Robert Chandler, who was a large coal and iron dealer from San Francisco, stepped in to help by advancing money to the South Wellington Mine. He also had a vested interest in the area, as he had earlier purchased 600 acres from the Westwood Estate with the coal rights; this became the East Wellington Mine. When Bate learned of this he was skeptical, thinking that Chandler must expect "to get the amount of his loan back out of the coal somehow."[12] The mine was opened and eventually turned out 200 tons in 24 hours. On the delivery of the first cargo in San Francisco, Chandler met with hot opposition from Dunsmuir; the wily veteran collier did not want more competition in the marketplace. In an effort to keep his customers in the face of this new competition, Dunsmuir allowed a rebate on his Wellington coal of 50 cents a ton.

In March 1879, however, Nicholas declared bankruptcy and the property was put up for auction. Chandler was the only one bidding. His agent, Ralph Wingate, was appointed to run the mine, but according to Bate it was a dangerous mine to work; it was full of gas and had "numerous disadvantages attached to it." Dunsmuir kept a close eye on the mine, which operated close to his lease. After only a few months Chandler sold out to Dunsmuir. On December 22, 1879, Bate advised Wild that Dunsmuir had bought the mine. He speculated on the financial difficulty his competitor faced:

> Buying out Admiral Farquhar and Capt. Egerton, and the acquisition of the South Wellington property, almost so to speak in one breath has in all probability necessitated a heavy loan from the bank, which must of course be repaid with interest. A certain quantity of coal has to be delivered to Mr. Chandler in a given time, and unless they do a large paying business it will not be a light job for them to meet all demands.[13]

Bate was curious about how much Dunsmuir had paid Chandler for the mine and later found out from Rosenfeld: "Mr. Robins was informed by Admiral Farquhar that the price was $6,000 cash down and 48,000 tons of coal to be supplied at the rate of 2,000 tons a month during two years."[14]

One land transaction put Bate in a personal financial predicament. A comedy of errors occurred when he asked Noah Shakespeare, a former resident of Brierly Hall, England, now living in Victoria, to bid on his behalf on the Rippon Estate in the Mountain District of Nanaimo. Bate and Shakespeare shared the same great-grandfather, Joseph Shakespeare, so were third cousins.

Noah emigrated in 1862, and after experiencing the Cariboo gold rush, he settled in Nanaimo, where he worked a double shift as a labourer in the Vancouver Coal Company mines to pay passage for his wife, Eliza Jane, and their son to join him.[15] Eliza travelled to Victoria aboard the clipper *Napoleon III* with her sister-in-law, Phoebe Elizabeth Raybould, and Phoebe's husband, William, in January 1864.[16] Noah was also a partner with William Raybould in the Nanaimo Emporium, which supplied apparel for men. After he moved to Victoria, Noah managed galleries for the photographers George Robinson Fardon and Charles Gentile.

Rippon had died intestate and his lawyer had taken charge of the estate. The auction for his land was held in Victoria. Bate told Shakespeare to keep their correspondence and intentions strictly private and confidential. He advised, "My name must not be whispered."[17] The sale was held on July 20, 1874. In a letter to John Bermingham, in San Francisco, Bate explained what happened: "I told him he might bid for the Rippon Estate in the amount of $5,000, if he liked, and if the land was knocked down to him at that figure I would take it." Bate was dumbfounded when he learned that "the stupid fool instead of bidding $5,000 bid $250.00 an acre for one hundred acres which amounts of $25,000. The fellow had been calculating one hundred acres at $250 as $2,500." Bate immediately repudiated the purchase but expected to hear from the auctioneer and the lawyer. As if to console himself, he concluded, "The land must be worth something to our Wellington neighbours when Dunsmuir, Diggle & Co. just bid $24,000 for it."[18]

Letters flew back and forth for months between Bate and his lawyers in Victoria and the transaction ended in court. This must have been a very trying time for him, for it was not until June the following year that he learned the judge had ruled in his favour. He reported to Wild on the outcome:

My opinion of the value of the 100 acres is being strengthened every day almost and without it and another patch or two adjoining them. Dunsmuir, Diggle and Co. would be very much hampered. I am told they are offering $6,000 for 40 acres off Chantrells lands, and Rippons lot, according not only to my judgment but that of nearly everybody who knows anything about it, is worth much more than Chantrells. Some persons or party I expect will be after it besides D.D. & Co.[19]

Bate later claimed the Rippon Estate was worth more money than Shakespeare bid for it; there was coal underneath and it was "both thick and good." He said if he had $25,000 he would have bought the 100 acres. In the end he had to pay $696 in legal fees.

Shakespeare entered politics in 1875 and became the city councillor for the James Bay Ward in Victoria. In 1878 he led the Workingmen's Protective Association, an early labour union whose primary goal was the elimination of Chinese competition. He was known for his anti-Chinese beliefs. Later he helped found the Anti-Chinese Association. His high profile led to a term as mayor of Victoria, beginning in 1882. The following year he was elected to the House of Commons; the height of his career was the tabling of a motion for a law to prevent further Chinese immigration, which led to the Chinese Immigration Act of 1885.[20]

FINANCIAL DIFFICULTIES

At this time Bate was personally in a serious financial situation. He had loaned his friend Clarke $1,000, money he had borrowed from the bank, which he promised to repay by April 1875. A year later Bate, embarrassed, asked Clarke for repayment. Clarke sent him a note, which Bate used to borrow $700 from his friend Tom Peck to partially pay the claim. Bate wrote,

> I have never before in my life had to ask for assistance from a friend, and it gave me no little uneasiness to have to do so. I do not like to owe Peck money nor anybody else, and the house expenses and other charges that fall on me, absorb all my income hence I depend on a refund from you to pay my indebtedness. Were I not fettered I should not be so urgent.[21]

Peck was the fireman who arrived in Nanaimo with the *Pioneer* locomotive, and was now a business entrepreneur. He partnered with James McKay Sabiston in the Nanaimo Saloon, site of today's Modern Café. Sabiston withdrew from the partnership and opened his own establishment in 1871, the Identical Hotel, on Victoria Crescent. Peck soon followed him to Victoria Crescent and opened up Peck's Hotel.

There is no indication when and if Clarke repaid his loan, but Bate continued to have financial difficulties for the next few years. In February 1879, he told Wild he was broke; a trip to San Francisco, doctor's bills for Sarah when she was ill, and improvements made on their property had absorbed any surplus funds he had.

THE PIONEER CEMETERY

Bate kept in touch with his former colleague, Charles Nicol. He had cared for the gravesite of Nicol's son James, and informed him that "the fencing around the grave had been given two coats of paint, cleaned inside and out, the brickwork repaired, and the headstone, which had fallen to one side, had been set firm and upright." James was born in October 1864 and died the following spring. In the early days of the colony it was left to family members to care for the burial sites. Bate commented, "Our little cemetery is now nigh well filled."[22]

13

FIRST MAYOR
OF NANAIMO

IN 1875, EVEN BEFORE HE was asked to run for mayor, Bate felt somewhat overwhelmed by all the civic duties expected of him. He wrote to his cousin David in England,

> I cannot describe to you on this small sheet the many duties which fall upon me—some of which I have voluntarily assumed but these unofficial positions take up all my leisure hour—at least what should be such. Only last evening a deputation was sent to ask me to allow myself to be placed in 'nomination' for the mayoralty of our town, which has been incorporated quite recently. I wonder, what next? President of the Literary Institute; Chairman of the School Board; Justice of the Peace; Leader of an Amateur Band etc. etc. etc. Surely they wanted to work me to death! This Mayor business I must decline. There are other gentlemen who want the office, and I don't want it.[1]

The city first had to achieve incorporation before it needed a mayor. Since the first attempt to incorporate, in 1866, Nanaimo had prospered. No longer just a mining village, it had a population of approximately 1,500 residents, not including the Snuneymuxw. In the new Canadian province, it was second to Victoria in importance. Its seaport rivalled Victoria's, with up to ten vessels sitting in the harbour at one time, and the four mines provided steady employment. The aerial tramway was being constructed from the Harewood Mine to Cameron Island. Nearby, Dunsmuir's colliery and the town of Wellington were growing, as Dunsmuir's mine produced coal for the California market. The Vancouver Coal Company was also expanding; it had found coal at Chase River and reopened the Fitzwilliam Mine, and it was building wharves at Newcastle Island. In addition to the company's large coal wharves, two other wharves provided access for freights and passengers— Gordon's Wharf and Hirst's Wharf, built by local entrepreneurs David Gordon and John Hirst. Bate noted, "All this and other stimulating prospects were encouraging to Nanaimoites."[2]

In a letter to Charles Nicol in the spring of 1874, Bate noted the changing face of the town. However, with the increased population came a few drawbacks:

> The town continues to grow and many new buildings are going up, some of them not wanted. I allude to the two new hotels. When those two are finished we shall have no less than six drinking places in a line within a distance of 450 yards. Licenses are granted by Capt. Spalding without any regard to the wants of the place, and it seems a great pity that there should be so many inducements put in men's way to drink. It is a great drawback to workers, and an injury to the community generally. A fine new public school is erected at the site promised some years ago on Crace Street, and we have an organization of militiamen—40 in number.[3]

The hotels Bate refers to were on Victoria Crescent: the Provincial, the Crescent, the Grand, the International, the Oriental, and the Identical. The last two, small wooden establishments, were actually next door to each other. The International became the Queen's Hotel, still in operation today.

The volunteer militia Bate mentions was formed in 1866. In 1872, the Nanaimo Rifles No. 1 Company was under the command of Second Lieutenant James Harvey, a popular local merchant who married Dunsmuir's daughter Agnes.[4] However, Nanaimo still looked toward Victoria for protection.

The area of town where business was conducted was confined to a rocky piece of land. A wooden bridge spanned the ravine, which ebbed and flowed with the tide. New residences sprang up across the divide. The Wellington and Departure Bay communities developed nearby, and entrepreneurs provided transportation services to connect them with Nanaimo. A small ferry ran twice a day to Departure Bay, and Joseph Ganner's passenger stagecoach service operated twice a day to Wellington. Ganner also carried the mail between the towns.

INCORPORATION

Many people believed incorporation was important to the health of the area, and it was again in the air in early 1874. During the mayoralty campaign the following year, detractors were quick to point out Bate's role in the defeat of incorporation in 1866 and the resulting negative effects on the town. In the news sheet *The Comet*, which emerged briefly in 1875 for the mayoral campaign of James Harvey, Dunsmuir's son-in-law, the paper remarked on lost revenue and other things the town missed by not incorporating back in 1866:

> If it had incorporated there would have been two members sit-
> ting in the provincial legislature, and one member in the House

of Commons . . . by the defeat on that occasion those political advantages have been lost, the first for years, the second may be for generations, these are prizes that other countries value and fight for.[5]

This was political maneuvering, to be sure; Bate's reasons for thwarting the initial proposal were likely misconstrued. On March 7, 1874, the MLA for Nanaimo, David Babington Ring, introduced a Nanaimo incorporation bill in the provincial legislature. No action was taken. In a third attempt, in December of the same year, Alex Dunsmuir and police constable William Stewart petitioned to reopen the debate in the new community newspaper, the *Nanaimo Free Press*. The two men successfully obtained 221 signatures of the approximately 260 eligible voters. Bate thought that the young Dunsmuir no doubt had the support of his father in this endeavour. The petition requested "that self-government be granted in order to prevent the further expenditure of town revenue in opening roads to distant parts of the district." It suggested local government would improve the streets and bridges in Nanaimo, which were in an unsatisfactory condition.

Bate was happy to see the *Nanaimo Free Press* published and said to Wild on April 15, 1874, "The first issue of the *Nanaimo Free Press* newspaper came out this morning. I sent copies to Mr. Robins." Later he commented with pride,

> The *Free Press* came somewhat suddenly upon us bringing a fresh germ of hopefulness, and by the energy and push of the editor and proprietor, George Norris, a splendid work was begun in disseminating intelligence of doing and happenings hereabout. Mr. Norris, as a publisher, did not dally with his duty.

Norris married Amanda Theresa Gough in 1869, the eldest daughter of Edwin and Elizabeth Gough from Dudley. They couple met on one of the Gough family trips to Victoria. Norris, originally from London, England, worked for the *Victoria Daily Chronicle*, which merged with the *Daily British Colonist* in 1866. They came to Nanaimo in 1874 with their three children to open a print shop on Front Street, at the site of today's Globe Hotel, and in April began publishing the *Nanaimo Free Press*.[6] In September, Norris moved the business to what became known as the Free Press block on Commercial Street. Amanda helped her husband in the print shop until their boys were old enough to take her place.

Norris's newspaper wholeheartedly endorsed the incorporation petition, stating that "one thing is certain, we want some change to lift us out of the muddy condition in which we are at present,"[7] referring to the unpaved roads. Alex Dunsmuir presented the petition to the government on December 21, 1874. However, some people thought he should have pushed for reimbursement for the neglect the town had suffered. On December 22, a counter-petition circulated that opposed incorporation unless a bonus of $40,000 was granted for the years of neglect. Since settlement began, the only roads, streets, and bridges in town were those built by the Vancouver Coal Company, now residents wanted compensation for those years of being ignored by government. While the counter-petition only collected 134 signatures, a number of people had also signed the incorporation petition. Whether for or against requesting the compensation for neglect, Nanaimo residents clearly wanted change. Bate, who had opposed the first incorporation attempt and still felt the same, signed the counter-petition. His opposition may have related to his work as manager of the Vancouver Coal Company. If and when incorporated, the municipality would levy taxes on property, and since Vancouver Coal Company was the largest landowner, it would clearly be an unwelcome outcome.

On December 24, 1874, the Lieutenant Governor in Council issued letters patent "incorporating the townsites of Nanaimo and Newcastle, and their approximately 1,500 inhabitants as the Corporation of the City of Nanaimo. Nanaimo became the province's eighth municipal corporation and third city municipality."[8] This change of decision from previous attempts apparently evolved after new legislation (the Municipal Act) in 1872 allowed the lieutenant governor and the Legislative Council to grant incorporation when they received a petition signed by two-thirds of the residents of an area of a certain size.[9]

The planning for Nanaimo's first municipal election, to be held on January 19, 1875, could go now ahead. When Bate heard who was the only candidate for mayor—Harvey, Dunsmuir's son-in-law— he decided to throw his hat in the ring. His antagonism toward the Dunsmuirs continued. Nominations for the election were scheduled for noon on January 18, at the old wooden Courthouse on Front Street, with the election to be held the following day between 9 a.m. and 5 p.m. The returning officer, Thomas Lea Fawcett, was paid $25 for his service. Fawcett provided many functions in the community—auxiliary police constable, collector and reviser of voters, registrar of births, marriages and deaths, returning officer, land commissioner, and government agent.

To qualify for a seat on council the nominee had to own property valued at $500 or occupy leasehold property valued at $300. All expenses for the first election had to be covered by the candidates and were not to exceed $100.[10] Only a man who had been a resident for two years, was a British subject, and was at least 21 years of age could vote. These requirements disqualified Chinese and First Nations people and women; Japanese people were added to this list of the disqualified in 1896.

Nanaimo's first election was held on a cold wintery day, the harbour frozen across to Protection Island. Interest in the city's first election was high. Fourteen candidates ran for council, though only seven could be elected, and two were running for mayor— James Harvey and Mark Bate. The cold weather did not deter the

219 voters from making their way through the rutted and frozen streets to cast their ballots. When the final results were tallied, Bate had edged out Harvey by a slim margin of only 17 votes. After the votes were counted, the *Nanaimo Free Press* reported that following the meeting, "the friends and supporters of the Mayor-elect lifted him shoulder high and carried him through the town cheering as they went." Afterwards he rewarded them with a champagne supper at the new Peck's Hotel on Victoria Crescent.

NANAIMO'S FIRST COUNCIL

What was Bate thinking when he trudged up the muddy road to the wooden courthouse on Front Street on January 22, 1875, to stand before Magistrate Warner R. Spalding and be sworn in as Nanaimo's first mayor? Perhaps he carried his walking stick and wore his top hat, the accoutrements of a distinguished gentleman. The young lad from Dudley had come a long way since arriving in Nanaimo. Was he excited about this new position and the responsibility about to unfold? He may have been anxious and justifiably worried about what he had undertaken to do. Could he serve two masters—the Vancouver Coal Company and the new City of Nanaimo?

At the first council meeting, Bate looked around the board table and viewed the men he would work with over the next year. Some had supported his opponent, but he hoped that political differences could be put aside in their deliberations. All were unpaid, including the mayor, and they would all have to seek re-election again in another year. One of the elected aldermen was his colleague, John Bryden, who the same year had been elected a Member of the Provincial Parliament (MPP). Bryden replaced John Robson who had resigned when he became paymaster and commissary of the Canadian Pacific Railway surveys. Bryden served only a year before resigning, to look after his business interests, he said. Bate never spoke of his mine manager's provincial duties.

Other council members included John Dick, the Scottish miner who helped find coal for Horne and Sabiston. Dick also discovered a coal seam for the Vancouver Coal Company that became the Chase River Mine. Another councillor was the businessman William Raybould, who with his wife, Phoebe, operated Raybould Millinery Shop and the Nanaimo Emporium. Phoebe, whose maiden name was Shakespeare, the sister of Noah Shakespeare, was a distant relative of Bate. John Hirst was a community-minded entrepreneur, who built the general shipping wharf known as Hirst's and a large stone warehouse, and he also operated a grocery store on Commercial Street. Richard Nightingale was manager of the Newcastle Quarry; John Pawson built the Old Flag Inn on Bastion Street and served on the first school board. A Welsh miner, Richard Brinn, rounded out the list of aldermen. Of the successful candidates, *The Comet* had endorsed three—Dick, Nightingale, and Pawson. The first items of business were procuring a seal for the city, taking a census of the city, and setting up an assessment roll.

Council meetings were held every Monday evening between 7:00 and 8:00 p.m, initially in the old courthouse, which was also used as a post office, harbourmaster's office, and government agency, and beginning in May of 1875, in a stone building on Front Street called the Council Hall. A few seats were provided for the public and one for the *Nanaimo Free Press* editor, George Norris, who reported on all the council's meetings in his newspaper. Under the rules of procedure, the mayor took his seat, and the minutes of the previous meeting were read and adopted; correspondence was read, then presentations made of accounts, committee reports, deferred business, and new business. According to a bylaw, no protests or disagreement were to be entered into the minutes, so it is unlikely that reading the minutes would show the debate or any disagreement. A schedule of new business was posted in the porch of the first council hall, and later, on the bulletin board in front of the new city hall.[11]

In his inaugural address to council, Bate asked the aldermen that in all their deliberations they would treat each other with courtesy and forbearance, and he advocated "economy in the expenditure of the City Revenue and urged the desirability of being mild with taxation."[12] One notable bylaw, the first of many such bylaws, passed in 1876, instituted Sunday observance, liquor sales regulations, and the suppression of gambling. Under the Municipality Act of 1872 city councils had the power to guide public morality, ensuring, for example, that residents observe the Sabbath and conduct themselves in a moral manner while in public. Later they were able to legislate the closure of saloons at night and on Sundays.[13]

Bate appointed the teacher, Charles Newton Young, as the first city clerk. Young had been a professor of English in the Netherlands before coming to BC in 1862 to take part in the Cariboo gold rush. He settled in the Victoria area, where he married Elizabeth Clarkson. Young taught at South Saanich School from 1865 to 1867, then resigned to become vice-principal of the Victoria Collegiate Institute. After the Vancouver Coal Company moved in 1867 from the Stone House to new headquarters on Haliburton Street, Young came to Nanaimo and opened a private school in the Stone House.[14] He next taught in the new Crace Street Boy's School. He was the first teacher certified after the Public School Act of 1872, which established the Nanaimo School Board, with Bate as chairman. The school was named after the first secretary of the Vancouver Coal Company. Young's salary was $75.50 a month; unfortunately, it did not always arrive on schedule. In December 1874, Elizabeth complained to Bate that her husband had not been paid for the month of November. Bate wrote to John Jessop, the provincial superintendent of education, telling him he should pay Young "two months salary" the next week.[15]

Not all children in Nanaimo attended school. Some parents felt that mining and the wage it brought into the household was more important than school. During the 1875-76 school year, attendance showed that out of 275 school-age children in the city, only 105 attended school.[16]

Young's salary as city clerk was $87.50 a month, slightly more than he made as a school teacher; however, after being on the job only two weeks his clerk's salary was reduced to $60.00. His duties included collecting road taxes and dog licenses as well as administering the daily business of the city; he also served as clerk of the county court. When council decided to reduce his salary even further, he recommended that the city advertise for a new clerk in both Chinese and English.[17] After yet another reduction in salary, he resigned and worked as an insurance agent and notary public. Two years later, Dunsmuir employed him as an accountant.[18]

SETTLING IN AS MAYOR

Bate found there was much to learn about running a city. He wrote to Mayor R. Dickenson of New Westminster for a copy of his city's bylaws, and asked for information about how police were paid, and how he managed police court business: "Have you as a council sole control and do you exercise it over those matters?"[19] Until this time Constable William Stewart had maintained law and order in Nanaimo with the assistance of Fawcett as an auxiliary police constable. Stewart had been hired in 1866, after the previous constable had been fired the year before and law and order had almost disappeared. Robberies and assaults were common, and bootlegging flourished. Stewart was appointed a special constable. After incorporation he remained on the job and became police chief, a position he held until his death in 1904. Magistrate Warner Spalding became county court judge, court of appeal judge, coroner, gold commissioner, and marriage registrar.

Bate did not inform Wild of his election as mayor until March 3, 1875:

I must tell you a word or two about the Municipal Election by the way. As you know, the incorporation of the Town was brought about by Dunsmuir's factors, mainly it is by now seen, to harass the company. They had things pretty much their own way and proposed this that the others considered themselves the chosen of the people and made sure of controlling the town. I told Bryden it would seem to [transfer] the Company's property to the tender care of his Father-in-law, Brothers-in law and their [--] and we must stop it. Hence, upon the request of our friend, I jumped into the [race] as a candidate for mayor when the Election was pretty near. You can imagine the nature of the opposition. I assumed money was probably disbursed but all to no purpose. Giving my opponent about 28 bought votes [from] the Wellington Mine. I had no [idea] then of it. You would have [loved] to see how [mad] old Dunsmuir was when the result of the poll was announced, though in half-an-hour afterwards he was cursing and raving like a maniac—insulted Bryden, who had not since spoken to him and the whole family unhappily are not [pleased] and only one or two on speaking terms. The election cost over $150 [sic], which I could ill afford to expend, and I mention this to you thinking probably the company might help me.[20]

Wild apparently ignored the mention of remuneration, but he did congratulate Bate on being elected mayor and expressed his opinion about some the councillors. Bate responded:

Your opinion of our Councillors, at least some of them, is quite correct. They have advanced notions of Municipal Government, and are growing as fond of Politics as the Canadians of the Eastern Provinces, who have the reputation of being thoroughly posted in the workings of Representative Institutions. The majority of the Council is our supporters I think, but I expect our taxes will pretty nearly come up to the old Real Estate tax. Whatever the tax

Mark and Sarah Bate. Photographs by Wilhelm Arthur Nahl, a German artist who immigrated to San Francisco in 1851. He worked in various media, with portraits and landscapes as his subject matter.
NCA, ARTWORK COLLECTION

Mark Bate with his second wife, Hannah, at their home on Hecate Street, Nanaimo. NCA, BATE FONDS

First Mayor of Nanaimo, by George Henry Southwell, gift to Nanaimo for its Diamond Jubilee in 1924. COURTESY OF THE CITY OF NANAIMO

Cornelius Bryant, teacher, Methodist minister, and cousin of Mark Bate. NM I1-251

Nanaimo Dominion Post Office building, 1884, designed by Thomas Fuller, chief architect for the Dominion of Canada's Department of Public Works. NCA 989.29 B5/135

John Bryden, mine manager, businessman, politician. MLA for Nanaimo (1875–76) and North Nanaimo (1894–1900). NM I1-250

Robert Dunsmuir, Scottish coal-mining tycoon, responsible for the E & N Railway and Craigdarroch Castle in Victoria. COURTESY OF CRAIGDARROCH MUSEUM SOCIETY

Nanaimo Courthouse, built between 1895 and 1896, designed by noted BC architect Francis Mawson Ratttenbury. NCA 989.25 B5/135

Nanaimo's first City Council: Mark Bate, centre. From top clockwise: John Bryden, John Pawson, John Dick, Richard Brinn, City Clerk Charles Newton Young, John Hirst, Richard Nightingale, William Raybould. NM J1-2

Wedding photo of Adam Grant Horne and Elizabeth Bate. NM 12-143

The Vancouver Coal Mining and Land Company mine called the No. 1 Esplanade
was sold to Western Forest Products in 1902. Photo circa 1890.

Sam Gough, a *Princess Royal* pioneer, served as clerk and in other positions for the City of Nanaimo for forty-five years. NM I1-38

Mine manager George Robinson, Mark Bate's uncle. NCA ROBINSON COLLECTION

Nanaimo's Silver Cornet Band. NM L1-4

The Black Diamond Fire Company in front of Fire Hall No. 2, built in 1893. NM F1-2

First St. Paul's Anglican Church on Chapel Street, between 1861 and 1865. Note roadwork being done in the foreground. NM C1-9

The Hospital, Nanaimo, B. C.

The Nanaimo Hospital at Franklyn and Kennedy Streets began
accepting patients in 1883. Author's postcard collection

Ashlar Lodge, Commercial Street, designed by A.E. Henderson, first opened in 1874.
Some alterations were made in 1963, and the building was restored in 1985. NM B-37

Ardoon, the Dunsmuir house, in the 1880s; it was built in 1858 and purchased by Mark Bate in 1890. He lived there until 1911 then sold it to the Merchants Bank of Halifax. NM B1-43

The Literary Institute Hall became Nanaimo City Hall, at Bastion and Skinner Streets. NCA

Franklyn House, built in 1862 on a site adjacent to the present City Hall, for Magistrate William Hales Franklyn. The Bate family lived in the house from 1886 to 1890. NCA

View of early Nanaimo from Nob Hill. NM A1-32

Esquimall & Nanaimo train station, Nanaimo. NM Q2-2

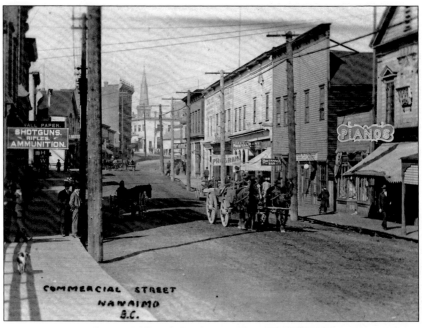

Commercial Street before the turn of the century. NM B1-10

Crystal glasses from Brierley Hill, England. Donated by Princess Royal pioneers for the 125th anniversary of their arrival in Nanaimo, in 1979. NM DISPLAY, 2012

Map of Great Britain showing Staffordshire and West Midlands as shown in Peggy Nicolls's pamphlets, FROM *THE BLACK COUNTRY TO NANAIMO*, 1854.

Collection of Mark Bate artifacts, including his cornet, walking stick, and top hat. NM DISPLAY, 1997

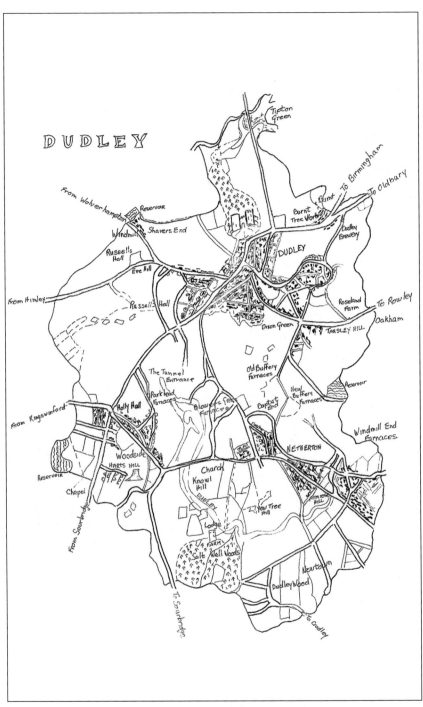

Map of Dudley and neighbouring villages, circa 1850. Author's sketch. FROM WILLIAM LEE,
*REPORT TO THE GENERAL BOARD OF HEALTH INTO THE SEWAGE, DRAINAGE, AND SUPPLY OF WATER, AND THE
SANITARY CONDITIONS OF THE INHABITANTS OF THE PARISH OF DUDLEY, IN THE COUNTY OF WORCESTER.*

Map of Esquimalt & Nanaimo Railway Company Land Grants, 1884–1925.

FROM W.A. TAYLOR, *CROWN LAND GRANTS: A HISTORY OF THE ESQUIMALT AND NANAIMO RAILWAY LAND GRANTS, THE RAILWAY BELT AND THE PEACE RIVER BLOCK*, P. 3.

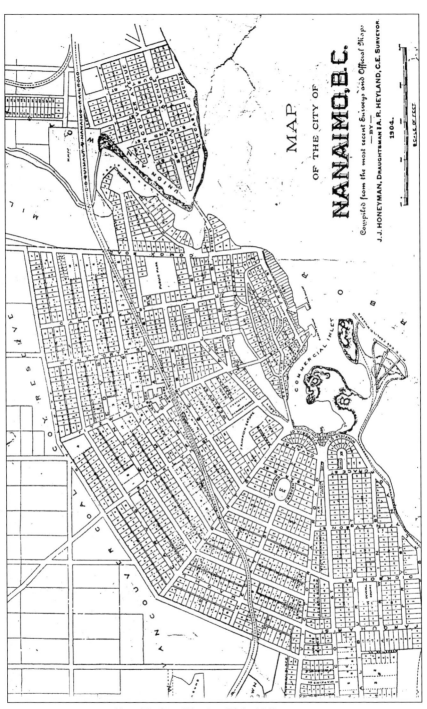

Map of the City of Nanaimo, BC, by J.J. Honeyman,
draughtsman, and A.R. Heyland, C.E., surveyor, 1904. NCA

may be, I shall not be backward in putting a good share of it (in as specious a manner as possible) upon tenants and purchasers of property. The Company can do as they please with the land outside the City boundary, of another town if thought advisable. It will be competent however, for the Council to enlarge the city as per Clause 46 of the Municipality Amendment Act. If we can keep a hold in the council as at present we shall not come off as badly as we otherwise would.[21]

Bate would have no influence over any land dealings of the city, because as the presiding officer, he had no vote except in the case of a tie. He explained to Nicholas Jones that "since incorporation, taxes would be severely felt." Jones was once a member of the Literary Institute and lived in Savannah, Georgia. He rented out two of his homes in Nanaimo. A bylaw was passed requiring property owners to put down sidewalks and keep them in order in front of their premises. Bate sent Jones a copy of the bylaw, which he said was only one of a number the council contemplated passing. Bate commented, "I am getting rid of the Company's building and property as quickly as possible to avoid the pressure of taxes."[22] Jones had written that he was not receiving rent as he should from his two houses, but, he said, "I think there is no fear about them paying up sooner or later." The next year Bate sold Jones's property to Captain Spalding for $1,800 cash. "I consider it a good sale in your interest, for really the buildings are in very bad condition."[23] Bate would get a commission on the sale.

A letter from Premier Walkem on April 29, 1875, brought some good news for Nanaimo. Bate commented on the "favourable tenor" of the letter, which he read before council. Walkem's good news was that Nanaimo finally would receive some provincial money—$3,000 to help defray the costs of construction of Bastion Bridge over the ravine, which had been a source of unhappiness for residents for years. The city would also receive funding to rebuild the Long Bridge, also called the Commercial Street Bridge. In reply to Walkem's letter, Bate wrote:

> You would readily understand the necessity of the city policeman being at hand to aid in carrying out the laws of the council—hence we thought the Government might be disposed to meet our wishes in that matter. Your advice on the subject of road tax, and the good news you gave us about the bridge across the ravine, were received with delight and appreciation. We have a big job before us as in the way of fixing streets and bridges.[24]

The Millstream Bridge that spanned Millstone (Millstream) River at the present site of the Pearson Bridge to the Newcastle townsite also received some repairs at this time. The Newcastle townsite was a suburb within the 1875 municipal limits, but had few residents before 1890.

A NEW CEMETERY

One of the first items to come before the council was the subject of the local cemetery. The old cemetery, known as the Pioneer Cemetery, at the corner of Comox Road and Wallace Street, was overcrowded and a new area had to be found. According to the Municipality Act of 1872, municipalities were required to establish and regulate their own cemetery. The council applied to the provincial government for a land grant to establish a new one but were told that all government lands were reserved for railway purposes. Their request for a grant to purchase land was also denied.

The refusal of the provincial government to grant land for the cemetery dated to 1871, when BC joined Confederation and the provincial and the federal governments agreed to build a railway from Seymour Narrows to Esquimalt Harbour. On July 18, 1874, the *B.C. Gazette* announced "a strip of land Twenty Miles in width along the Eastern Coast of Vancouver Island between Seymour Narrows and the Harbour of Esquimalt, is hereby reserved." The Railway Reserve Land became known later as the Esquimalt and Nanaimo Land Grant. Not even five acres for a cemetery could be taken from this land. The railway land did not include land already owned by the Vancouver Coal Company.

At Bate's suggestion, the council petitioned the Vancouver Coal Company for a piece of land. The company granted the city five acres, adjacent to but outside the city limits on the south side of Comox Road, near the present-day intersection with Howard Avenue. The new site for the cemetery required fencing and clearing, and the funds to do so, so the council appointed a cemetery committee. In 1877 the province finally stepped in with some assistance to prepare the site. The committee sent the site plans for the cemetery to England, where a concert raised $170 toward their cemetery fund. By July that year the site had been surveyed and two acres cleared. The deed for the cemetery was given to the city in 1878. It was up to the city clerk to manage it, supervising the gravedigger and the sale of plots and burials. For this service he received an additional monthly pay of $5.[25]

By 1895, interment in the old Pioneer Cemetery, as it is now known, at the corner of Comox Road and Wallace Street was considered "prejudicial to public health." The medical health officer officially closed it, and the new cemetery continued to grow over the years.[26]

HELPING FAMILY

The family in England was never far from Bate's thoughts; he was especially concerned for the health and wellbeing of his mother. He wrote to her in April 1875 after having sent copies of the newspapers announcing his election as mayor and enclosing a $20 greenback to "relieve a little of the tightness you feel owing to hard times. Greenbacks can be easily obtained here." Greenbacks were paper currency issued in the United States during the American

Civil War. They were printed green on one side. As always, he included information about his family:

> I must tell you that we are all well. Sarah Ann gets stouter every day and never, thank God, has any serious complaint to make about illness. The children continue healthy and strong. Mark still goes to school and he really is a bright chap. He is 15 years old . . . Sally also is a regular attendant at school and would not miss a lesson on any account. She is learning to play the piano and bids fair to become as fine a performer as Emily.[27]

Bate's mother died on November 6, 1875. She had been in ill health for some time, so it would not have come as a shock to her son or other family members in Nanaimo. Bate had a close relationship with her even though they were oceans apart. He faithfully wrote letters to her and sent support money, making sure she was well cared for in her declining years. Elizabeth was interned beside her first husband, Thomas, and their daughter Sarah, in St. Thomas's Churchyard, Dudley. (The Bate headstone no longer exists. The bodies were removed from the churchyard and re-buried in Dudley Borough Cemetery to make way for a road and buildings.)

Bate and Sarah had healthy children, so when their son George (Georgie), aged ten, got a sore throat and runny nose around Christmas in 1875, they probably thought little of it. Within days, however, the boy had difficulty swallowing, and as the illness progressed they would have realized it was quite serious. The boy died January 3, 1876, of diphtheria, a bacterial infection that was once a major childhood killer but today is very rare owing to worldwide vaccinations. The report of George's death in the *Nanaimo Free Press* on January 5 said the boy had died due to "membraneous croup." He had been ill for only ten days. Few believed at that time the disease was infectious, nor was there any knowledge of the cause, so there was no quarantine. Fortunately, none of the other Bate children caught the disease.

Nothing is more devastating for parents than the death of a child. The weather, one of the coldest winters recorded to date, matched the chill that settled over the Bate household after George's death. The Nanaimo Harbour was frozen all the way from Protection Island through to Departure Bay. Bate penned a memorial verse for his beloved son:

> Shall we meet thee, dearest Georgie,
> Who wert torn from our embrace;
> Shall we listen to thy sweet voice,
> And behold thee face to face?
> Yes, we'll meet thee, darling Georgie,
> When the burden we lay down;
> We shall change our cross of anguish,
> For a bright unfading crown.

The young boy was buried in Nanaimo's Pioneer Cemetery. A beautiful gravestone drawing was sketched by the cartographic draftsman James Benjamin Launders, a member of the Royal Engineers who drew many of the early maps of the province. The boy's headstone read: "In Memory of George Arthur Bate / Beloved son of Mark and S.A. Bate / Who died 3rd January 1876 / Aged 10 years and 8 months. / He shall gather the lambs with his arm and carry them in his bosom."[28]

Words of condolence came from family and friends, including the company agent in San Francisco, John Rosenfeld. Bate thanked him for his "kind sympathy upon the loss of my poor boy. He was a fine little fellow, nearly 11 years old, and his death has been a sad blow to me and Mrs. Bate. I have not been well since he died."[29] Later that year he asked a personal favour of Rosenfeld: could Rosenfeld order a fence for "my poor boy's grave." He sent a plan with a note about the ironwork and stone coping he wanted. "The makers will see the size I require by the plan. The fence and gate I wish complete, nicely bronzed, and ready to put together on arrival here."[30]

The death of his son spurred Bate and his council to appoint a contagious disease committee to confer with the "medical men of the city" in an attempt to enact a health bylaw. The sanitary committee ultimately assumed responsibility for contagious diseases since the cause was often poor sanitary conditions. Although a first attempt was made to enact a contagious diseases bylaw in 1876, it did not pass until 1885 during a smallpox epidemic.[31]

Sarah took the death of her son hard. However, her grief was soon mixed with joy when she gave birth to another son on September 10, 1876. John Augustus (Gussie)'s birth was announced in the Nanaimo Free Press on September 13. His arrival must have been difficult for Sarah, as she was reported to be seriously ill in November of that year. Bate was very concerned about her health. The next year Sarah was still unwell. In Bate's report to Wild, he thanked him for his "kindly mention of Mrs. Bate." He said he found it difficult to find the language to tell him how thankful he was that she was getting along so well. "Although her general health is not as good as it was before her terrible illness . . . she seems to be taking great care to be gradually gaining strength. She goes about her usual house duties but is rather easily fatigued."[32] Bate gave no indication of what the serious illness might be. The next summer she continued to be unwell. He wrote, "I am very sorry to state that Mrs. Bate has not enjoyed good health since her painful illness nearly two years ago. She is now confined to her room and I am writing this by her bedside."[33] As Sarah's illness continued, their daughter Sally took over many of the household chores. Bate noted, "Sally has grown quickly and is valuable to her mama and the management of the house and family." Sally was 18 years old.

A NEW PUBLIC HOSPITAL

The death of his son also prompted Bate to take action to establish the town's first public hospital. The original building, cobbled together a year earlier and located on the west side of Chapel Street, catered only to sick or injured men and would have been no help for Sarah or her son. Two miners' cabins, once belonging to the *Princess Royal* pioneer John Biggs, each provided ten beds. Water came from a spring nearby. It was a modest beginning, a step up from the hotel room previously used but not adequate for the needs of the growing community of families.

On July 14, 1876, Bate chaired a meeting, assisted by the secretary, Mr. C. Walmsley, to establish a committee consisting of David William Gordon, Richard Nightingale, John Pawson, and two doctors, Daniel Cluness, and Loftus R. McInnis, who were charged with finding a way to create a public hospital. The Nanaimo Hospital Association was eventually formed to build a new hospital, with Robert Dunsmuir as president and Bate as a government appointee.[34] Once again the two adversaries joined with others to meet their community's need. The hospital was built with government aid and private subscriptions at a cost of $3,000. On November 5, 1881, the Nanaimo Hospital opened on Franklyn Street on a site donated by the Vancouver Coal Company.

LORD DUFFERIN'S VISIT

The announcement in 1876 that Frederick Temple Blackwood, Lord Dufferin, the Governor General of Canada, would be visiting the province caused some excitement in British Columbia, as this would be the first viceregal visit. It would be an opportunity to discuss the failure of the federal government to build a rail line west of the Rockies to Esquimalt on Vancouver Island—a promise that had convinced British Columbia to join Confederation in 1871. In March, the Nanaimo Railway Bill, established to fund the construction of the railway, had passed in the House of Commons in Ottawa, only to be defeated in the Senate. During the federal election campaign in 1874, Prime Minister Alexander Mackenzie declared publicly that the terms of union with British Columbia were "impossible" and that Sir John A. Macdonald's commitment to bring the transcontinental line across to Vancouver Island could not be fulfilled.[35] When reports reached Ottawa that the province was threatening to break away from Confederation, Lord Dufferin was sent to appease the dissenting voices.

Bate was among those unhappy with the way the province was being treated by the federal government. He told Nicolas Jones,

> Everybody (is) disappointed on account of the do nothing policy
> of the Canadian government. They are treating the country
> shamefully. You will perhaps bear in mind that a railway was to
> be built over the mountains, and the agreement was to start with
> the work in two years. Four years have now gone and there is no
> beginning yet.[36]

This was a troubling year for Bate, losing his son in January and Sarah still ill and pregnant, so perhaps the letter he received in July 1876 from the mayor's office in Victoria was a distraction from his personal life. He was invited to a meeting in Victoria on July 13 to discuss the "most appropriate manner" of receiving Governor General Lord Dufferin.[37] He likely did not attend the meeting, because he wrote to Government House to find out if Dufferin intended to visit Nanaimo. The reply, dated August 18, states,

> In reply to your letter of the 14th inst. that it is the present inten-
> tion of the Governor General to visit Nanaimo, where he expects
> to arrive, weather permitting, on the 24th August. His Excellency
> will arrive in HMS *Amethyst* in the evening, disembarking if con-
> venient to you about 10 on the 25th, sailing northward at 1 p.m.
> the same day.

Lord and Lady Dufferin had already arrived in Victoria on August 16, so the visit to Nanaimo may have been an afterthought, prompted perhaps by Bate's letter. They had travelled west by train through the United States before boarding the *Amethyst* for the final part of their trip to British Columbia. Bate and his council must have scrambled, having only six days to put together an official reception for the Queen's representative. A brief overnight visit was allotted for Nanaimo before they sailed to the Queen Charlotte Islands and other points along the coast.

Dufferin need not have worried about the reception he might receive in the west. Instead of rebellious angry forces, he found a friendly carnival-like atmosphere in both Victoria and Nanaimo. Everyone seemed prepared to show respect and loyalty to the Governor General. In Victoria, however, an arch over a street warned, "Carnarvon Terms Or Separation." Seeing the sign, Dufferin smiled and ordered his carriage to take another route to his viceregal quarters at Government House. The Carnarvon Terms were a set of proposals ordered by the British colonial secretary Lord Carnarvon in 1874 to settle the dispute between the province and the federal government so that "the railway from Esquimalt to Nanaimo shall be commenced as soon as possible."

After the initial warm welcome in Nanaimo, Bate and his council informed Dufferin of their grievances and the way in which the city had been neglected. In his speech, Bate pledged loyalty to the Queen, then outlined the chief attributes of Nanaimo: its "spacious harbour, which is navigable for the largest vessels and safe at all seasons . . . and receives more tonnage than any other port in this Province. As a site for a dry dock our harbour is unrivalled." He added that Nanaimo was "the seat of the most important industry in British Columbia and in a most prosperous and progressive state; . . . But we regret to say that our coal trade is carried on under the serious disadvantage entailed by the heavy duty imposed in the United States upon our large exports to that country—our principal foreign market."[38]

An attentive audience listened as Bate continued to outline the wants and needs of his community. "We have a long felt and pressing need of direct communication with the Telegraphic Systems of the world, and there is an entire absence of suitable buildings for the Customs, Post Office and other federal departments at Nanaimo." Normally, Nanaimo did not take part in discussions of a political nature affecting the province, he said, but asked that for "the peace, progress and satisfaction of the people of British Columbia, we believe what are known as the Carnarvon Terms should be fulfilled intact by the great Dominion of Canada." Bate concluded by thanking Dufferin for his "liberal patronage and encouragement of education and the arts."[39]

Following the presentation, Lord and Lady Dufferin and their entourage proceeded along Church and Commercial Streets, passing under six large arches built for the occasion. After inspecting the coal mines at Harewood and at Chase River, they received a salute from the cannons at the Bastion before continuing their journey.

Lord Dufferin sent Bate a letter in which he thanked the mayor and council for the visit to the harbour and the City of Nanaimo, adding that he was able to appreciate "by personal observation the satisfactory indications of the mineral resources." He regretted the heavy duties imposed by the United States, which he would bring to the attention of the proper authorities, along with the lack of telegraphic communications and public buildings, of which Bate had complained. He said he sympathized with the anxiety about the

"Carnarvon Terms," more especially as the performance of one of them you consider yourselves so deeply interested, viz., the construction of the Nanaimo and Esquimalt Railway, has, through the actions of one branch of the Canadian legislature, become extremely problematical. I can only hope that a friendly consideration by the parties concerned of the difficulties which have arisen out of this disturbing incident may lead to the substitution of some equivalent which may be found acceptable by the province. With regard, however, to the principal feature, of the original agreement, namely the construction of a railway to the Pacific Ocean, although it is no part of my business to give you any assurance on that point, I sincerely hope that your just expectations may be realized.[40]

Dufferin returned to Victoria on September 19, and gave a "magnificent speech" lasting two and a half hours, in which he praised the resources of the province, then explained the federal government's railway policy, and concluded with a plea for patience. At no time did he give any hint as to whether he sympathized with British Columbia's cause.[41]

After touring the province, Dufferin returned to Ottawa. He had listened and formed an opinion of the grievances. Right or wrong, the province wanted money spent on Vancouver Island and the matter of the railway terminus settled. He noted that only in Victoria was there serious discontent. "The brute expenditure of construction money on the Esquimalt and Nanaimo railway would satisfy their craving,"[42] but he said he was inclined to agree with the people of New Westminster that "a line connecting a little town of five thousand people and a village of one thousand would be a useless and extravagant expenditure of money." The suggestion of bridging the Strait of Georgia seemed absolutely impracticable.

Nanaimo and the province had made the case and waited for action. Nanaimo, meanwhile, went back to doing what it did best: mining.

EARLY RECOGNITION

Bate and his council moved into new headquarters at the old Stone House on May 19, 1875, after renovating the interior. This was a much more substantial building than the one previously occupied by the city. Built by stonemason William Isbister in 1852, its walls three feet thick, it was constructed of stones from the beach and lime made from crushed clamshells. Bate described its history:

> The building was occupied by Captain Charles Edward Stuart, who was officer in command of the [HBC] "Nanaimo Establishment," and served as the Pay Office and contained the Officers' Mess Room, where many a way-farer was handsomely regaled by the generous hospitality of the gentleman in charge, whose table always was bounteously supplied. The Mess Room was used, now and then for a dance when the Governor's daughters, and other ladies; Mr. A.G. Dallas, Dr. Tolmie, Mr. Blenkinsop, and several others who might be named, paid Nanaimo a call.[43]

Residents may have felt that the first city council was working as well as could be expected, considering everyone was new to the job. However, Bate was frustrated by the divisions within it: "Our city council does not work very smoothly. The old sectional jealousies are as rife as ever, one part of Town and people against the other, and every body disappointed."[44] While these divisions were troubling, Bate was acclaimed to a third term as mayor in 1878. Constituents appreciated how he managed the affairs of the city and paid tribute to him during a celebration of the Queen's birthday on May 24, 1878. He was presented with an English gold watch with an inscription to "Mayor Mark Bate," and a silver-plated tea and coffee set of six pieces, and an epergne and tray for Sarah Bate. The items were placed for all to see at Hirst's store. William Rayould read the testimonial before a large crowd enjoying the Victoria Day celebrations on the Green.

> In public recognition of your just and able conduct in the Civic Chair and in Court as Chief Magistrate of the City . . . and in high appreciation of your sterling worth as a gentleman, both in your business and private life as evidenced by your sound judgment, far

reaching sagacity, earnest industry, tenacity of purpose, integrity and firmness in action and withal your imperturbable urbanity and courtesy in the performance of your duty in every walk and relation of your life. In conclusion we trust that Mrs. Bate, yourself and children may be long spared to enjoy an unmeasured share of the highest happiness and prosperity.[45]

While the Nanaimo Brass Band played "Hail to the Chief," the various items were presented to the Mayor and Mrs. Bate. A copy of the address was printed in gold on satin and given to the couple. In accepting the gifts Bate thanked everyone for the beautiful presents, and added: "Let me say that I have desired no other reward in the performance of public duties than the appreciation of my fellow citizens." He said the gifts would be handed down to his children and would be treasured long after the social gatherings were over.

Bate may have had greater aspirations than city hall. In his September 1878 report to Wild, he broached two ideas for which he sought the company's permission. At the last provincial election he said he had been "strongly pressed" to become a candidate, but he felt it his duty to decline, though local businesses had a vested interest in the election's outcome:

I was induced, however, to give a tacit support to Mr. G.A. Walkem's nomination, i.e. to a gentleman who he could depend on in the House, and in consideration of that support, Mr. Walkem promised me he would, if it lay in his power, abolish the dual system of taxation in Municipalities, a system inaugurated by the late Elliott government.[46]

In the 1878 provincial election, he supported James Atkinson Abrams, who was elected by only 15 votes over his opponent, David William Gordon. Abrams owned and operated the Nanaimo Tanning

Company. Although no party designation existed at this time, it was known he supported the interests of the government. Premier Walkem announced in the legislature that there would be a repeal in the next session of the dual tax collected under the Assessment Act. Bate believed the repeal would save the company about $4,000 a year. He wrote to Wild, "The present member is a staunch friend of mine, a friend of the town, and a friend of the Company, and he will at all times do anything he can for our united interests."

Bate observed that in the next provincial general election, Nanaimo would be allowed two members in the legislature, and he asked Wild if the company would allow him the time to be a candidate:

> I fully expect I should be requested to represent the city-portion of the district, or at least to become a candidate for the honor. Of course, I could not consent without the Board's sanction. May I take the liberty to ask to you kindly inform me if it is probable I might be permitted to attend to the duties, which would devolve upon me in the event of my election? My great aim in entering Parliament would be to benefit the Company if I saw an opportunity, as well as to attend to the interests of the District.[47]

He got his answer; the board said "no" to him accepting a nomination. If he was disappointed, it did not show in his reply to Wild:

> I have no particular desire to become a candidate for Parliamentary honours, nor do I wish to be pestered by politicians, hence I promised to ascertain from the directors if I may be permitted to stand at the proper time in the event of a written request being presented to me.[48]

In the next provincial election, held in 1882, Nanaimo did indeed have two seats, as Bate had predicted.

14

BUSINESS
OPPORTUNITIES

O N THE AFTERNOON OF APRIL 20, 1878, a strong north-westerly wind fanned sparks from a chimney fire, setting ablaze buildings along the lower side of Commercial Street. The dire consequences of the situation were immediately apparent, as most of the buildings in town were of wooden construction, and the town had neither a fire department nor a ready supply of water. A few wells had been sunk and pumps erected, but most people still drew their water by bucket from springs. As the conflagration quickly spread, volunteers began drawing water from the ravine in an effort to douse the flames. Residents gathered to help or watch but there was little anyone could do except look on helplessly as building after building went up in flames. The owner of the Millstream Sawmill, Chauncey Carpenter, gave his employees the rest of the day off to go and see the blaze. He viewed it as a business opportunity and a ready market for his lumber, but it was a devastating blow to the city and business sector of town.

Bate would have been dismayed the fire destroyed so many buildings that affected much of the town's business economy, but it inspired the small town to make some changes. The rebuilding of Commercial Street began almost immediately and new businesses soon opened. Businessmen John Hirst and Josiah Walter Stirtan donated a lot on the east corner of Commercial and Wharf Streets for the city's first fire hall, to house the newly organized volunteer Black Diamond Fire Company. Carpenter donated lumber for the fire hall, which opened on January 21, 1879. By the fall, enough money had been raised to purchase a Button and Blake fire engine from the fire department of Portland, Oregon.

In the aftermath of the fire, city council ordered the excavation of cisterns around the community to hold reserves of water for use in case of fire. In 1881, it also authorized Stirtan to lay a system of wooded water pipes to be used in a new waterworks system, the first attempt to provide the city with a regular water supply. In return Stirtan was to supply the fire company with free water. By 1884, the Nanaimo Water Works Company Limited was formed and took over Stirtan's system. It was not until 1901, after a board of arbitration fixed the price at $104,000, that the city formally purchased the Water Works Company and transferred its plant to the city.

All that was needed were bells to alert the population when a fire erupted. Bate inquired of Rosenfeld if he knew the name of a company in San Francisco that made bells. The fire chief had asked him to find out the price of "good bells about 150 to 200 tons steel and bell metal." Bate eventually placed an order for one of the #192 bells made of bell metal. He requested it be sent direct to the *Idaho* sailing for Nanaimo. By August 1878, Bate reported that the firemen were pleased with the bell, for which the council paid $95.85.

DUNSMUIR COMPETITION

Trying to keep abreast of all possible business opportunities for the company, Bate became involved in a venture that belonged to his two brothers-in-law, Adam Grant Horne and Peter Sabiston. Adam and Elizabeth Horne's return to Nanaimo in 1878 was precipitated by the closure of the HBC post at Comox. Educational opportunities were also better in Nanaimo for their children, and Elizabeth wanted to be closer to her sister Lucy. In addition, their eldest son, Henry, aged 19, now lived and worked in Nanaimo. They built a house next door to Lucy and Peter on Wallace Street.

In the venture that drew Bate's attention, the two men purchased 400 acres south and east of Chandler's property. John Dick, known for his ability to find coal, did some prospecting for them and found a seam. The *Nanaimo Free Press* congratulated them on the coal discovery in its edition of December 24, 1879:

> This proves the richness of the property of Messrs. Horne and Sabiston for it also demonstrates the pleasant fact that about 2000 acres belonging to the Vancouver Coal Company in the immediate neighbourhood is rich in coal. It is somewhat surprising that the Company have not extended their prospecting to that portion of their property for it has been the impression among practical miners that vast beds of coal exist between this city and the Millstream.

Neither Horne nor Sabiston had the knowledge required to open a mine, so they entered into a partnership with Dick and Jacob Blessing. Jacob handled the accounting and Dick supervised the operations of the Millstone Valley Mine. The mine operated from 1879 to 1881.

Bate explained how his company lost another opportunity:

> Mr. Beaumont has been negotiating with Sabiston & Horne with a view of "bonding" their coal land for 18 months, and in the meantime it was intended to well explore our own ground adjacent to

that of Messrs S & H: but while Mr. Beaumont is arranging terms, Dunsmuir, Diggle & Co. offer $30,000 cash! Which put an end to the bonding. It is strange how young Dunsmuir could have learned so soon what Mr. Beaumont was after, as he hoped to get things settled before the move he was making became generally known. The fact is we did not want to buy Sabiston and Horne's mineral rights and Dunsmuir, Diggle & Co according to my estimates have paid "too much for the whistle." If the bond had been executed we could probably have traced the seam from Sabiston and Horne's place to our ground not far away.[1]

Once again Dunsmuir had shown how he could act quickly and make a decision, which Bate could not do; he had to wait for the Vancouver Coal Company's corporate directive from London. Dunsmuir closed the mine and used the equipment elsewhere. A decade later it reopened as Wellington Collieries No. 2 slope. Coal was mined for just over a year. It was this mine that earned the nickname Jingle Pot Mine. According to local folklore it was so named by a worker constantly bringing buckets of coal to the service remarking "someday there may be jingles in these pots."[2]

After giving 27 years of service to the HBC, Horne returned to retailing. He opened up a store on Victoria Crescent, Horne & Son, selling dry goods such as "fashionable" hats and "the finest and cheapest underclothing," plus grocery items. Sabiston continued operating the Commercial Hotel.

THE MINE AGENT'S VISIT

The company's agent in San Francisco, John Rosenfeld, paid a visit to Nanaimo in 1879. His visit may have unsettled Bate, for he raised questions about the mine operation. The company books and the director's diaries were closely examined, and after inspecting the wharves, the weight house, and the railway bridge, he concluded that the Nanaimo coal operation was "far behind the times" with its pithead arrangements. Bate found him very inquisitive. Rosenfeld wondered why they "tip nearly all [the] coal on the ground and have to take it up again. Why don't you put up bunkers like other people? Bulkley had bunkers!" He was referring to the Harewood mine. Bate agreed, he said he had talked about bunkers and improvements for years and had repeatedly suggested to Bryden that would improve shipping. Once more Bate shifted the responsibility to his mine superintendent: "Bryden preferred wagons before bunkers."

After looking at the books and the director's diaries, he noted that Bate had made suggestions where improvement could be made. Rosenfeld confided, "Mr. Bate tell me privately does not Mr. Bryden take notice when you make suggestions about anything." Bate replied, "Well, he perhaps notices what I say but he takes his own course nevertheless." Rosenfeld concluded, "He neglects things and I shall tell them so. Your wharves will cost three or four times as much to fix as they would if repaired in time."[3]

The next day they visited Newcastle Island and while there Rosenfeld quickly discovered, and pointed out to Bate, that Dunsmuir, Diggle and Co.'s South Wellington Mine had bunkers to store coal. The island lay across Departure Bay and the Wellington wharves were clearly visible. His point was made that the company's loading facilities could be improved, particularly regarding bunkers, locomotives, and wharves.

There were two mines on Newcastle Island, the Newcastle and Fitzwilliam mines. On Rosenfeld's visit, he and Bate discussed reopening the Fitzwilliam mine, which had been kept free of water since it closed following a gas explosion in 1876 that killed three miners. At that inquiry coroner Warner Reeve Spalding found negligence on the part of the company, officers, and superintendent. He also found that the men were as much to blame. This was Bate's first fatal mine accident while working as manager for the Vancouver Coal Company. The mine closed the following year due to poor sales and problems with ventilation, but the company continued working the pumps to keep it de-watered. It reopened in 1880 for a short time.[4]

The Newcastle Mine was being mined privately in 1868 by *Princess Royal* miners Jesse Sage and his son-in-law, Edward Walker. It had ceased operations by 1876, according to the Ministry of Mines report of that year.

MANAGER AND MAGISTRATE

Bate had a lot on his mind when the Coal Mines Regulation Act came into effect in 1877. Like other mine managers, he was always concerned about safety as well as keeping the mines open and productive. However, the new Act placed the onus for safety on the miners rather than on the managers; it was up to the workers to keep the mines secure. This placed Bate in an awkward position, for he did not want to be accused of interfering with a miner's ability to earn a living, although he did have the authority to remove someone if danger was present.

Another provision in the Act could have been interpreted as prohibiting Chinese from working underground in the mines. "No Chinaman, or person, unable to speak good English could hold any position of trust or responsibility." However, mine managers appeared to have ignored this interpretation. In 1878, 300 Chinese lived in Nanaimo, 87 of them employed in the Nanaimo mines.[5] Many had businesses and were productive members of the community.

A movement to deny Chinese the same liberties as those enjoyed by other residents was advanced in Victoria by Noah Shakespeare. He strenuously opposed immigration to any part of the Dominion. Bate knew that the previous year changes made to the Municipal Act prohibited Chinese from voting in any municipal election. While he never expressed an opinion about the Chinese in any of his writings, however, he must have appreciated their labour in the mines and in his home. Ah Ling, aged 16, worked as a cook/domestic in Bate's home.[6]

One of Bate's Chinese helpers was involved in a burglary that resulted in Bate testifying on his behalf before the Magistrates Court. The crime happened in his brother-in-law's business, Horne & Son, on Victoria Crescent, in January 1881. Burglars had broken into the shop during the night and stolen expensive items of clothing, boxes of tobacco, and grocery items. Police constables immediately searched Snuneymuxw and Chinese houses, and in the home of Ah Jake and his wife Fook Loye, they found the couple asleep in bed with two blankets covering them, which Horne identified as two of the stolen items.

Ah Jake, Fook Loye, Young Dok Leet, Lee Hung, and Ah Klung were arrested and marched off to jail. Some of the goods were later found on Cavan Street in front of Tom Peck's residence and close to the company's office on Haliburton Street. On January 29, 1881, the *Nanaimo Free Press* called it an "audacious burglary," with a follow-up story about the clever capture of the burglars. The trial was held in March. Bate was the only person to testify on behalf of one of the accused. "M. Bate swore—I have known Ah Jake from 7 to 8 years, he was 6 years at my house during that period, got sick after he got married, came back and stayed about 15 days and was taken ill again: always looked upon him as a very good man indeed."

The jury returned a guilty verdict against Young Dok Leet and Lee Hung for housebreaking, and Ah Jake for receiving stolen property. Jake's wife, Fook Loye, was not charged. The men were sentenced to three years in the New Westminster penitentiary.[7]

As mayor, magistrate, and mine manager, Bate held conflicting positions. Such was the case when Mike Manson related a story that illustrated the general attitude toward Chinese workers. A railway was being built to the Chase River mine and Manson was in charge of a night gang of Chinese. One man insisted on sitting down on his wheelbarrow to have a smoke. Manson did not fault him for smoking but insisted he run the wheelbarrow as soon as the cigarette was lit; this he refused to do. After repeated orders the man began to "curse him in Chinese fashion," so Manson whacked him with a stick a couple of times and broke two of his ribs. Other Chinese co-workers got involved in the melee and came after him with shovels. Manson took refuge on top of a tree stump and held them off until they calmed down, then he told four of them to take the injured man home. "I got down among them and they surely worked that afternoon."[8]

The next day a lawyer representing the Chinese worker came to Magistrate Bate's office asking him to sign a warrant for Manson's arrest. This Bate refused to do but he warned Manson not to leave the country until he looked into the complaint. The next day Manson gave Bate a full explanation of the incident. Bate let him off "with a smile" and told him "not to hit them so hard next time but get the road built as quickly as you can." Meanwhile, Bate the mine manager paid the Chinese man his wages while he was recovering, and as soon as he was well he returned to the road gang. Manson had no further trouble from him, and said the rest of the men "worked like Trojans until the road was finished."

The magistrate's court took up a lot of Bate's valuable time. Many of the offences were minor in nature but indicative of the frontier nature that was then Nanaimo. The court's calendar was divided between seven justices of the peace. Sometimes only one JP heard a case, while at other times there were several. Many of the cases reviewed were linked to First Nations or Chinese residents, or were liquor related. This is not surprising considering the number of liquor outlets in the city.

The night watchman, Pargeter, was a regular in court as he patrolled the streets in the evening and brought many of the offenders into court. Such was the case with one man charged with "being drunk and riotous on public streets," who had no problem pleading guilty to being drunk but objected to the charge of riotous conduct. For minor crime, prisoners could spend a few nights in the uncomfortable and unheated Bastion jail, and for longer sentences they were shipped off at the city's expense to serve their sentence in Victoria.

MINE EXPLOSION

Bate lost one of his staff in 1877 when Edward G. Prior resigned to accept the appointment as BC Inspector of Mines, following the passage of the Coal Mines Regulation Act. At age 24, it was up to him to enforce the new rules, but Prior found it an uphill battle. As mining companies increased production, safety issues were sometimes ignored, resulting in dangerous conditions.

This was the case with the Wellington mine, owned by the Dunsmuirs. When Prior warned about explosive gas in the tenth level of the Wellington mine, his concern was not taken seriously, as there had been few issues of afterdamp (gas) in the mines. The explosion in the mine on April 17, 1879, which took the lives of 11 men, was a wake-up call for all mine operators. Prior described the incident in his report: "The year 1879 was visited by the heaviest calamity that has ever overtaken the mining community of this province."[9] He had drawn attention to the problem with gas but had been ignored.

Bate, meanwhile, kept a close eye on his competitor and reported to Wild: "Some of the Wellington miners are afraid to go to their stalls in the lower part of the mine—they do not consider it safe, and a few of the men have applied to Mr. Bryden for work but he does not employ them."[10] The explosion and deaths of fellow miners obviously unsettled all miners. The Wellington mine gained the reputation for being the most dangerous of all the island mines.

At the time of the accident Robert Dunsmuir's son, James, was mine manager, but unlike his father, he did not warm to the miners and was perceived as cold, haughty, impatient, and demanding.

Watching, perhaps waiting in the wings, was Robert's son-in-law, John Bryden, a likely candidate to replace James.

Bate kept a close eye on the Dunsmuir operation. When he heard that James's brother Alex had moved to San Francisco, he wrote to Rosenfeld:

> It is understood that young Dunsmuir (a silly sort of fellow) is to join Berryman in partnership and that the firm name will be "Berryman & Dunsmuir." They are to open coal yards in various localities—at Oakland right away. Whether the assistance Diggle and young Dunsmuir will afford Berryman will be of any value or not you will be able to judge. I agree with you they must be kept out of harm's way, and to prevent their rashness from materially injuring us, as you will know how to push them and in what direction and to what length our opposition should run. Please don't let them get any of the Pacific Mail SS Co. business if you can prevent it.[11]

What Bate did not know was that the Alex Dunsmuir went to San Francisco with a mission. His father suspected Berryman of using his position as sales representative of Wellington coal for his own advantage. It irritated Dunsmuir to share any profit with him, and he wanted to make new arrangements and needed someone he could trust to keep a watchful eye on Berryman's activities. Who better than his son Alex! Alex quickly found a way to end the partnership, essentially accusing Berryman of embezzlement.[12] Robert Dunsmuir announced he had "successfully adjusted partnership affairs" by taking over Berryman's business. Alex settled in San Francisco and to oversee family operations in that city. Another partner, Wadham Diggle, also moved to San Francisco, to manage the company's marine operation.

The year 1878 was not a good year for the coal mines of Vancouver Island. Prior, the mine inspector, reported the year was one of "unprecedented discouragement." Coal prices in San Francisco, the island's main market, were the lowest ever. "Indeed," wrote Prior, "while subjected to so much depression, only the most able commercial management, and the utmost economy in carrying on the works, have saved this important industry from entire cessation."[13] Prior said the BC producers were at a terrible disadvantage over those in the Puget Sound, saved only by the "superior quality" of Nanaimo coal. He explained, "Every ton of BC coal going into San Francisco has to pay a duty of 75 cents. Seattle coal of course escapes this . . . Ships coming to Nanaimo are compelled to pay pilotage dues," he said, but all US vessels are exempt.[14] On this point Bate agreed with him, when he voiced his concern about the coal industry with his insurance agent in Victoria. "Prices were never as low before at San Francisco as they are now. Such a ruinous statement is more than any of our Island mines can stand under for any length of time. I fail to discern the slightest prospect of an improvement."[15] The outlook for Nanaimo coal was gloomy.

15

BRYDEN
RESIGNS

WHILE BATE RESPECTED BRYDEN'S KNOWLEDGE of the coal mining operation, Bate seemed besieged with suspicion about Bryden's loyalty to the company. Since Bryden's marriage to Robert Dunsmuir's daughter Elizabeth, Bate constantly watched and checked up on him. He also monitored every move of the Dunsmuir operation. In monthly reports to Wild, he regularly questions Bryden's decisions, suggesting they were made less on behalf of the company than at the advice of the Dunsmuirs:

> With respect to the question of wages it puzzles me greatly to understand why Mr. Bryden should say we cannot mine coal as cheaply as our neighbours. I do not recollect making such an admission . . . he appears to avoid and seems totally mixed up with his "Father-in-law" and crowd that he can hardly be expected to do anything against their interests, to go against their wishes.[1]

Perhaps Bate was trying to find a way of getting rid of Bryden when he wrote to Rosenfeld in 1879, questioning Bryden's lack of qualifications in light of requirements in the new Mining Act and wondering who might replace him. He asked that the discussion be kept "strictly confidential":

> In the event of an accident to Bryden, or his absence, or retirement from the company, could he [Bate] employ one of the miners, or work managers? In this country, the person responsible for the safe conduct of the Colliery must be certificated [sic] by a Board of Mining Engineers, and it is he and not the general manager who is called to account if an accident occurs. If this is so, what was done when the Act came into operation to qualify Mr. Bryden? In the event of any of the contingencies just mentioned i.e. in the case of Mr. Bryden ceasing to act for the company from any cause whatever, could you find a man (now) in the service whom you could with full confidence select to act in Mr. Bryden's place? I informed the secretary that we could at once make a temporary appointment pending the employment of a thoroughly competent man.[2]

DISAGREEMENT OVER STRIKE

Bate need not have worried about getting rid of Bryden, however, for changing circumstances caused Bryden to resign. Those changes began with a strike in March 1880, after the company's board of directors ordered a reduction in wages. Bryden was determined to hold firm, but as was often the case, the two men disagreed on how best to resolve the problem. A frustrated Bryden recommended that instead of hiring "white" miners to do the work of the striking miners, they bring in independent-minded Italians (who were not considered white) from San Francisco. Bryden wrote, "I think we should try them as they are a class that would not be easily advised or intimidated."[3]

No one thought the striking miners would resort to arson. One morning shortly after the strike began, fire destroyed the company's workshops and large store, a devastating blow to the Vancouver Coal Company. The old steam engine, the "Lady McKay," that had been brought from Scotland and lovingly cared for by engineer Andrew Hunter 30 years earlier, was also destroyed in the blaze.

Bryden reported the incident and his investigations to Sam Robins in London:

> The fire was discovered in the machine shop, and as there was a high wind blowing at the time it soon spread to the other buildings. And it was with some difficulty that the Railway Bridge was saved, and had it not been for the plentiful supply of water from the fire engine a portion of it must have been burned down . . . In the machine shop there was an ordinary fireplace built of stone and brick for warming the room. But on the day previous there was but little fire in it, as the day was fine, so that little fire was required. And it has always been a rule with us that previous to the men quitting work at night to see that the fire was safe, and to bank it well with dead ashes and tamp it hard down.
>
> I examined the fireplace after the buildings had been burned down, and found the fire heavily banked with dead ash and well tamped down . . . I think it was hardly possible for fire to have communicated to the building from the fireplace. No lights had been used in the shop the evening previous to the fire. And I passed the shops that night at about 11 o'clock and all was then dark and quiet. It was about 5 o'clock in the morning when the strong glare from the fire woke me up.[4]

Bryden lived nearby on Esplanade and could see the machine shop from his window. He too suspected the fire had been deliberately set. Nothing could be proved, though, so its origins remained a mystery. There was no hurry to rebuild the workshops until it was known where the next mines were likely to be located.

Bryden told Sam Robins that management had failed to negotiate a reduction in wages. He implied that Bate's lack of firmness had strengthened the miners' conviction that striking would allow them to negotiate on their own terms.[5] Bate, meanwhile, told Rosenfeld he tried everything in his power to get the men to work. He had paid agents working among the miners to try to influence them, but he feared that as long as they had hope of obtaining work elsewhere, they were encouraged to continue the strike. "I should exceedingly like to bring the men to terms, either by starving them out or getting new men, and the only way we can do it is by being firm, even if we have to buy a cargo or two from the enemy."[6]

The final straw came with Rosenfeld's telegram to Bryden, saying that the company directors in London authorized Rosenfeld to make the decision. This confirmed the instruction Bryden had received from the directors. Rosenfeld's advice: "Resume work immediately, on best terms."[7] Bryden, however, believed the only way to proceed was to break the strike, restore colliery discipline, and resume production. He suspected Rosenfeld of panicking then intervening with company directors on his own behalf, without considering alternative sources of coal supply, such as from Dunsmuir, at least until management won the dispute. He felt he had no other option but to resign. He wrote to Robins:

I was very much surprised when the telegram reached us. I was led to believe the company was prepared to stand by us in the event of a strike. Giving way to the men at this time, and under the present circumstance, they have placed themselves and us in a false position ... The Wellington company would have sold, and offered to supply it at the same prices at which Mr. Rosenfeld were returning to the company; an offer which I think was very fair. You must see I have been placed in rather a strange position. A reduction of wages was ordered, and the men came out on strike. The decision in the matter has been left to Mr. Rosenfeld, and he orders work to be resumed, and we have had to resume it at the miners' terms. I fear that my influence with our men will be very much lessened, and consequently my usefulness to the company very much impaired. And seeing this I do not think that I would be doing justice either to the company or myself by remaining in my present position. I therefore beg to place my resignation in your hand. And in doing so, I do it with the best of intentions, and in the hope that the change may be beneficial to both parties.[8]

The strike ended when miners accepted a reduction in wages that was less than the company had initially proposed.

Bryden's resignation came as no surprise to Bate. While Bryden told Bate he resigned because the company had left a settlement with the men virtually in Rosenfeld's hands, Bate told Robins, "I do not think his head has been in his work for a long time and I think there is not the slightest doubt we can be better without him than with him." Bate said that during the years of his association with Bryden, never had "an angry word passed between them."[9] When leaving, Bryden remarked that the company should have "but one head . . . as the full management."[10] Robert Dunsmuir quickly replaced his son James with the much more experienced Bryden as manager of the Wellington mine. James was shuffled off to the less demanding job of loading coal at the Departure Bay wharves.

The board was not in any hurry to replace Bryden. When his letter of resignation arrived in London, on the morning of the general meeting, it was held over until the next board meeting. He had sent his letter in April of 1880, but it was not until July 25 that the board notified him they had accepted his resignation, which would take effect on November 17.

Bryden's resignation coincided with rumours that Dunsmuir, Diggle and Co. was negotiating with the directors to purchase the Vancouver Coal Mine. Wadham Diggle was suspected of buying a large number of shares to gain control. Bate writing to Rosenfeld in

April 1880, hoped the company would never let the estate fall in the hands of Dunsmuir: "It will be a bad job for me and the whole place if they now get possession of the Nanaimo mines."[11] Wild instructed Bate to sketch a map of the company's land; his map showed it had over seven thousand acres. No reason was given for this directive, although Bate suspected it had to do with Dunsmuir's initiative.

THREAT OF A DUNSMUIR TAKEOVER

Rumour and innuendo fuelled Bate's obsession with Dunsmuir. At 55, Dunsmuir was twelve years Bate's senior. He had been employed by the Vancouver Coal Company as mining supervisor several times since its inception, until he began his own mining concern in direct competition with the company. Dunsmuir was also well acquainted with the Vancouver Coal Company's directors:

> The old gentleman seems to be turning attention to me, and appears to think I am in their way. I understand he or his friends are complaining to the directors about me. He may rest assured I shall put nothing in his way, and I know he can hardly bear the idea of my being so placed as to prevent his having partial control of our mine as well as his own.[12]

In September, he was notified by telegram that John Wild would visit Nanaimo with a Mr. Jeffcock, and for him to arrange accommodation. Jeffcock was to arrange the appointment of a substitute for Bryden, and would be armed with "full power in respect to all matters concerning the company."

Bate could not resist another swipe at Bryden when he next wrote to Rosenfeld: "Bryden is cleaning up and making things look as well as he can in various directions—attending in fact to some little matters that have been neglected for years."[13] Bate suggested that Archibald Muir would make a good superintendent, "and we have other good men among our miners," he added, "but they all perhaps lack the degree of technical information which may be considered essentials."[14]

Privacy seemed paramount with the threat of a Dunsmuir take-over looming. Bate began communicating using Slater's *Telegraphic Code*,[15] and he suggested Rosenfeld do likewise. He offered to send him a copy of the code if he did not have one. He explained to Rosenfeld privately how to use the code:

> We can always use the name of a Mine when necessary, and in fact I suppose we need only use the code when secrecy is required. If you please we will add 88 to the words we wish to have read—thus: I want to say "man struck" I do not find the word "men" in the book so I send that as if it is, but opposite the word struck there is 21755, to which I add 88, 21843 and opposite 21843 we find the word "succeeding" so that I would wire, for "men struck" men succeeding.[16]

There is no indication Rosenfeld understood the bafflegab explanation or even if he wanted to use it, for he continued to write as openly as before.

RESPONDING TO CRITICISM

The board of directors in London received negative comments about Bate. When Bate heard about this, he reacted angrily in a letter to Rosenfeld, while thanking him for his strong friendship:

> My calumniators are well known, and I can truthfully say that where I drink one glass of beer they drink a dozen glasses of whiskey. I never neglected a day's business in my life through drink. I have always considered myself a moderate and a small drinker, and can do quite well without taking intoxicants at all. As to my playing the fiddle, I do help once or twice a year, at our local concerts and other entertainments, but surely there can be no harm in that. I also play a cornet with our amateur Brass Band and pass a few hours pleasantly

in that way. Surely that can't be wrong. I shall act upon your very kind advice—shall let Mr. Jeffcock see that I am not over fond of the glass, that I do not care for it at all and there give him an opportunity of carrying to the directors information which will disprove the reports which may have reached them. I think I have mentioned to you before that it is a son-in-law of old Dunsmuir, Col. Houghton, they call him, who writes to Mr. Irwin, but it is amazing the directors, or any one of them, would notice anything emanating from such a quarter. The Col. is a lazy fellow who has nothing to do and he occupies his time in slandering and similar evil practices. Houghton is a worthless fellow and I do not think he is worth noticing further.[17]

Irwin was one of the directors of the Vancouver Coal Company. He and Colonel Charles Frederick Houghton had corresponded for some time. Houghton first came to Nanaimo with the militia in the spring of 1877 when he was asked to assist in suppressing a coal miners' strike at the Wellington mine. Dunsmuir appreciated the military intervention, so when Houghton, 39, asked for the hand of Dunsmuir's 22-year-old daughter, Marion, he was welcomed wholeheartedly into the family. They married on March 27, 1879. Bate remembered Houghton from two years before when he applied for 1,200 acres of prime land in Nanaimo Harbour. Marion, who has been described as "tight-lipped and bad-tempered," with "a kind of petulant attractiveness,"[18] may have had a disability or illness of some sort, for Bate remarked, "he married the daughter who has been a cripple for some years." They "sailed lately for England to see if his wife can be benefited by some skilled physician."[19] The Houghtons went on a European honeymoon. Bate later indicated that Houghton and Irwin were related. Bate thought Irwin might as well be writing directly to Dunsmuir, who sometimes talked about "hearing from the directors." Bate presumed it must be through his new son-in-law.

Jeffcock, visiting Nanaimo and examining the company's operations, began making changes that according to Bate were improvements he had wanted for years. Jeffcock also satisfied himself that Bate was not the dreadful character he had been led to believe. In October 1880, Jeffcock interviewed Robert Dunsmuir. Bate quipped, "I don't think Mr. Jeffcock is a man that Dunsmuir could deceive." Afterwards he told Bate in confidence that Dunsmuir had made an offer for the company's mines and property. Bate immediately notified Rosenfeld:

> The offer was to pay three per cent per annum on the paid up capital of the company and buy the whole concern in 10 years at the same price I believe as the shareholders have paid up. Mr. Jeffcock does not think the offer will be acceptable in London, but as no returns to speak of have been forthcoming for some time it is hard to say what the proprietors may do. Dunsmuir's three per cent would only amount to about $12,000 per year and it may pay our opponents to keep the place at a standstill at that figure, that is, to buy off the opposition. I hope Dunsmuir will never get the property on any condition, and I feel sure you will spare no effort to prevent him.[20]

Dunsmuir showed he was serious about buying the Vancouver Coal Company and its properties. If the first offer was not acceptable, he was prepared to make another. Bate suggested the company should turn around and offer to buy the Wellington mine on the same terms. He expressed his concern to the directors about local businessmen being alarmed "because it means ruin almost to some of them who have invested largely in town property," and urged them to restore confidence and stop Dunsmuir short by "flatly putting down their feet" to the scheme: "The constant talk of buying out the Vancouver Coal Company can have no other effect than to depreciate the value of the company's town property."[21] The manager of the Bank of British Columbia, W.C. Ward, was reported to have said he hoped Dunsmuir would get the Nanaimo mines. Bate, however, suggested that gentleman had an eye to business: "I have no doubt the bank, one way and another, is doing well out of our opponents."[22]

COMPANY EXPANSION

Weeks of speculation and rumour were finally put to rest on December 17, 1880, when Bate received a cablegram from the directors in London, who had decided to sink new pits. They inquired about applying to the provincial legislature for a right-of-way to build a railway in front of city property. Bate also received a letter from Jeffcock reassuring him that everything was satisfactory to the directors and that he had recommended they proceed with new pits. This was a good day for the Vancouver Coal Company, for Nanaimo, and for Mark Bate.

The BC Mining Report of 1880 stated that the mines of the Vancouver Coal Company were in good order and safe to work in, and that the company was contemplating opening an extensive mine near the town. The mines operating were Chase River, Douglas, and Fitzwilliam. Archibald Dick was appointed the inspector of mines following the resignation of Edward G. Prior, who opened an iron and hardware store in Victoria.

The new mining engineer arrived the following spring. James Beaumont had worked for 30 years as a mining engineer in Yorkshire.[23] Bate noted, "Mr. Beaumont has had great experience in opening new pits, and I have no doubt he will put things in good shape to start with in beginning a fresh mine." His contract with the company was for three years.[24] With Bryden gone, Bate continued to manage the business of the company with the help of Beaumont and William McGregor, who was appointed general manager in the mines. McGregor was the son of pioneer miner John McGregor, who had the altercation with Bate's uncle George Robinson in 1856.

MORE LABOUR DISPUTES

Another strike, or series of work-related incidents, occurred in 1881.

The first was in March when the Fitzwilliam miners walked off the job over a dispute about free coal for miners' homes. Then in September, a spontaneous combustion fire in the Chase River mine burned for four weeks and cost the company orders that were promptly picked up by Dunsmuir. In yet another incident some miners wanted compensation for dirty coal. Bate explained to Rosenfeld in September how the miners were making demands, which he said Beaumont advised should be strenuously resisted: "I am very much adverse to strikes and hope we may by reasoning with the men get them to continue working. Having already been idle three days they will probably take a further rest."[25]

Three weeks later the men were still not back to work. Bate seemed resigned about the work stoppage: "Our men are not making any move for work. Before long a number of them will be leaving the place I expect and it will be a good job for us if a number of them go. There are some very bad fellows among them."[26] Bate also criticized Dunsmuir again, probably for taking advantage of the strike and luring the striking miners away with higher wages. He wrote that Dunsmuir's people

> do not scruple to use every endeavour to embarrass us, and I should feel glad to see them get a requital. Dunsmuir Sen. talks a good deal, and is as deceitful and as designing as ever. He requires very careful watching. I am in hopes we shall shortly get men to work at Chase River Mine. We have shown no anxiety to resume operations and have not said a word on the subject; because we did not propose any alterations to give the men grounds to "strike." They wanted to make changes which we could not agree to.[27]

Bate gave in to all the miners' grievances, but the board had wanted him to take a tough stand. With coal stockpiled, the board felt a strike would free up capital for development of the big new mine that hopefully could solve all their problems.

The miners had settled down by October, but Bate remained angry with Dunsmuir:

> We have a tremendous "Bill" to settle with Dunsmuir, Diggle & Co. for the manner in which they have done their best to embarrass us during our trouble with the miners. Not only have they employed our "strikers" but they have actually endeavoured to entice away our men from the new shaft by offering them increased wages etc![28]

In the meantime Bate revealed that his "Nanaimo Railway Bill" had passed the provincial legislature. With this approval for a right-of-way, Bate's company could construct a railway through city property to the coal wharf at Cameron Island. The passage of this bill had not been easy. Bate said Captain Spalding, "a friend of our opponents," did everything he could to prevent it passing. He did not mince words when he described Spalding to Rosenfeld in his letter of January 6, 1882:

> I am glad to hear you met Capt. Spalding who is considered here a great "gas pipe" "blow hard" etc. He very likely does not wish me well, only because I happen to have been opposed to him and one or two of his friends politically, and because he was prevented, by myself, from defeating through his lawyers, our Railway Bill. Had he succeeded we could not have sunk the shaft in the place, which Mr. Jeffcock selected. Our Company has not a greater enemy than Capt. Spalding; that is well known.[29]

Under Beaumont's direction, the engineer, E.B. McKay, began exploring the new coal seam using the steam-powered diamond boring machine. Before long a large body of coal was found close to the beach. This would become the No. 1 Esplanade mine, the mine that would change the fortunes of the coal company.

16

CITY
IMPROVEMENTS

W HILE BATE WRESTLED WITH THE personnel changes
taking place within the Vancouver Coal Company, he also
dealt with structural changes in the city and its harbour. Since the
city's incorporation, management of the Nanaimo Harbour took
on new importance. This was the city's prize asset, although now
managed by the Dominion government.

ADVANCES IN TRAVEL AND COMMUNICATION
Bate was appointed to the Pilotage Authority of British Columbia
in 1875, then four years later to the Pilotage Authority for the
Port of Nanaimo. This governing body's mandate was to "maintain and administer in the interest of safety, an efficient and
economical pilotage service." It also prescribed pilotage charges
on ships entering the harbour. His friend Captain John Sabiston
became the port's first harbourmaster and also its first harbour
pilot, and Tom Peck was appointed deputy customs collector.

Bate's list of public service appointments continued to grow.

The status of the port was upgraded in 1884 to an independent Port of Entry. Bedford H. Smith, a graduate from the University of New Brunswick, became the Collector of Customs with a salary of $1,200 per year. He replaced Tom Peck, who returned to the hotel business, opening the East Wellington Hotel. The first year's revenue as a port was $51,581. Smith may have been the first person of Canadian birth to be appointed to a position of authority in Nanaimo, which was still predominantly British.

The Entrance Island lighthouse, built in 1874, greatly improved navigation for ships rounding the northeast end of Gabriola Island. The movement of ships within the harbour improved in 1888 with the blasting and removal of a shipping obstacle known locally as "Little Rock," situated off the coal wharves at Cameron Island. But it was not until 1890 that the first legal survey of the harbour was undertaken. The first series of lights and bells was installed at Gallows Point at the entrance to the harbour in 1900.

The *City Directory* for Nanaimo of 1882 showed a population of 2,000 and 51 retail outlets. The burgeoning city was no longer isolated; new lines of communication had opened. A regular ferry, the *Leviathan*, operated by Joseph Foster, ran between Nanaimo, Newcastle, and Departure Bay.[1] Joseph Spratt's ferry company, the East Coast Line, which operated between Comox, Nanaimo, and Victoria, used the *Maude* and *Wilson G. Hunt* to provide regular passenger service to these growing coastal communities.[2] And in May 1879, a telegraph line hung on brackets on trees connected Nanaimo to Victoria.[3] Bate may have been heartened by the new technology, but he continued to use Slater's *Telegraphic Code* in private correspondence.

REORGANIZATION OF ELECTORAL AREA

The electoral face of Nanaimo changed in 1879. A committee of council recommended the city be divided into three wards to allow different areas to be equally represented in council on the basis of taxation, making a more diverse council. The North Ward and South Wards elected two councillors, and the Middle Ward elected three. The North Ward extended to the northern city limits on Newcastle Townsite from Bastion and Fitzwilliam Streets. It included the old wooden courthouse on Front Street, the Bastion, the Stone House, St. Paul's Anglican Church, a Methodist church, the Literary Institute, the Old Flag Inn, and St. Ann's Convent on Wallace Street, which had just opened. The Middle Ward lay between Victoria Road, Bastion, and Fitzwilliam Streets. It comprised miners, Chinese, businessmen, and professionals, and hosted a strip of hotels and saloons along Victoria Crescent.[4]

The South Ward, the area south of Victoria Road, was home to the largest number of miners. Some lived in boarding houses, others in small cottages. The Dew Drop Inn had just opened, and would figure prominently in community horse racing events. Manson's General Store was a popular shop at the corner of Haliburton and Farquhar Streets. The South Ward was also the headquarters of the Vancouver Coal Company, on Haliburton Street, and the home of Mark Bate. As the city grew and new buildings were constructed and businesses started, the ward divisions became unnecessary.

In 1879, Bate was acclaimed mayor for another term, in the first election held under the ward system. William Earl and Richard Nightingale were elected to the North Ward: James Harvey, John Meakin, and John Sabiston to the Middle Ward; and Thomas Miller and Thomas Morgan to the South Ward. Many of the councillors were familiar to voters. This was Nightingale's fourth election and Sabiston's third, and it was Harvey's first time running as a councillor. His first foray into municipal politics was his battle against Bate for the mayor's chair back in 1875. Other first-time councillors included William Earl, who had taken over from James Harvey in handling the mail; his second-hand store served as the community post office. John Meakin, a miner and *Princess Royal* pioneer, was the first to buy a lot on Esplanade when the company put lots on the market. Bate referred to him as a "progressive citizen, well read and well informed."[5] Miller and Morgan were also miners; Morgan would eventually succeed Archibald Dick as Inspector of Mines.

EXPANSION OF SCHOOLS AND BYLAWS

Incorporated only five years earlier, the community slowly began to see improvements. The Bastion Bridge was probably the greatest advancement, for it gave easy access to land across the ravine. This is where the Roman Catholic order, the Sisters of St. Ann from Victoria, built a two-storey wooden convent and day school on Wallace Street. The school opened in 1879 with 35 students, only a small percentage of whom were Catholic. Both Bate and Dunsmuir supported the initiative.

Bate was the first chairman of the Board of Education, which began in 1878. Three schools operated in the community at that time: a boy's school on Crace Street, a girl's school at Selby and Franklyn Streets, and the day school at St. Ann's Convent. Joseph P. Planta, former vice-principal of Victoria College, became principal of the Crace Street Boy's School following Young's appointment as city clerk. Planta and his wife, Margaret, and their children Amelia, Jess, Albert, and Walter came from Adelaide, Australia. In 1878, girls got their own school, and Margaret Planta was appointed principal, the first female teacher to hold that position in Nanaimo. Other district schools opened in Wellington, Gabriola Island, and North Cedar. On July 1, 1881, a motion to re-elect Bate by acclamation for another three-year term as chairman of the Board of Education could not be carried out due to "absurd provisions of the School Act." Votes had to be cast. The results were 63 votes for Bate, and one each for Robert Dunsmuir and D. Jones.[6]

Nanaimo may not quite have had the bright lights of major cities, but the city council worked hard to improve the quality of their streets. When oil lamps were mounted on lampposts for the first time in 1879, it seemed like the town was beginning to realize its potential. The streets also showed improvement when Bate ordered ashes from the mine workshop to be spread on city streets, providing a dry hard surface. Later the Street Committee obtained a road roller and a rock crusher. This equipment improved the roads still further during the wet season. The council required owners of lots on those graded streets to construct a sidewalk along the front of their lots. They were given a time limit; if they failed to comply, the city would construct the sidewalk and charge the property owner.

The frontier aspect of the town, with dogs, horses, cattle, goats and sheep running at large, was somewhat curtailed when council introduced Bylaw No. 6, which taxed dogs and horses, and ruled it against the law to keep farm animals within the city. One of the first committees appointed dealt with a nuisance caused by the carcass of a dead pig. It became the sanitary officer's responsibility to enforce what became known as the nuisance bylaws. Eventually these bylaws became part of the public health provisions in the city.

Bate took a break from civic duties and did not run in the 1880 election. He may have been preoccupied with developments over the possible Dunsmuir takeover of the Vancouver Coal Company. Before he left the councillors praised him for the manner in which he had carried out mayoralty duties. The Nanaimo *Free Press* recorded council's laudatory speech: "We take this opportunity of congratulating you upon having achieved the enviable distinction of filling the honorable position of mayor of the city during five successive years to the full satisfaction of the public generally."[7]

John Pawson filled the mayor's chair until Bate returned the following year. Bate then dismissed Young, the city clerk, and hired Samuel Gough on July 19, 1880. Young had been unhappy for some time and had been quite vocal with his complaints about the reduction in his salary while serving as city clerk, assessor, collector, city constable, and night watchman.

The year 1881 dawned with wedding plans in the Bate family. Sally Bate's wedding would be the second in the family. The first was Emily's unfortunate elopement with Charlie Alport. In December 1880, Bate proudly boasted about the upcoming nuptials to Rosenfeld:

> Sometime early next year I expect a marriage in the house. Sally I think will leave us to join "heart and hands" with a young gentleman who lately arrived from England, and who I believe called on you in San Francisco. He is a worthy fellow as far as I have seen of him, and I have every confidence they will be happy.[8]

Sally was 19 when she wed William J. Goepel on February 24, 1881, at St. Paul's Church. It was a morning wedding, and guests were served breakfast at the Bate residence.[9] The groom came from London, England, in 1875 and had worked as a clerk in the Vancouver Coal Company office.[10] Bate knew him to be an accomplished pianist and had accompanied him when he played violin at the opening ceremonies when the Literary Institute's hall was enlarged and reopened on August 18, 1877.[11]

In March, Bate noted the newly married couple had returned home after a pleasant trip on the *Victoria*, the Pacific Coast Steamship Company's ship that operated between Nanaimo and San Francisco.[12] The Goepels moved to the James Bay area of Victoria, where William went into business with Richard Hall. The couple gave Mark and Sarah their first Canadian grandchild. The family later settled in Nelson, BC.

A year later, Sarah's sister, Elizabeth, and her husband, Adam Grant Horne, also celebrated their first family wedding, when son Henry married Emily Cooper on May 17, 1881. They were to have three children: Harry, Gertrude, and Edith. Henry became Nanaimo's postmaster after William Earl retired in 1890. He served as postmaster until 1928.

Two years later Mark and Sarah enjoyed another family wedding when their eldest son, Mark, Jr., married Amelia Agnes Planta, daughter of the school principal. Reverend Good married the couple in St. Paul's Church in Nanaimo on August 16, 1883. Mark, Jr., who had previously worked in the office of the Vancouver Coal Company, was now employed as an agent for the Dominion Savings Bank.[13]

Bate's cousin, Cornelius Bryant, now an ordained minister of the Methodist Church of Canada, returned to Nanaimo in 1881. It had been 25 years since he and Mark had left England and shared their long journey around Cape Horn to Vancouver Island. Both were married with children and held positions of authority within the community. Bate would have enjoyed the camaraderie of a close friend and family member. Cornelius visited England in 1886 and met with his younger brother, Thomas, a teacher in Dudley. In the course of their conversation they discussed the possibility of Thomas converting his English teaching certificate to a Canadian one. On his return, Cornelius was successful in obtaining a teaching position for him at Sumas. Thomas then joined his brother and cousins in British Columbia.

BATE'S BAND

Music continued to be part of Bate's life. He took time off from the business of managing the mining company and his duties as mayor to play in the Nanaimo Brass Band. In September 1882, the band played at the launching of the ship *Nanaimo*, built by Chauncey Carpenter, the owner of Millstream Sawmill. Band members included Bate, his sons Mark, Jr., and Tom; the Morgan brothers, Thomas and John; Joseph Randle; and David Nebb. He recalled that special day many years later:

The members, with other guests, boarded the vessel while on the "ways" and remained on board as the barque glided gracefully with colours flying into the harbour off Dobesons Foundry. As the anchor was dropped, the band struck up "A Life on the Ocean Wave" and played one or two other seasonable pieces on the deck. It was a great day in Nanaimo and the band did much to enliven the occurrence.[14]

The band was always available for charitable events, church concerts, and other public occasions. Bate especially remembered the annual reunion of Foresters (AOF), held on a clearing near the Millstone River, where a large dancing platform was erected; "the band was always there joining in the festivities," he recalled.

DUNSMUIR LAYS PLANS FOR RAILWAY

Bate and Dunsmuir may have been adversaries in the coal mining business, but when it came to serving on committees that influenced or improved life in Nanaimo, they were united. Many times they worked together for the betterment of the community. Their antagonistic approach toward each other regarding work was well known, but they respected each other's dedication to the community. Seldom did Bate speak of their private conversations. People began referring to Dunsmuir as "the Old Man," probably differentiating him from his sons James and Alex.

In July 1881 Dunsmuir told Bate he was going to travel next spring and indicated he would be spending more time in Victoria than in Nanaimo. He did not tell Bate that on visits to Victoria he had been slowly acquiring land in anticipation of a move to the capital city. Feeling somewhat financially secure, Dunsmuir hinted he could afford to "go around a little now" and did not see why he should not enjoy himself.[15]

Dunsmuir had also begun to think seriously about building an island railway, taking up the mantel of the promise made at Confederation to link Nanaimo to Esquimalt by rail. No doubt the canny Scot was also thinking about the coal and mineral wealth that lay underneath the railway land reserve. After securing financing from investors in San Francisco, he went on his European tour. It was his first trip back to Scotland since he left in 1850. On the way he stopped off in Ottawa to meet another Scot, Prime Minister Sir John A. Macdonald, to present his railway proposal. The two men shared a common heritage; they were born only miles apart and they shared a love of good Scotch whisky.

Macdonald, however, was on the eve of an election and decided it would be in his best interests if the provincial legislature made the decision about the railway. There were two proposals being put forth, one by Dunsmuir for the Victoria, Esquimalt and Nanaimo Railway Company, the other by Lewis Clement, for the Vancouver Land and Railway Company of San Francisco. Dunsmuir's partners were Charles Crocker, Collis P. Huntington, and Leland Stanford of California; Dunsmuir was president and owner of half the shares.

Bate kept abreast of developments, and noted on April 21, 1882: "Dunsmuir's Railway Bill has been defeated in our Local Legislature, and at present Standard [sic] Crocker & Co. are not likely to obtain a franchise to build a Railway from Esquimalt to Nanaimo."[16] But Bate had overlooked the tenacity of Dunsmuir, who was in Glasgow when he heard that his bill had not passed. The provincial legislature rejected his proposal in favour of Clement's plan. Dunsmuir was unconcerned and prepared to wait until Clement's contract collapsed, for he knew the American did not have the financing to carry out the project.

Before Dunsmuir left for Europe, he indicated an interest in running in the provincial election on July 24, 1882. The most important issue of the day was the railway. Dunsmuir was probably the most influential of all the candidates and certainly had the most recognizable name, but other locals decided to run and made it a contest. They were William Raybould, merchant; Edward Quennell, butcher; William Hinksman, miner; and John George Barnston, lawyer. Dunsmuir garnered 229 votes and Raybould

185 votes of the 770 votes cast. Nanaimo had become a two-seat riding, and it now had two new representatives.

When Dunsmuir returned in September he received a warm welcome from a crowd gathered at the Nanaimo dock, and the Wellington Brass Band played "Home Sweet Home." In his absence he had become an MPP, never having campaigned or solicited votes. Everyone knew he was a man with a mission to build a railway.

Before a scheduled visit to British Columbia by Canada's Governor General, John Douglas Sutherland Campbell, the Marquess of Lorne, and his wife, HRH Princess Louise, the daughter of Queen Victoria, Dunsmuir planned ahead by purchasing the Albion Iron Works in Victoria from its founder, Joseph Spratt. The foundry was a necessary component if he had to manufacture rails. He also bought out his partner, Wadham Diggle, for $600,000[17]; then he changed the name of his company to R. Dunsmuir & Sons. He now had total control of the mining company, and no one was better prepared to build a railway than he was.

GOVERNOR GENERAL LORNE'S VISIT, 1882

Governor General Lorne and his wife arrived in Victoria on September 20, 1882, with the goal of resolving the serious railway situation. Today, the position of Governor General is mostly ceremonial, but then the role had some political clout. Lorne was 33 years of age and the youngest Governor General in Canadian history. The visit to British Columbia was supposed to last two weeks, but they stayed three months, attending tours, parties, and official ceremonies throughout the province. Lorne knew of the great unhappiness in the west; Ottawa had heard rumours that the province might secede from Canada and join the United States. It had been six years since the last visit by a Governor General, who had also been sent to quell dissension in the province regarding the railway. When Lorne announced in Victoria that the transcontinental railway would be completed by the year 1887, he anticipated the news would be greeted with widespread applause. To the contrary, instead of receiving this news with joy or diplomacy, Premier Robert Beaven asked if Princess Louise could become Queen of the Kingdom of Vancouver Island. It was a crazy idea but it clearly indicated the isolation felt by Vancouver Islanders. The transcontinental railway would help the mainland but would do nothing for the island. His statement showed that the rivalry between the island and the mainland still existed.[18]

The Governor General visited Nanaimo a month after his arrival in Victoria, a visit that was to play a particular role in securing the settlement of the Esquimalt and Nanaimo Railway. There was disappointment all around when Princess Louise did not accompany her husband, who arrived on October 20, 1882. The flag-decorated steamer *Alexander* made its way into Departure Bay, where Dunsmuir was taken on board, and proceeded to Johnston's Wharf in Nanaimo Harbour. Before the official welcome by Mayor Bate and local dignitaries, Constable William Stewart fired a 19-gun salute from the five historic guns next to the Bastion. Did Bate know Dunsmuir would be picked up before arriving in Nanaimo, and how did he feel when he saw his nemesis standing side by side with the Governor General?

In Bate's welcoming speech he expressed regret that Princess Louise was not present. Then he broached the subject of the railway; his speech was printed in the Nanaimo *Free Press* on October 21:

> We have repeatedly urged the Dominion Government by every constitutional channel available, it was the general public opinion that the Island Railway should be constructed by the Dominion Government as a Government work project in fulfillment of its obligation to do so under the Carnarvon Terms of settlement.

This was obviously not what Dunsmuir was hoping to hear from Nanaimo's mayor. At the conclusion of Bate's remarks, the Silver

Cornet Band played "God Save the Queen," children sang the national anthem, "The Maple Leaf Forever," and two members of the Snuneymuxw performed a feast dance.

Before leaving the wharf, Lorne chatted briefly with Andrew Hunter about his memories of Scotland. Lorne was also the future Duke of Argyll in Scotland. Hunter was the engineer who brought the steam engine from Scotland to Vancouver Island in 1850; it had burned during the strike of 1880. Lorne, Dunsmuir, and Hunter shared stories of their homeland.

The community gave a tumultuous royal welcome to the visitors as Governor General Lorne, Mayor Bate, and MPP Dunsmuir boarded carriages and toured along Commercial Street, which was decorated with seven large arches built for the occasion, including one from the Chinese community. While Dunsmuir hosted Lorne at his home, Ardoon, on Albert Street, his party officials settled into the Provincial Hotel. The two men had ample time to discuss the terms and conditions of building the railway. In the evening, they were treated to musical renditions by the Wellington Brass Band at the Dunsmuir residence.

During the Governor General's overnight stay in Nanaimo, Bate and his mining engineer, James Beaumont, escorted him on a tour of the two Vancouver Coal Company mines in operation, the Esplanade and the Chase River. Later he visited the Wellington mine with Dunsmuir. He was told the coal from the Nanaimo mines led the market in San Francisco, and he was impressed. A report in *The Times* of London, repeated in the *BC Mining Report* for 1882, quoted his forecast, made at a Victoria banquet held during his visit, that "before long Nanaimo will become one of the chief mining stations on the American continent."[19]

The Governor General reported back to Prime Minister Macdonald that while Dunsmuir wanted to build the Esquimalt to Nanaimo railway, his decision was conditional on the acquisition of all the Railway Reserve Land from Esquimalt to the Seymour Narrows.

Dunsmuir also said he preferred to deal with the Dominion of Canada government rather than the provincial government.

DUNSMUIR LANDS RAILWAY DEAL

Dunsmuir got his wish. The railway land was transferred to the federal government who in turn conveyed it to Dunsmuir. Sir Alexander Campbell, Minister of Railways and Canals, and Dunsmuir signed the contract on August 28, 1883. The railway line was to be completed by June 10, 1887.[20] The canny auld Scot would receive a subsidy of $750,000 and a land grant of almost two million acres along the east coast of Vancouver Island, including all the coal and minerals that lay under the land and the timber that grew on top of it. Only the land already occupied by settlers was excluded. Where First Nations reserves, Crown grants, military reservations, and leases existed, he was given an equal area of land in the Peace River Block. All this free of taxation, just to construct 73 miles of railway.

When details of the massive deal became known, there was outrage in both British Columbia and Ottawa. Macdonald shrugged off all criticism. In the provincial legislature, in the non-party system, MPP Dunsmuir had forged an alliance that held the majority of seats, thus assuring the Settlement Act would pass on March 28, 1884. The Albion Iron Work employees were elated to know their jobs were secure. They marched to Fairview, Dunsmuir's new Victoria home, to offer congratulations. There was equal excitement in Wellington when the news reached there. The Wellington Brass Band led a torchlight procession to manager John Bryden's home, where they cheered Dunsmuir and the Settlement Act. A jubilant Dunsmuir said "it afforded him the greatest pleasure to be able to state that the matter of building the Island Railway had been placed wholly in his hands and the work would be begun at an early day." He hoped to be able to raise "the whole Island from a dormant state."[21]

Some of Dunsmuir's severest critics in Nanaimo invited him to a public meeting to discuss the monopoly that would be created by the deal. He could not make the meeting but sent along a letter that was read before a packed house. In it he outlined the history of the island railway, the Settlement Act, and his determination to build the line, and made a veiled threat: the railway might just bypass Nanaimo. "Having put my hands to the plow," he wrote, "I am not the man to turn back. I have the contract and I am going to build the roadway and telegraph, and operate them too, in spite of any opposition emanating from jealous individuals who act the part of the fabled dog in the manger."[22]

Construction began on May 6, 1884. The building of the railway took two years. It was a giant work project that put hundreds of men to work, logging, preparing the railway bed, laying tracks, and constructing bridges and trestles. They even built a wharf at Oyster Harbour, Ladysmith, to unload rails and equipment, including the first locomotive. And the rail line did pass directly through the heart of Nanaimo. Bate never publicly voiced his feelings about the Esquimalt and Nanaimo Railway. He had earlier stated his opinion that it should be a government project, but knowing Dunsmuir, he probably realized the job would be completed as promised.

Another provincial election, held July 7, 1886, returned MPPs Dunsmuir and Raybould to represent Nanaimo electoral district.[23] Raybould's second term in office was short, for he died December 3, 1886, at the age of 50, following an accident at his home. A by-election held on January 3, 1887, returned George Thomson, an Independent candidate.

JOHN A. MACDONALD OPENS THE NEW RAILWAY

Bate invited Prime Minister Sir John A. Macdonald to visit Nanaimo for the opening of the Esquimalt and Nanaimo Railway. This was Macdonald's first journey to Vancouver Island, even though he had represented Victoria for four years after he lost his

Kingston seat in the general election of 1878. He accepted Bate's invitation. The important date of August 13, 1886, is enshrined in Vancouver Island history, when Prime Minister Macdonald drove the last spike of the Esquimalt and Nanaimo Railway at Cliffside Station, Shawnigan Lake, where the north and south construction crews had met. Lady Agnes Macdonald joined the invited guests and a happy Robert Dunsmuir and his wife, Joan, for this historic occasion. Macdonald congratulated Dunsmuir on the completion of the railway: "Everyone must admit the pluck and energy of Mr. Dunsmuir, which has brought this important work to a successful conclusion."[24]

A special train took the guests north to Nanaimo where Bate and his councillors hosted a civic reception in the Royal Hotel on Wharf Street. Bate gave a welcoming speech:

> The Esquimalt and Nanaimo Railway, over which we anticipate you have had a delightful run, is now very nearly completed, and we feel it our duty to draw your attention to the great benefits that would accrue to us from the establishment and maintenance of ferry communication between the Mainland Terminus and Nanaimo so as to make the Island Railway a branch of the transcontinental Line and Esquimalt the Ocean Terminus.

Bate refers here to his desire for a regular ferry service between Vancouver and Nanaimo, to meet up there with the new Esquimalt and Nanaimo Railway, south to Victoria or north to Comox. A ferry service had been running a triangle route between New Westminster, Vancouver, and Nanaimo since 1883. The ferry, the *Robert Dunsmuir*, was nicknamed "Dirty Bob" because on its return trip from Nanaimo it carried coal.

Bate could not resist reminding the prime minister how the mining industry was still hampered by an import duty of 75 cents per ton charged on foreign coal entering the United States. He said he looked forward to a time when a reciprocity treaty would be adopted between the United States and Canada. Bate concluded, "We sincerely trust that your visit to British Columbia will be beneficial to yourself and Lady Macdonald, and we hope your return to Ottawa will be pleasant and safe."[25]

One man present at this meeting, William Lewis, who died at the age of 105 in 1968, reported seeing the prime minister walking back and forth on the verandah of the hotel. Lewis concluded that the prime minister and Dunsmuir were dismayed by the "ladies keeping too close tab on their actions, so arrangements were made for the party to visit the Wellington mine."[26] Lady Agnes and Joan Dunsmuir declined. When Macdonald and Dunsmuir reached the bottom of the mine, Dunsmuir produced two glasses and a bottle of Scotland's finest, and together they toasted the completion of the railway.

Dunsmuir continued to acquire more land in Victoria, this time to build a spectacular castle for his wife. Until it was built, they continued to live in Fairview, across the street from the legislative buildings.

17

CHANGE OF JOB
AND HOMELESS

IN 1883, SAMUEL ROBINS DECIDED the time was right for an inspection tour of the company mine in Nanaimo. No one knew more about the Vancouver Coal Company operation than he did. He had followed, offered advice, guided, and reported on the Nanaimo mines since 1862, when he became secretary to the board of directors. Bate anxiously awaited his arrival, no doubt anticipating some changes ahead for the company, with a new mine about to be developed.

A NEW POST OFFICE BUILDING

As Robins approached the Nanaimo Harbour, he would have noticed a large construction project underway on Front Street. This was the new Dominion Post Office building, designed by the chief architect for the Department of Public Works, Thomas Fuller. His reputation as an architect preceded him, as he had designed the Parliament Buildings in Ottawa as well as numerous post office buildings across the country. Nanaimo was finally getting the government building, something Bate had lobbied for during Governor General Lord Dufferin's visit to Nanaimo seven years before. Dufferin had promised Bate he would take the city's complaint to the proper authorities, and this he had done. Nanaimo expected a building that would show progress and confidence in its future prosperity.

The sum of $10,000 was designated from the federal government toward the project in Nanaimo, for a "building suitable for a Post Office, Custom House, etc." On July 25, 1882, Bate arranged the purchase of the site from the Vancouver Coal Company for $1,000. On September 18, 1882, the city awarded the building contract to Smith and Clark of Victoria. The contract price was $23,250.[1] The two-storey building was constructed using Newcastle Island stone, and was 48 by 24 feet, with a staircase wing of 12 by 24 feet, with wooden basement, floors, and roof. No provision was made for approaches to the front or rear of the building, nor for office furniture. The contractors expected to be finished by October.

By 1884, George H. Frost had completed his contract for the office furnishings, and for the outhouses and fencing, at a cost of $3,066.54. After the furniture, stoves, safes, and so on were installed, the building was considered ready for occupancy. George Norris, the editor of the *Nanaimo Free Press*, expressed the hope that "the dark day of slow mails will soon give way to the brighter of receiving and dispatching mails three times a week." The mail from Victoria came by ship until the Esquimalt and Nanaimo Railway opened. The first postmaster in the new building was rightfully William Earl, who had served the community in that position from his second-hand store since 1878. This beautiful building became one of the city's most loved and recognizable of that period.

MINE INSPECTION

Robins was expected to make some improvements to the mining company during his visit. Robins was born in Cornwall, England,

and was only three years older than Bate. He had worked with his father in business with large mining and manufacturing enterprises before joining the VCML in London.

In 1882, the Southfield mine had opened, four miles south of Nanaimo. The BC mining inspector, Archibald Dick, predicted it would be "an extensive and valuable mine." He noted that at some places the coal was 7 feet thick and 250 tons of coal a day were being mined. This meant employment for more miners. However, the prospects for "the big shaft," as the Esplanade mine became known locally, were even greater. Dick reported:

> On October 26, 1883 the news was sounded from the bottom that coal was found. As the rock was cleaned off, they found the coal was hard and good quality, and seven feet four inches thick. The people of Nanaimo are to be congratulated on such a finding, and the Province in general, but the Vancouver Coal Company in particular, as they have the prospect of a good and extensive mine.[2]

James Beaumont, the company's mining engineer, received credit for his engineering skill and for his caution and eye for safety. Everyone was excited at reaching coal in this new location, and it seemed the tide had turned, as if better times were ahead for the Vancouver Coal Company.

Four days later, during a "Winning the Coal" banquet, a bullock was roasted to feed 300 employees and guests, who filled the upper and lower levels of the Institute Hall. Robins's speech referred only briefly to the company's past record: "It would be a gloomy task, and we will let the dead past bury its dead." He said the opinion in Nanaimo seemed to be that the Vancouver Coal Company was "a stupid old Company and the proprietors had more money than brains."[3] Robins promised things would be different in the future. After his inspection of the mines was completed, he returned to England. He and Bate would have had time to assess the situation and plan for the future, and it was clear Robins planned to return. In what capacity, however, it was not revealed.

An editorial in the *Nanaimo Free Press*, January 1, 1884, referred to major events of the previous year:

> The sinking of the Esplanade shaft to the coal can be reckoned as the principal local event of the expiring twelve months. The visit of Mr. S.M. Robins, the energetic and capable Secretary of the Vancouver Coal Company, has inspired more life into our city, and from the works and measures inaugurated by the Directors and Mr. Robins, the brightest hopes are felt that in the near future Nanaimo will again have a front rank in shipping coal.

FIRE DESTROYS THE BATE HOME

Early in 1884, Bate's family life changed dramatically. On Monday, April 28, a fire broke out on the roof of the offices of the Vancouver Coal Company, which also served as his residence on Haliburton Street. The building stood only a few feet from the coal trains on their way to the shipping wharf. Several times in the past Bate had to extinguish fires on the roof of the building when sparks flew off the passing engine, and only two years before, in August, sparks from the train set fire to the roof of the kitchen attached to the offices. Mark Bate, Jr., discovered the blaze and sounded the alarm. He and his father climbed on the roof and managed to put out the fire using buckets of water.[4] This had been the Bate family residence for quite a few years and many of their children were born in it, so they had a great personal attachment to the building.

However, on this day, the wind blew in from the northwest, carrying sparks from the train to the highest part of the building. The flames spread rapidly across the roof. Several neighbours tried to extinguish the fire using buckets of water. The Nanaimo Fire Company arrived with its fire engine and hoses, but the fire had already enveloped half of the large roof. They first thought they could save the lower part of the building, but when the water supply from the first well ran out, and before the fire engine could be moved to another, the flames had spread and the building was destroyed. The fire engine was hooked up to the company's water tank and so managed to save the adjoining home of Richard Richardson.

Nothing of the Bate home remained standing but the chimneys. All the contents, including the three safes from the company offices, had been removed from the building as well as all of the Bate family household effects on the ground floor. All the family's clothing, however, which had been on the second floor immediately beneath where the spark had ignited the roof, was lost. The building had been insured for $1,000.

Fortunately, most of the Bate children were in school, but it must have been a troubling situation for Mark and Sarah, wondering what they would do for accommodation and clothing. Two weeks later Bate publicly thanked the Nanaimo Fire Department, Nanaimo citizens, and the captains and crews of the ships in the harbour for their help in saving property during the fire. He then added, "Mrs. Bates respectfully asks that any persons who may have picked up stray valuables, books, papers, etc, would be kind enough to return them."[5]

Of the children living at home, three were now teenagers, Lucy, Mary, and William. The two youngest were Charles, seven, and Lizzie, ten. Tom lived on Irwin Street and Mark, Jr., lived on Finlayson Street. This would have been a difficult transition for the family, having lived at the "boarding house" for most of their lives. The city directory for that year, 1884–85, shows the family living in a home at the corner of Esplanade and Crace Street.[6] On May 1, 1886, Bate leased the Franklyn House, owned by Dr. Edward James Franklyn, of Ardrishaig, Argyleshire, Scotland, on Wallace Street. The home had been built for Magistrate William Hales Franklyn in 1862. This was a large fashionable house located on five acres of land on the west side of the ravine, adjacent to the present site of city hall. The lease was for a three-year term, for $12.50 per month.[7] The coal company moved its office into a building at the corner of Farquhar and Esplanade Streets.

NEW MINE MANAGEMENT

Robins returned to Nanaimo on May 6, 1884, via the mail steamer *Princess Louise* and accompanied by his nephew Mr. F.W. Stead, from London, England.[8] After receiving a warm welcome from friends in the city, he immediately took charge as superintendent of the mines and began working to put them on a paying basis. Bate remained as his assistant and office manager for the next two years. From the beginning it was obvious Robins would have total control of decisions and would not have to wait for directives to come from San Francisco or London, something that had always hampered Bate in moving quickly and forward. Bate no doubt felt a load had been lifted from his shoulders, and he would have more time to devote to the business of the city.

As superintendent, Robins controlled a vast territory, a large part of which had accumulated when Bate was manager. On behalf of the company, Bate had spent over a quarter of a million dollars in the construction of new works and the exploration and development of its vast property in Nanaimo. The Vancouver Coal Company was now one of the largest private landowners in British Columbia. It owned the Nanaimo Estate, that is, all of the City of Nanaimo plus thousands of acres adjoining it, and included Newcastle Island and its renowned stone quarry, as well as Protection Island. The company added other properties to its inventory—Dolholt's Peninsula (John Dolholt farm) and the Frew Estate (David Frew farm), both located south of Nanaimo in the Cedar area, as well as the Harewood Estate of about 9,000 acres in the Mountain, Cranberry, Douglas, and Nanaimo Districts. The company purchased the Harewood mine, along with its aerial tramway and shipping site, and the wharf at Cameron Island, from the bank on April 22, 1884.[9]

Robins had only been mine superintendent for two years when he was called to testify in Victoria before the Royal Commission on Chinese Immigration. In 1885, 600 people worked for the company, and of these 100 were Chinese and Snuneymuxw.[10] He testified that the agitation against the Chinese began about two years ago,

> chiefly fostered by the white trading classes, who saw large sums of money paid in wages to people who never entered their stores. White miners also, who found it difficult to secure employment for a relative (whom they had induced to come to the province by descriptions of their own prosperity), whilst they see the Chinese fully occupied are eager to do all they can . . . [I]n my opinion it is not necessary to retain Chinese in the province, but their removal should not be sudden.[11]

The Vancouver Coal Company had in fact removed almost all the Chinese stores and businesses from the Commercial Street business area to View Street south of the city on eight acres of land it owned. Each Chinese employee was charged a dollar a month for rent. Far from being segregated or downtrodden, the Chinese thrived in this new location, especially during the building of the Esquimalt and Nanaimo Railway. Chinatown officially became part of the City of Nanaimo on January 13, 1887.

Bryden and Robert Dunsmuir also testified before the Commission on Chinese Immigration. Both were complimentary about their Chinese workers. Bryden believed that "the presence of the Chinese has contributed very much to the development of the province." Dunsmuir acknowledged, "If it were not for Chinese labour, the business I am engaged in, specially coal mining, would be seriously retarded and curtailed."[12]

The final report of the Commission determined there was little evidence to support claims against Chinese immigrants.

Nevertheless, it recommended moderate restrictions on new Chinese coming into Canada and proposed a $10 duty on entry.

BATE LEAVES MINING COMPANY

Bate's association with the Vancouver Coal Company ended in 1886, when he was appointed provincial assessor and collector for the District of Nanaimo. He was elected again for an eleventh term as mayor, and joining him on the council was his brother-in-law Adam Grant Horne; the carpenter Charles Wilson; William Webb, owner of the Nanaimo Bakery; Walter Wilson, a tinsmith; John Hilbert, undertaker and furniture maker; James Knight, a company engineer; and George Bevilockway, owner of a general merchandise store on Victoria Crescent.[13]

The city council moved into new headquarters that year. The need for a new city hall had been discussed for about two years, and one idea was to purchase the Literary Institute. The year before, ratepayers decided against a bylaw that would allow the city to raise the $2,000 needed to buy the building. However, the next year the bylaw passed, though by only one vote. The city raised the money and purchased the building. After some renovations, council moved into the upper front room. Bate held the first council meeting in the new chambers on October 4, 1886. The bottom floor of the hall was rented out. From 1888 to 1894, the Salvation Army rented it, except when the hall was reserved for council use. The Army's drum disrupted the council meetings upstairs, however, so the group was asked to withdraw their Monday evening use.[14]

Bate chose not to run in the 1887 mayoralty election. The new mayor was a miner, Richard Gibson, who worked for the Vancouver Coal Company in the No. 1 Esplanade mine. Neither Bate nor Gibson could have foreseen the difficult year ahead. Robins, clearly in charge, closed the old Douglas Mine, the New Douglas mine, also known as the Chase River mine, and the Fitzwilliam and the Harewood mines. Machinery, rails, and dumps were taken out and the mines filled with water. He concentrated all effort on the No. 1 Esplanade and the Southfield mines. The company spared no expense in making sure the No. 1 was in good working order. He installed a large fan to improve ventilation and prevent the accumulation of gas.

Archibald Dick, in his mining report of 1886, commented on this strategy:

> It is to be hoped that this valuable mine, after all the expense the company have been put to, will yet be a financial success, which will be good for the company, the people of Nanaimo, and the Province in general . . . Last, though not least, it may be a reward to the Vancouver Coal Company, which has been so liberal in furnishing the means to search for and find such hidden treasures.[15]

The miners grew to like their new superintendent. Robins was judged a "kindly gentleman, a lover of trees and his fellow men."[16] He collected trees from all over the world. Ship's captains brought him exotic specimens to add to his collection. His former home became known as Robins' Gardens. Evidence of his passion for trees remains in the exotic and unusual specimens that still beautify the town. Robins was partially deaf and miners remember his "hearing aid" was an enormous "ear trumpet." The deafness affected his health, and he regretted the loss of sound: "One of my great troubles has been that I could not hear the waves beating on the shingle and the wind blowing through the beautiful forest, but most of all, the prattling of the children. I often meet little boys and girls upon whose lips I read, ''ow do you do, Mr. Robins?'"[17]

Robins made a point of never discussing anything but mining during business hours. After work he would discuss sports or any other subject except mining. The miners regarded him as a fair man, although they were not always satisfied with the answer they got from him.

18

OUR GREAT
DISASTER

T HE VANCOUVER COAL COMPANY DOCK was usually a busy place with ships loading coal. This was the case on July 29, 1886, when the *Queen of the Pacific* took on a shipment. As the coal slid down the chute, it pushed forward a draught of air heavy with coal dust, which ignited in an immense sheet of flame. The forward section of the boat exploded. Twelve men were severely burned. They were taken to the Nanaimo Hospital where doctors fought to save their lives. Eight died from extensive burns and shock. The subsequent inquest concluded that coal dust was explosive and was the cause of the explosion.[1] This was not news to the former manager of the coal company.

DANGERS OF COAL DUST

At this time in British Columbia the mining industry seemed unaware of the explosive potential of coal dust. Archibald Dick's annual mining reports warned about the danger of noxious gas in the mines; he reported eight explosions of gas in 1886. Dick always checked on the ventilation in a particular mine, but made no references to coal dust or its explosive nature, for that subject had only recently been raised in the coal mining industry in Europe and the United States.

However, Bate knew about this issue, having kept up with the industry literature. Since his earliest days in Nanaimo, friends sent him mining journals from England and the United States, and he also read the periodical magazines available at the Literary Institute. In one, he read about an explosion in France that occurred 1875, and he conveyed a summary of this incident to Norris at the *Nanaimo Free Press*, which appeared in an editorial about coal dust explosions. In the Campagnac Colliery in France, an engineer had explained,

> No firedamp had been detected at any time but as the floor was covered with very fine, dry, coal dust and as the shot was fired at the bottom of the face, and would consequently raise a cloud of dust, it was concluded that nothing but the instantaneous combustion of coal dust under the influence of the shot could account for the accident . . . Very fine coal dust is a cause of danger in dry working places in which shots are fired. In well-ventilated workings it may of itself alone give rise to disasters. In workings in which firedamp exists it increases the chance of explosions. And when an accident of this kind does occur it aggravates the consequences.[2]

WORST MINING DISASTER IN BC

A year later, another coal dust explosion, the worst mining disaster in BC history, devastated the island. On the afternoon of Tuesday, May 3, 1887, about 154 men, both white and Chinese, were working on the No. 1 Esplanade mine, deep beneath the city and about a mile out under the harbour. A fireman on each shift examined all the workings and everything seemed to be in good order, and all apparently safe.

About 5:55 p.m., just as people were sitting down for dinner, a tremor shook the entire city. Everyone realized immediately an explosion had occurred in the mine. A second blast, caused by coal dust igniting on other slopes, quickly followed, shooting through the underground shafts for almost a kilometre. The pressure blew burning debris hundreds of feet into the air. The mine's steam whistle sounded the alert and sent fear into the heart of every mining family.

Nanaimo was in shock, as wives with children, brothers, fathers, friends, and off-duty miners went to the mine site, anxious to hear if loved ones were safe. Crews from ships in the harbour and shopkeepers who closed their doors rushed to the scene to help combat flames pouring from the mine face, rising high into the sky. Men bore buckets of water to keep the fire back until the fire engine from the city arrived. Ship crews helped work the fire engine. The fire had spread throughout the mine. After a day, the flames near the main shaft were finally extinguished sufficiently so that rescuers could proceed a short distance into the mine.

Many of the town's early pioneers and prominent citizens died in the explosion. Only seven men who were in the mine when the explosion occurred escaped with their lives. The foreman and mayor of the city, Richard Gibson, was at work that day on the afternoon shift.[3] Somehow he managed to make his way through an airshaft to the stables where the mules were kept, where he and six companions were found by one of the first rescue parties. William McGregor, Archibald Dick, and Sam Robins all worked tirelessly, and were joined by miners and managers from Dunsmuir's Wellington mine, including John Bryden, who knew most of the men. Edward G. Prior, who was a member of the legislature, also helped in the rescue attempt.

McGregor joined an off-duty miner, Sam Hudson, in another

rescue attempt but both were overcome by afterdamp (the deadly gas emitted by the fire). Hudson could not be revived, and his name would eventually be added to the death toll. McGregor was taken home to his wife, Amanda. Sometime later, when she checked on his condition, William had returned to the mine site, where their relatives worked. Amanda lost her father, John Meakin, and her brother Arthur, and William had lost his cousin, Archibald Muir.

There is no record of where Bate was during this nightmare in the mine. He would have heard the alarm, and he knew most of the miners trapped inside, many of them friends, so it is unlikely he sat idly by while others risked their lives to reach the trapped men. There would have been a need to co-ordinate with the community for places to bring the injured men and the bodies that eventually emerged. Schools were closed for two weeks, and the Crace Street School became a temporary morgue.

The headlines in the *Nanaimo Free Press* on May 7, 1887, told of the drama unfolding in the community: "Our Great Disaster! Total Loss of Life in the Mine Will Reach 148! 96 White and 52 Chinamen: 46 Widows and 126 Orphaned Children." Flags were lowered to half mast. A special train with medical supplies and mining experts arrived from Victoria to assist.

A relief committee was established to raise funds for the families left behind. Mayor Gibson chaired the committee that included Sam Robins as treasurer, Dr. Emil Arnold Praeger as secretary, Mark Bate, and Robert Dunsmuir. Donations came from across Canada and the United States. Victoria's city council sent $1,000, as did John Rosenfeld in San Francisco. The money helped sustain widows and children.

Many of the victims were buried at a mass funeral in the new cemetery, though local churches held funerals as well, one at St. Paul's Anglican Church on May 15, followed by another at the Methodist church on May 22. The bodies were carried to the cemetery by horse driven wagons. As the drivers approached the cemetery, a man on horseback met them; each driver gave the rider a list of names, which he carried back to the mourners waiting by their final resting place.

The final recovery of bodies occurred December 10—two Chinese men, labelled simply as numbers 139 and 140 (employers were not yet obliged to register the names of Chinese workers).[4] Seven men remained entombed until their remains were found 20 years later during a mining operation. Their bones were collected and buried.

The coroner's inquest, conducted by Dr. William W. Walkem, lasted two weeks. Its deliberations filled pages of the *Nanaimo Free Press*. The jury blamed the explosion on the firing of an unprepared and badly planted charge that ignited accumulated gas fuelled by coal dust. No criminal negligence was attributed to anyone. The inquest recommended "all firemen, or shot-firers, pass a qualifying examination." Amendments were subsequently made to the Coal Mines Regulation Act.

McGregor eventually got the No. 1 Esplanade mine back into working order. However, not all miners returned to their jobs. Some left for good, and others took time to return, due to the trauma and shock. The town tried to get back to normal, if there could be anything normal about losing so many men in a town with only four thousand residents. Gibson recovered enough to fulfill his duties as mayor for the remainder of the year.

BATE RUNS FOR MAYOR AGAIN

Early the next year Bate let it be known he would again seek the mayoralty office. The newspaper report judged this municipal election as "very exciting" and a hard fought one, as Gibson was reluctant to give up the position. He and Bate had fought a previous election in 1886 in which Bate edged out Gibson by 33 votes. In this election, initially Gibson took the lead and gained a majority of 24 votes; then Bate took the lead. "During the counting the candidates tied no less than five times, the highest majority was attained by Bate, and at the close Bate held a majority of sixteen."[5] The final vote count was Bate 167, Gibson 151.

Bate thanked the electors for their confidence in him and said he would do all in his power to advance the best interests of the city. "I have lived here for many many years in this city and all my interest is here. It is only natural that I feel a keen interest in all that appertains to the welfare of Nanaimo."[6]

On January 18, 1888, Justice of the Peace Joseph P. Planta administered the oath of office as he had so many times before. Bate gave a short speech saying he hoped the business of the council "would be conducted harmoniously and that all questions could be brought to a ready and proper result." He trusted "that expenditures would be kept within proper bounds, and be distributed equitably and economically," and he hoped "there would be no reflections on past actions, and that each councillor would drop all personal feelings and act in all matters for the benefit of the public and the city."[7]

DUNSMUIR MINE EXPLOSION

John Bryden, who had worked so hard trying to rescue the miners trapped in the No. 1 Esplanade Mine, was suddenly thrust into another tragic situation as manager of Dunsmuir's Wellington mines. On January 24, 1888, at eight o'clock in the morning, an explosion in the No. 5 shaft at the Diver Lake mine killed 77 men, 46 of them Chinese; they left 10 widows and 22 children. This was the newest and best ventilated mine in the Wellington collieries.

When news of the mine explosion reached Nanaimo, Sam Robins shut down all the Vancouver Coal Company mines to enable workers to help in the rescue. He and William McGregor and a number of employees went to assist. Robins personally stayed at the Wellington mine the entire time. When Dunsmuir received a telegram in Victoria advising him of the explosion, within 15 minutes he had commandeered a train to Wellington. The train made the run in one hour and forty-two minutes from Victoria, a record for that time. Dunsmuir remained at the mine entrance until the next morning, through the heavy rain, supervising rescue operations and comforting weeping family members gathered there waiting for news. After all the miners' bodies were recovered and arrangements made for their interment, Dunsmuir returned to Victoria.

As with the Nanaimo mine disaster, the inquest into the Wellington tragedy assigned no blame. The miners obviously thought differently, however; they thought the Chinese miners were the cause. In early February, a number of meetings were held to consider steps to secure greater safety in the mines. Managers and miners alike attended these meetings held in Nanaimo and Wellington. At the first meeting, Robins and McGregor came prepared with a list of recommendations they thought were fair, and resolved that "the coal operators be allowed time to get rid of the Chinese from the underground workings of mines."[8] There were lots of suggestions from the floor; then someone voiced what everyone was thinking—that Chinese workers should be banned immediately from the mines. Robins said he would if other companies did likewise, and on that point Robins and Bryden agreed. Thinking there was a consensus, someone suggested a statue be erected on Mount Benson commemorating the anniversary of the abolishment the Chinese in the mines on this date February 6, 1888. Only one mine owner, Robert Chandler, was reluctant to dismiss his Chinese workers, but when the miners in his East Wellington mine refused to work until they were gone, he caved in.

The two explosions within a few months of each other caused some debate in the provincial legislature. What could be done to ensure safety in the Nanaimo area mines? Again the blame fell with the Chinese workers, and attempts were made to ban them from the mines. Dunsmuir, in his role as MPP and alert to the ramifications of the proposal, was quick to respond. Despite the earlier agreement with his miners to remove the Chinese from his mines, he said the Knights of Labour had started the anti-Chinese agitation because they were looking for new members. He argued that genuine miners had not attended the meetings nor had they taken part in any campaign. The British Columbia Knights of Labour organization in Nanaimo was spearheaded by an Irish coal miner, Samuel H. Myers, who described himself as "combating the Chinese curse." The Knights were initially successful in organizing white miners who felt threatened by the Chinese.

However, Myers was among the men trapped in the Vancouver Coal Company explosion of May 3, 1887. He died intestate and the pay due to him was used to erect a marker over his grave in St. Peter's Roman Catholic cemetery in Nanaimo.[9] The organized agitation he had begun against Chinese workers had no power, for the next Ministry of Mines report, in 1889, showed that the mines of Robins, Dunsmuir, and Chandler continued to employ Chinese workers. However, changes had been made to the Coal Mine Regulations Act, which required that a deputation of men examine each mine, and the condition of the mine be recorded in a book kept for that purpose, and a notice be placed where everyone could see it.

DUNSMUIR DIES

The walls of Craigdarroch Castle were still going up when the Scottish miner and coal king, Robert Dunsmuir, died on April 12, 1889. Like everyone, Bate was shocked to learn of his death, for Dunsmuir had been ill only a few days and was considered in no danger. Norris's *Nanaimo Free Press* expressed the feelings of the community: "The whole province mourns as if each had lost a friend and here in Nanaimo where for years he had made his home among us, the feeling is that a good man has run his race and has at last been called home."[10] The *Nanaimo Free Press* published a whimsical tribute to Dunsmuir, entitled "The Old Man of the Mountain." By assigning Dunsmuir's nickname to a mountain, the newspaper created a personification that embodies a sense of veneration:

> That more people were to be seen on Commercial Street this afternoon, than for some weeks past, [demonstrates that] Nanaimo is beginning to resume its former air of rush and business which is very interesting to the Old Man who has taken a paternal interest in the City for many, many years.[11]

Robert Dunsmuir lived life to the fullest. He was an astute businessman who took advantage of every opportunity, and he died the richest man in the province. Perhaps his biggest achievement was the building of the Esquimalt and Nanaimo Railway; however, Craigdarroch Castle, completed the year after his death, remains as a lasting memorial to the Scottish miner. Joan inherited her husband's estate, estimated to be 15 million dollars. The two sons, Alex and James, may have been directors and held shares in the company, but their mother held the purse strings. James became president of the Wellington mines and Alex became president of the Esquimalt and Nanaimo Railway Company. Before Joan left on a visit to Scotland, she signed over power of attorney to her sons and turned over the family home in Victoria, Fairview, to James, who moved from Departure Bay. On her return in 1890 Joan moved into the castle with her daughters, then shocked everyone, including her sons, by announcing she was selling the Wellington mines. The Dunsmuir family saga was just beginning. James Dunsmuir took the company north to Cumberland and opened up another coal operation, the Union Colliery Company, then south to the Extension mine. He became premier of British Columbia in 1900, the same year Alex died. John Bryden, Robert Dunsmuir's son-in-law, completed Dunsmuir's term as MLA.

Miners either loved Dunsmuir or hated him, but they never denied his achievements. He and Bate had had many battles, mostly over mining issues, but they were a dynamic duo when fighting for improvements in the community. Bate would later acknowledge Dunsmuir's legacy. In 1907, in an article for the Nanaimo Free Press about some of the original pioneers of Nanaimo, he wrote:

His remarkably successful operations at the Wellington Colleries, his bold enterprise in building the Island Railway, and his adroit management of that and other large undertakings have won for him a lasting fame. With a mind commercially comprehensive, quick to perceive and act, he evinced great courage and pertinacity in all his ventures. His good fortune was exceptional. Like Midas, he could not touch anything that did not, in his hands, turn into gold. Energy, hope and will were his, and by them he conquered. The wealth he gathered materially enriched the Country. Hundreds partook of his affluence, through the free distribution he made, in various ways of his ample means. He was a gentleman of most generous disposition—a staunch friend, outspoken, one who would at all times fearlessly express whatever opinion he might entertain. His death was a heavy loss to the province, and was very generally regretted.[12]

19

DEATH OF
LOVED ONES

SINCE BATE'S ARRIVAL IN NANAIMO in 1857, the town had grown from a few cottages along Front Street into a vibrant municipality with its future firmly entrenched in the mining industry. Bate's life and that of his family were woven into the town's historical tapestry through their involvement in church, school, and community. Bate served another year as mayor in 1889 before declining to run for mayor in the 1890 election, but he continued to keep a close watch on the affairs of the city.

John Hilbert became the next mayor, after campaigning for better roads and improved sanitary conditions. At the first council meeting of the new administration, Bate commented on the improvements made in the city and praised the Street Committee for "doing its duty to the city in every respect." He was thanked for his long service as mayor and for his strict attention to duties and also for the manner in which he continually assisted the aldermen of the different wards. He recalled that during his long service as mayor he had missed only two meetings, and those were due "to a little illness."[1]

MORE SIGNS OF CITY GROWTH

Nanaimo's population had grown to over 4,500 and, according to one reviewer, the town was "destined to attain a position of commercial and industrial importance only second to any of the Pacific Coast." Nanaimo now boasted an opera house, on Church Street, which opened on November 16, 1889, with a grand ball. It had a large auditorium, two galleries, four spectator boxes, a dress circle, and a long bar. Bate welcomed this new addition to the cultural life of the community, for it provided a new venue for local and visiting performers, and served a dual role as hotel on the upper two floors and theatre on the ground floor. Next door, a new wing of the Windsor Hotel was just completed, and on Victoria Crescent, Frederick Rowbottom proceeded with the construction of his Crescent Hotel.

Adding to the ambience of the town around Dallas Square, a new courthouse was being built on Front Street with a grant of $25,000 from the provincial government. The building, designed by the Victoria architect Francis Mawson Rattenbury and faced with Newcastle Island sandstone, opened in 1896 and remains a prized heritage building today. Positioned on the west side of Front Street, across from the Dominion Post Office building, and adjacent to the Globe Hotel built by Alex Henderson in 1887, the new courthouse presented a picture of a young, prosperous, and growing city.

Bate had cause to be proud of the accomplishments of past councils. He said the improvements "may be recorded to the lasting credit of those persevering and doggedly determined men who abhorred debt and went, in public matters, by the good old rule of 'cutting the cost according to the cloth.' It is surprising what was done in about 10 years with a revenue of from less than $6,000 or less to $12,000, per year."[2]

The geographic configuration of early Nanaimo made progress difficult. Bate could look back and see where all the progress was made. Where once were trails or pathways, streets and walkways now defined the town. Rock formations that were barriers to traffic had been cut through and graded. Such was the case on Front Street, where part of a rock face was blasted away to allow Front Street access to Comox Road. Wharf Street was raised from the beach up to the level of Commercial Street. And one very early council, he acknowledged, had ordered the excavations for cisterns to hold reserves of water for use in case of fire.

He also remembered the giant trees that were logged and cleared along Selby Street from Albert to Fitzwilliam Street. But he cautioned it was not always entirely the work of Nanaimo City Council; "Sometimes persuasion helped get assistance from others." The provincial government provided financial assistance for the building of the first Bastion Street Bridge over the ravine, and the Vancouver Coal Company donated land for the Nanaimo Cemetery.[3] Bate saw all these changes and felt proud to have been part of the city's transformation.

In referring to errors of past councils, he felt the greatest mistake had been made on May 5, 1890, when the city passed a $50,000 loan bylaw for street improvement: "For 30 years ratepayers have been paying $4,000 a year and will continue to do so for twenty more years."[4] He reminded everyone that for 25 years the mayor and aldermen served without salary. He would not reap the benefits of a bylaw passed in 1900 giving the mayor $300 and aldermen $120 per year, for by then he had retired from municipal politics.

THE VANCOUVER COAL
COMPANY RESTRUCTURES

The Vancouver Coal Company changed its name to the New Vancouver Coal Mining and Land Company on January 30, 1889.

Business was declining, in the face of competition with the Dunsmuirs' burgeoning company.[5] Changing the company's name by restructuring and adding "New" to its title helped remove any burden of debt from its shareholders.[6] It also put a new face on the company following the tragic mining accident of 1887. William McGregor remained as works manager while his brother James managed the Southfield mine. Rosenfeld stayed on as the company agent in San Francisco. In 1891, the New Vancouver Coal Company employed 1,464 men.[7]

The company's extensive land holdings, which included the Harewood Estate, came under Robins's direction. Plagued by the constant threat of fire in the undeveloped land to the west, to protect the town Robins initiated an innovative scheme to clear and subdivide the area into five-acre lots, which were offered to miners to lease or purchase. His plan was to assist miners in becoming independent. There were conditions, however. The land had to be cleared and made suitable for cultivation, fenced with post and rail—and only miners need apply. Around seven thousand trees were logged, the wood used for pit props and the remainder burned. For weeks black ugly smoke hung over the town as the clearing continued. Roads were built into the estate, much of the work done by a chain gang from the Nanaimo jail. The first to lease and build was former mayor and survivor of the 1887 mine tragedy Richard Gibson, who built the first home on Howard Avenue.

In 1892, the job of real estate agent for the company's development project went to James Hurst Hawthornthwaite, whose ties to the company's management were firmly established. Previously, he had served as an agent for the United States, a position that propelled him into the intricacies of settlers' rights and competing mineral claims on Vancouver Island involving Robert Dunsmuir. "Big Jim," as he was known in Nanaimo, got along well with the miners and had a good relationship with Robins and Bate.[8]

In 1890 Bate purchased Robert Dunsmuir's large home, Ardoon, at the corner of Wallace and Albert Street. The family had enjoyed living in the Franklyn House for several years, but the lease may have expired or had to be renewed, and the opportunity arose to move into a permanent home. Archival records show Bate also owned several lots in the same block, as well as property in the South and Middle Wards, plus acreage in the Cedar area. The Franklyn House did not sit vacant for long, for it became the home of the Reifel family, who operated a brewery from the site next door.

Hawthornthwaite married Bate's daughter Elizabeth Ada (Lizzie) on June 7, 1890.[9] She was 18; he was 28. After their marriage they lived with his parents in Cowichan for a short time, where his father, William, was "a gentleman farmer."[10] The couple moved back to Nanaimo the following year. The couple would contribute ten grandchildren to the extended Bate family. In 1901, Hawthornthwaite was acclaimed as an independent Labour candidate for Nanaimo City in a by-election to replace Ralph Smith, who had resigned to run federally. He was the first socialist elected to the provincial legislature and would become one of BC's controversial figures through his career as a pioneer socialist.

Two more of Bate's children married in 1891. Lucy, 17, married Montague Stanley Davys on April 18, and then moved to Nelson where Montague worked as a mining engineer and assayer. The two Bate sisters Lucy Davys and Sally Goepel became prominent residents of Nelson, BC.[11] Their husbands were members of the Nelson Club, an exclusive gentlemen's club in the city, described as "a refuge in which men could relax by reading newspapers and magazines while enjoying their favourite cigar or drink, play cards or billiards, or even lawn bowling in the summer."[12]

William Charles also wed. His bride, Bridget (Edna) Jones, was from Harbour Grace, Newfoundland. They married on May 20, 1891, in St. Augustine's Chapel, on the reserve land of the Snuneymuxw in Nanaimo. Reverend Ernest G. Miller officiated at the ceremony, assisted by Reverend G.H. Tovey.[13] The chapel was an unusual venue for a Bate wedding, but Edna may have had First Nations heritage; she may have been a Mi'kmaq from Newfoundland. The chapel opened in 1891 and closed in 1903 when the congregation united with St. Paul's Anglican Church. Edna was two years older than Charles at the time of their marriage. She was a seamstress, and Charles, a mechanic. Bate gave the young couple a lot and a house when they married.

It is unknown when Thomas married Anabella Beatrice Dixon. In the census of 1891, the couple lived in Wellington, where Thomas worked as a machinist. They had seven children. After Anabella's death on November 16, 1906, in Cumberland, Thomas remarried a young Australian girl, Jean Muir Liddle, on April 7, 1909. He was then the proprietor of Magnet Cash Store.[14]

The weddings left two Bate children still living at home, Mary Beatrice and John Augustus (Gussie). Mary married a young Englishman, George W.B. Heathcote, on June 15, 1895, in Nanaimo, then joined her sisters Lucy and Sally in Nelson, where George worked as a clerk for the Bank of British Columbia.

About this time Aunt Maria, or as the Bate children liked to call her, "Auntie Snow," after her second husband, came to live with them in Nanaimo. She had been living in Victoria and had been unwell for some time. Cornelius Bryant, who had since retired to a small cottage at Mount Tolmie near Victoria, kept a watchful eye on his aunt, but as her mental and physical condition deteriorated, he wrote to Bate: "At times Aunt talks rational but only at intervals. I have written Snow to come and care for her, but I question if it will be of any use. I believe that this Snow has got hold of all that she had, no matter how she hid it."[15] She became more than Bryant could handle at this stage in his life, so the family decided to bring her to Nanaimo, where Mark and Sarah could care for her.

Maria's second marriage had not been a happy one. Her husband, Henry Snow, was away prospecting in the interior much of the time, and he was not a nice man. Stories abound about "Old Man Snow," a gold prospector who liked to stretch the truth. In 1889, he reportedly shot and killed a man in Fort Simpson by accident after the two got into a fight and a gun went off. Whether he was charged for this offence is unknown, but in 1895 he was charged in Victoria Provincial Court with failing to support Maria. Magistrate Farquhar Macrae presided over the case. When Snow agreed to provide for her, the charges were dropped, but her nephew Bryant implied that Snow had married her for her money, and some say he looked to his dying wife for gold.[16] Marie had inherited substantial property from her first husband, but she had failed to do due diligence and transfer the properties to her name. Bryant discovered that on one of the lots supposedly owned by Maria, the occupant had planted potatoes and paid Snow seven dollars a month in rent.

Maria died in Nanaimo on October 17, 1896, at the age of 78. In her will she requested her estate be divided equally between her nephews and nieces, leaving nothing for her husband.[17] After her death Bate and Bryant had difficulty finding Snow to finalize her estate. Bate inquired of the government agent in Fort Simpson, but no one there had seen or heard of him. Then in Victoria, Noah Shakespeare told Bryant he had seen Snow in town, and if he heard "aught" he would let them know. The cousins scanned the Victoria papers looking for his name. Bate was adamant; "I intend to get someone to keep track of him for a while as I may have more administrative business if it cannot be done here."[18] Bate contacted Fred Brown, a friend of Snow, asking him to get Snow to sign a form renouncing his executorship, which would allow Bate to deal with the administration of Maria's estate. "Make sure the form is witnessed by a Justice of the Peace," he advised. Both Bryant and Snow legally renounced their executorship in November 1897, giving Bate full authority to finalize her estate.

Bate had experienced many tragedies in his life, but the loss of his beloved Sarah was devastating. On May 5, 1897, while Aunt Maria's estate was being finalized, Sarah died, at the age of 57. They had been married 38 years. The cause of death was "valvular disease of the heart." Bate and his family mourned the loss deeply.

Whenever a pioneer of Nanaimo died, it was usually Bate who wrote the obituary, for he knew many of the people personally, no doubt from his years as mine manager and earlier as payroll clerk. At other times when a difference of opinion would develop, it was Bate who was called upon to render a decision.[19] Sarah's obituary would have been a difficult one to write. The community and members of societies to which Bate belonged rallied with an outpouring of sympathy and respect for Bate and his family.

At the council meeting of May 11, 1897, Mayor Joseph Davison and council signed a resolution conveying their "sincere sympathy in the recent bereavement which has overtaken him in the loss of his estimable wife who deservedly occupied a high place in the esteem and affections of the citizens of Nanaimo."[20] The Brethren of Ashlar Lodge wrote to Bate, acknowledging how much "harder the work of their world will be to you without the cheering sympathy of her who was for so long your dear companion." The Brethren of Court Nanaimo Foresters' Home, No. 5886, A.O.F., also offered their sincere sympathy: "You have been deprived of one of the truest and best wives, and the community of one of its noblest citizens."[21]

Later in November Bate confided in his cousin Cornelius Bryant: "I am feeling better than the weather but am lonely, and, despondent at times, when I think of my lost one. Only the hope, the blessed hope of meeting her again consoles me."[22] Bryant offered him comfort: "I note your personal references to your own great loss. True it is, that the hope of an immortal reunion with our departed is our only consolation."[23]

Sarah's funeral on May 11, 1897, was the final tribute to her memory. Her hearse was literally covered with emblems, wreaths, anchors, hearts, and crosses as the funeral procession, which extended over two blocks, moved to the Nanaimo Cemetery where she was interred next to her son George Arthur and Aunt Maria Snow.

BATE THE MAYOR RESCUES COUNCIL

It was the Fraser River gold rush that had enticed the young Mark Bate to travel halfway around the world to start a new life on Vancouver Island. Now, at 61 years of age, his black beard traced with white, Bate returned to the mayoralty in the wake of another gold rush.

When gold was found in 1896 on the Klondike River near Dawson in the Yukon Territory, the rush was on. Gold fever swept the country as if carried by gale force winds. Between 1897 and 1899 hundreds of gold seekers raced to the region. Nanaimo was not immune. Miners outfitted themselves by pooling resources. They filled the SS *Islander* on its trip north on July 27, 1897, encouraged from the docks by crowds of friends and family members. Each trekker was a potential millionaire. Bate's Silver Cornet Band sent the ship on its way with celebratory music.

The names of people from Nanaimo who went to seek their fortune are familiar ones. Jack McGregor, the son of William, the mine manager, and several family members went to Victoria on July 22 and boarded the SS *Queen* the next day for the trip to Skagway. The city council lost three of its members to the Klondike. Two aldermen were the first to leave; they left abruptly mid-term, then Mayor John Davidson took a leave of absence for the remainder of his term, which was only one month, leaving Acting Mayor George Campbell in charge of city affairs. Also joining the exodus was former mayor and miner Richard Gibson, he who had escaped the No. 1 Pit mining disaster.

At the final council meeting of the last term, Campbell disclosed that the council of 1897 was in a rather peculiar situation: "The goldfields of the far north had attracted the mayor and two aldermen, while another alderman had gone to the neighbouring city expecting to find a better field."[24] Considering all the difficulties, trials, and temptations of the year, he believed the council had made a good showing, but he hoped the incoming council would be able to straighten things out and get the city cleared of its debt.

Nothing seemed to be going right for the 1897 council. Sometime between the evening of November 24 and November 26, someone broke into the Collector's Office and "tore to atoms and completely destroyed" five of the most important city assessment rolls and special rates books.[25] After an emergency meeting of the council, they decided to ask the superintendent of the provincial police in Victoria to send "an expert detective immediately."[26] The council left the office in the disarray in which it was found, for the detective's perusal. The next day a reward of $500 was offered for information leading to the arrest and conviction of the perpetrator. A week later the city clerk, Adam Thompson, was arrested and convicted after shortages were discovered in the accounts he kept as city treasurer.

Who could bring order out of chaos—accounts in disarray, clerk arrested, aldermen and mayor absconded to the gold fields? The public had no interest in having a municipal election, so the next council's aldermen were all elected by acclamation. So Bate, still grieving the loss of Sarah, was petitioned to take over as mayor. He brought his years of experience to the troubled city administration. He immediately reappointed Samuel Gough as his city clerk/treasurer. Gough had been city clerk from 1880 to 1896, when Mayor Davidson demoted him to assessor, collector, and police court clerk and appointed his assistant, Adam Thompson, to the position of city clerk. With Gough, who would serve the city for a total of 45 years, again beside him, Bate began charting a course of stability for the city.

Bate's new council brought diverse abilities. All but one had previous council experience. Edward Quennell, the local butcher, had served as alderman and mayor, so would have been a valuable addition to new council. Thomas Brown, William Manson, Henry McAdie, James Knarsten, and Albert Planta all had council experience. The only new alderman was Frances LeFeuvre, who worked for the Vancouver Coal Company. The council also appointed two men: John H. Cocking and William E. Webb. Of immediate concern to everyone was restoring the mutilated real estate rolls of the city for the years 1896 and 1897, and bringing order to the city records in general.

For the next three years Bate led the council in a variety of different issues affecting the city. He had firsthand knowledge of how devastating a fire could be, so safety was a major concern; many of the buildings in the city were of wooden construction, and adding to the problem was the lack of an adequate water supply. Those cisterns that were constructed at various places around town to store water should a fire erupt were ineffective in a major blaze. This was evident in a fire in 1878, and was confirmed in 1894 when fire destroyed a portion of Commercial Street businesses, including the Nanaimo Hotel and Fire Hall No. 1. The next fire hall was constructed on Nicol Street using brick construction. The city investigated the possibility of a better alarm system, too: perhaps the telephone lines that connected businesses and residences could be connected through the telephone exchange office to the fire alarm whistle.[27]

But the water supply was an ongoing problem. There was a growing consensus that the municipality should control its own water supply. Previous councils had tried to purchase the existing waterworks plant now owned by the Nanaimo Water Works Company Limited. Over the years the city tried to negotiate the purchase, but the company repeatedly rejected the city's offer. Bate's council reentered negotiations. A board of arbitration fixed the purchase price at $104,000, but it was not until June 19, 1901, that the water works company formally transferred its plant to the city.

Nanaimo's council, like many councils of the time, was closely involved in regulating the morality and actions of its citizens. It passed bylaws against gambling, swearing, drunkenness, vagrancy, begging, and cruelty to animals. Bicycles had become a popular mode of transportation, and the council prohibited fast driving on bridges. It also vetoed horse riding on the sidewalks of Haliburton Street and the firing of guns. In 1898 it enacted a curfew bylaw to prevent children under the "tender" age of 14 from roaming the streets after nightfall.

In February 1899, the ward system also came under scrutiny by Bate's administration. A municipal council could abolish the ward system if it received a petition signed by the owners of more than 50 per cent of the value of the real estate. This would have meant hiring someone to circulate the petition, and due to the large number of absentee property owners and the large portion of the city vested in companies and estates, the council felt such a petition would be unrealistic. A referendum was therefore put to the electorate in 1902, asking, "Are you in favour of the ward system?" A very small majority answered negatively.[28] The ward system remained.

The council also changed the term for aldermen; up to this time they were elected for a one-year term. The council approved a two-year term; vacancies caused by retiring members could be filled through an annual election. A resolution also passed allowing active members of the volunteer fire brigade to be exempt from the payment of Revenue Tax and Road Tax.

ANOTHER MINING TRAGEDY

In 1898, the New Vancouver Coal Company had grown to over 1,100 employees; no Chinese, Snuneymuxw, or Japanese people were on the payroll.[29] As well as the No. 1 Esplanade mine and the two Southfield mines, the company had expanded and opened a mine on Protection Island in 1891 at Gallows Point (known earlier as Execution Point). The workers all lived in Nanaimo so were transported back and forth on the company's steamer, the *Mermaid*, from the Nanaimo wharves. The first shipment of coal from the Protection mine went out on August 2, 1892.

William McGregor was still manager at the Esplanade mine. Billy, as he was affectionately called, was well liked by the miners. Once, so the story goes, when business was slack due to competition from American coal, a grave threat to the industry, the company asked the miners to take a wage cut. A mass meeting was called. Sam Robins explained the situation. The miners were quiet and thoughtful, then one of them cried out: "What's Billy McGregor got to say?" McGregor asked for a three-month trial. After that, he said, he would see they got their wages restored. "That's all we want to know, Billy," someone shouted. And the men went back to work.[30]

Bate's history with the McGregor family went back to the time when his uncle George Robinson had an altercation with William's father, John, a pioneer miner during the HBC era. As earlier noted, John and his family left Nanaimo and did not return until after the HBC had sold its holdings. When John returned he went back to work at the mine that had become the Vancouver Coal Company, then under Nicol's management. Bate probably got to know the family from making up the payroll sheets for the company and later as mine manager. After John's death, 11-year-old William went to work as a "door boy" in the mine. (The boy was employed to sit by a light stopping, open it when necessary, and make sure it closed again.[31]) William studied hard and worked his way up to become mine manager under Bate. Their lives interconnected through work and community service; William also served as chairman of the school board.

On November 12, 1898, there was a fire in the Protection Island mine, and despite being seriously burned himself, McGregor helped carry out the fire boss, George Lee, whose legs were broken. Six other miners were also burned in the explosion and another fireman was injured. McGregor worked among the injured for hours before submitting himself to treatment. He was taken home. As at the fire of 11 years earlier, his wife, Amanda, once again nursed him, only this time he died, five days later. She and their six children mourned the loss of father and husband.

Bate was no stranger to death, having just buried both his wife and his aunt, and now he felt the grief of losing a friend. Once again the community mourned. Schools and businesses closed. An estimated three thousand people attended McGregor's funeral. Four railway coaches were filled with people from Wellington. The funeral procession was one of the largest in Nanaimo's history to date. Bate joined other mourners, including James Dunsmuir and John Bryden with his son Robert. Memorial services were held in several churches, including St. Andrew's Presbyterian Church on November 22, 1898.

Meanwhile, back in the Klondike, Jack McGregor learned the news about his father. All his plans for a nice trip home in a few months' time, and money enough to see him through college, were blasted away.[32] He left in the dead of winter on a 600-mile walk to Skagway, where he boarded the steamer the *City of Topeka* for Seattle. He arrived home in Nanaimo 27 days after leaving the Klondike. His experiences and epic journey home became the fodder for a true-life adventure story. Jack worked for 20 years as a master mechanic with Pacific Coast Coal Company in South Wellington, and was later chief engineer with Canadian Collieries No. 5 mine.

Bate fulfilled another year as mayor in 1900 and then retired from municipal politics, having served a total of 16 terms, elected several times by acclamation.

20

BEGINNINGS
AND ENDINGS

WITH ALL HIS CHILDREN MARRIED, Bate had time to spend with his grandchildren, and there were lots of them. He never wrote about this time in his life, so the recollections of his grandson Darryl Bate, Thomas's son, then living in Cumberland, provide a poignant glimpse into this period. In his speech to the Nanaimo Historical Society on November 8, 1966, Darryl described a visit to his grandfather when he was just a boy:

> It was quite an experience for a lad to step aboard the train at Cumberland, get cinders in your eye looking out the window heading for Union Bay; passing those blazing coke ovens that were going at that time; getting aboard the *City of Nanaimo* or the *Charmer*, for the cruise down to Nanaimo. My sisters accompanied me on those trips . . . The waiters would treat my sisters like princesses, and myself like a prince while they waited on me, at least that's what it seemed to me at that time. Then later, crawling into the

top bunk of the boat . . . listening to the slap of the waves at night and the roll of the boat . . . Then the thrill of hearing the whistle as we entered Nanaimo Harbour, blasted away. I recall one time when the propeller was whipping up the herring in the harbour; I felt awfully sorry for those herring . . . I recall tramping up the old plank wharf—it was very steep, from the old wharf up to the post office.

Who met us, I don't recall exactly, but we had so many relatives in Nanaimo. There was the Hawthornthwaites, the Plantas and the Martindales. My sisters used to go and stay with Dorothy Bate, or the Plantas, or the Martindales (the latter was a practicing chiropractor and businessman who married Lillian Planta), but my favourite spot to go was always to my Grandma Dixon's. Grandma and Grandpa Dixon and Uncle Arthur's home (mother's parents and brother) was at the mouth of the Millstream . . . Uncle Arthur was always my favourite uncle because he could tell tales about old Nanaimo . . . I remember a lot of the oldtimers would sit around in a summer evening and chew the fat about old Nanaimo.

When I visited Grandpa Bate, I would go to his house . . . I think the home [Ardoon] was originally built by Dunsmuir! On Sunday afternoon, I can see Grandpa today, standing at the head of the table sharpening that knife, perhaps there was a leg of lamb, or a leg of beef, I don't know, but I had to remain very careful. I had to watch my manners. One peculiarity I remember about Grandpa Bate was that I wasn't to drink, or we weren't to drink water with our meals. That was something—I don't know why—but I remember that as a youngster . . . I remember the coal-grate fireplaces that were in the dining room; they looked like very comfortable days when I look back now. Grandpa was a pretty busy man, there's no doubt; occasionally we'd take a walk and we'd talk. His main thought to me was always particularly about books. I recall later he used to take me into the library and before I left he'd always give me a book to take home to read: I wish I'd kept them. But

I remember one book that I did keep, it was Elbert Hubbard's notebook and one that I memorized, that I liked very much and it carried through with me for many, many years: Quote:

> If thou art worn and hard-beset
> With worries that thou woulds't forget,
> Go to the woods and hills
> Breathe the sweet air that nature gives.

Those are the impressions that Grandpa passed on to me.

Other walks I remember looking up toward Mount Benson and then we'd turn around and look over the Nanaimo Harbour. I think Grandpa had in the back of his mind, once upon a time, that as his background as a youngster, his father was in the iron and steel business in Birmingham. I think he had a dream that someday we would have an iron and steel business in this area, either here or in Union Bay, because my Dad used to talk about it also. At that time the complaint was we don't have enough iron-ore. I would say the essence of everything that Grandpa told me—live right and your days on this earth shall be many.[1]

A VISIT TO ENGLAND AND A NEW BEGINNING

In 1900, Bate was in the middle of his last term in office as mayor when he decided to take a trip back to England. What precipitated this sudden travel is unknown; possibly it was to visit his sister Ann, who still lived in Droylsden, in Lancashire, the only member of his immediate family left in England; his sisters Elizabeth (Horne) and Lucy (Sabiston) lived in Nanaimo, and the whereabouts of his brother Joseph was unknown. The timing of his visit also coincided with his daughter Emily's journey from South Africa to London with her husband, Charlie Alport, who was ill and needed an operation. Bate had not seen her since their elopement in 1873. Did he know she would be in England? Did they meet? These questions remain unanswered, but the Alports were certainly in London at this time. They left for Cape Town, South Africa, in January 1901. Sadly, Charlie died at sea.[2]

Bate travelled aboard Cunard's *Campania* from New York, arriving in Liverpool, England, on July 21, 1900. His daughter Sally Goepel accompanied him. This was his first visit home since leaving in 1857. At the age of 63, he was still a relatively young man. Thoughts of marriage and companionship through his later years may have crossed his mind, because he met the widow Hannah Harrison in England, and after a whirlwind courtship, he and Hannah were married on September 25, 1900, in the parish church in Droylsden. He gave his residence at the time of their marriage as Fairfield Road, and Hannah's as Edge Lane, both in Droylsden. Rector Fred Knight conducted the wedding ceremony. Witnesses were Owen Lee and Alice Chambers, Hannah's sister.

On their marriage certificate, Bate still gave the profession of his father as managing partner in the Woodside Iron Works.[3] Why would Bate still hold to the conviction about his father's profession at this stage in his life? Did he really believe his father was a partner in the Iron Works, and not a skilled glasscutter, as was the case? He was only eight years old when his father died; perhaps this was the story he was told as a young boy and he never had reason to doubt it.

Hannah was born September 5, 1856, in Pilkington, Lancashire, the eldest of six children born to Thomas McVitty and Selina Haworth. She had two brothers and three sisters. Lancashire was once the home of the world's cotton industry, so it is not surprising that her father was employed as a cotton finisher and her mother as a weaver. At the age of 15, Hannah also worked as a weaver. She married Philip Harrison in 1877 and they settled in Droylsden. He was a mechanic in an iron works. They had four children, Joseph, Elizabeth, John Harvey, and Selina. Philip died in 1898.

The history of the family of Bate's new wife is a sad tale of mental illness and an unhappy marriage. Hannah's mother, Selina McVitty, died in January of 1876, murdered by her husband, Thomas. Hannah was one of the main witnesses at his trial. He was judged not guilty on the grounds of insanity and spent the rest of his life in the notorious Broadmoor Prison in Berkshire. The murder was a sensational news story at the time and was carried in newspapers around the country. The account below is taken from the *Manchester Courier*, published January 22, 1876.

The McVitty family lived in a small house with two bedrooms. Hannah's brothers, John and William, occupied the back room, while Hannah and her sisters, Alice, Lucy, and Clara, aged four, slept in the same room as their parents. There were two beds in the room, and Clara, the youngest, slept with her parents. Thomas and Selina often quarreled and occasionally he struck her. Two weeks before the incident, the family had tried to get him committed to an asylum. He thought Selina was being unfaithful, which she vehemently denied. He began keeping a razor under his pillow. One night, Clara's screams awoke everyone, including a neighbour, who came running to see what had happened. Thomas was sitting up in bed and Selina was on the floor between the beds, bleeding from the neck; she died the next morning.

What impact this incident had on Hannah is unknown, but she was a mature young woman of 20 years when the incident happened. She married the following year and raised four children with her husband, Philip, and it appeared to have been a happy marriage.

Bate returned to Vancouver, British Columbia, with Hannah and her 15-year-old son, John Harvey Harrison. For a short time they lived in East Vancouver, according to the Vancouver census of 1901. They remained there for a few months before he introduced his bride and her son to his family and friends in Nanaimo.

During Bate's absence, his son Gussie had married. Bate may not have known his son planned to marry. Gussie worked as a bookkeeper when he married Edith Perchet on October 5, 1900, in the parlour of the Windsor Hotel, now the Dorchester Hotel. She was 21, he was 24. She and her sister Annie were born in St. Catherines, Ontario. Their mother, Annie, was a widower when she moved with her daughters to Nanaimo to work as a live-in housekeeper in the hotel then owned by the Irishman Hugh Dempsey, who had married their mother on January 14, 1892.[4] Gussie and Edith moved to the United States.

Hannah's son John continued to live with them while he worked as a warden in the new Nanaimo jail on Skinner Street.[5] On June 27, 1911, he married Annie Sarah McKenzie in St. Andrew's Presbyterian Church.[6] The couple settled in the Victoria area.

DEATHS IN THE FAMILY

Bate's return to Nanaimo was timely, for he was present to offer comfort to his sister Elizabeth. Her husband, Adam Horne, died on August 9, 1901, at the age of 72. The Masonic Lodge took charge of the funeral, for which Reverend C.E. Cooper, the rector of St. Paul's, officiated. Elizabeth died in 1905. Five sons and two daughters survived her.

Horne's granddaughter, Mildred Simpson, remembered one of her uncles going to Horne's house when he passed away. It was a scene he never forgot, she said: "Several of the local Indians were on the front lawn with a fire going and they were dancing around the fire and playing on a drum and chanting." Mildred's uncle was the eldest son and went with his mother to the funeral. She said "he was terrified when he saw the Indians there, but my grandmother explained that they were just showing their respect as they were very fond of him."[7] The *Nanaimo Free Press* reported Horne's passing, and elaborated on his connection to the First Nations people and the Nanaimo pioneers: "His personality was a link between the first settlements and the living present."[8]

Horne and Bate were close, as were their families, having shared many family gatherings throughout the years. Horne Lake was named in his honour after he discovered it on one of his many expeditions across Vancouver Island. Adam in turn named the mountain overlooking the lake Mount Mark for his friend and brother-in-law.

Reverend Cooper of St. Paul's officiated at another funeral for another member of Bate's family. On December 13, 1903, Bate's son William Charles died suddenly in his sleep at the age of 32, from heart disease. He had not been in the best of health for some time. A hunting incident several years before affected his heart, then two years later he had a paralytic stroke, though he was able to resume work.[9] His wife, Edna, and their six children mourned his passing. A large number of relatives and friends, along with the Native Sons of British Columbia, Post No. 3, attended the funeral.

Bate began liquidating his property investments as early as 1899. He sold 30 acres in Cedar to the New Vancouver Coal Company for $10,300; this included all the surface and mineral and coal rights. He also sold his 285-acre farm in Cedar for $1,425. But the biggest sale of all was Ardoon, known as the Dunsmuir house, which he sold to the Merchants Bank of Canada. Bate and Hannah moved into their new home at 522 Hecate Street, where Bate also owned several lots.

THE OLD WARRIOR RETIRES

In 1907 Bate began writing a series of articles about his memories as a pioneer Nanaimoite. The articles were published weekly under the heading, "Mark Bate's Reminiscences of Early Nanaimo Days," in the *Nanaimo Free Press* during February and March of that year. In promoting the series the newspaper noted, "Mr. Bate has a remarkable memory, an easy, fluent flow of language and is a veritable storehouse for facts, figures, historical lore and amusing and interesting incidents of the strenuous earlier days of the city's life."[10]

Bate wrote about a wide range of subjects, from his arrival in Nanaimo to the location of various places connected with the first coal mines, as well as the people and where they lived and interesting incidents that happened in the town. Unrelated to his Reminiscences articles, he also wrote what was to become his most memorable article, "A Stroll around Nanaimo in 1874." In this he recalls interesting sites and some early pioneering retail strategy:

> On Church St. opposite St. Paul's Schoolhouse, there was a row of rooms built by Carl Bossi, used for a brief period as a soap factory, a store building adjacent, which for a while, served as the Public School Room. It had been put to various uses: a butchers shop, beer saloon, drug store and general trading establishment. William Copperman, a Polish Jew was proprietor of the latter. He had a branch house at Victoria and did a big business with the Indians. For their special information he advertised his wares in Chinook! As the Indians could not read, the Chinook posters were the cause of some little merriment, but Copperman shrewdly observed someone would tell the Natives what he had printed, and so their attention would be drawn to his shop.

During his 50 years Bate noted he had seen amazing discoveries and inventions:

> Electrical cables circled the globe, railways have spanned continents, and dozens of other great achievements applied to everyday service. No need to enumerate great wars, earthquakes, revolutions, slave emancipation, etc. "Peace hath her victories, so less renowned than war."

Bate had a wealth of sayings in his repertoire and produced them at will, whenever they seemed appropriate. These articles have become a valuable resource for people interested in the early history of the city.

He and Hannah visited England again in 1909 for an extended period, but returned with plenty of time before retiring his government appointment in 1913. They visited again a year later, sailing on July 26, 1914, from Quebec to Liverpool on the *Calgarian*, returning on the *Missanabie* on August 19, 1916. Bate faded away from the public spotlight, as old warriors are allowed to do, but he kept a watchful eye on happenings in the community.

MINING COMPANY LAND FOR NANAIMO

Of particular interest to Bate was the sale of the New Vancouver Coal Company. By the turn of the century the use of fuel oil in California had cut into the market for Nanaimo coal. After the HBC sold the mining enterprise, the Vancouver Coal Company mined coal for 40 years, but it did not have the financial resources to get into the coal-oil market, so they decided to sell to a group of San Francisco capitalists, the Western Fuel Company, registered in California. The company registered in BC in December of 1902 as an extra-provincial company. The agreement for sale was dated December 15, 1902, and the company took full title on February 11, 1903.[11]

The New Vancouver Coal Company made sure its directors were well compensated for their loss of office. Six directors divided the proceeds from the sale among themselves. Samuel Robins received a severance of $10,000.[12] He stayed on for another six months, then resigned in June 1903. Before he and his wife, Maria, returned to England, the community showed its appreciation by fêting the couple with a "Samuel Robins Day" held on the Green. Mayor William Manson delivered the address before the large gathering. Maria received a silver tray and Robins was given a copy of the farewell address designed and inscribed by local artist J.W. Jemson.[13] It was a fitting tribute to Robins, who had successfully increased the production of the mines from 50,000 tons in 1882 to 500,000 in 1902. During that time he managed to maintain a harmonious relationship with the workers; no strikes occurred during his 20 years as superintendent.

In 1915 the city council negotiated with the Western Fuel Company over the ownership of the town's parks and squares. This caught Bate's attention, even though he was visiting in Birmingham, England. Both countries were in the midst of the First World War and Bate was thinking about Nanaimo's parks and squares. He addressed his personal recollection on the subject to the city clerk in Nanaimo, and indicated the subject as "Nanaimo City Squares." Bate undoubtedly knew the history of the town better than anyone especially regarding the details of the purchase of the "Nanaimo Estate" from the HBC in November 1862. He explained:

The following year, 1863, about 500 acres were set off and surveyed as Nanaimo Townsite. Two plans were designed at that time, one by Robert Homfray and one by Andrew Hood. Homfray's draft showed more open park-like spots, and in certain parts of the town, straighter streets, than Hood's, but the plan by Homfray was discarded, and that by Hood, showing the squares, except Deverill, as they are today accepted, we finally adopted as the official Map of the Town and, as such, deposited in the Land Registry Office.

On a plan made subsequently by Mr. Edward Mohun, mostly copied from Hood's though on a larger scale, a few alterations of minor importance were effected, but no change whatever was made in the position or description of the "Squares." Here let me say that neither Mr. Mohun, nor his partner Farwell, made any survey of the town excepting in one or two places where a few additional lots and the original plotting had been laid out about Bridge Street. Mohun's Plan was also deposited in the Land Registry Office, after the Incorporation of the City. A complete check survey of the Town was made by Mr. Stephens, C.E.[14]

Bate wanted the people of Nanaimo to know that from the beginning, public spaces had been planned for the town:

The Squares, Parks, and Milford Crescent were assuredly absolutely resigned and set aside, "dedicated," if you like, in 1863 by the Vancouver Coal Mining and Land Company Limited, just as definitely and decidedly as the streets were, for the common use of the public. Consequently, and in verification of what I have said, the Squares (save perhaps Deverill, which was surrendered latest) are shown as town breathing places on the first, and on every other official plan deposited in the Land Registry Office, and in accordance with those plans, lots have always been sold, and conveyed.[15]

Bate confirmed that when the town lots were put up for auction in Victoria in May 1864, these areas were clearly outlined on the map. Deverill Square was not named on the original map, but the green space was clearly marked for park purposes. He concluded, "I could go much further and give other details, but with the circumstances as I have stated, what more is necessary to prove that the city owns the squares for common utility as much as it does the streets."

There is speculation that the one new square, Deverill, was named for George Charles Deverill, an assistant manager under Nicol. Deverill married Mary Franklyn, the daughter of the magistrate. The young couple's baby daughter, Laura May, died in 1866 and George died two years later in September 1868, at 30 years of age. The tragic circumstances of his young assistant apparently led Nicol to name the square as a memorial to him.

When Bate wrote his letter from Birmingham, the First World War was a year old and Nanaimo had survived two difficult years of a prolonged miner's strike, during which the militia arrived to ensure public safety.

Few people were left unscathed by the war. Bate lost his grandson, Douglas, son of William and Edna. After William's sudden death in 1903 at the age of 32, Edna had raised the couple's six children. Douglas had enlisted in the navy on April 18, 1918 and served as a ship's cook aboard the Canadian naval patrol steamer *Galiano*. Prior to this he was employed as a cook in New Westminster. On October 30, 1918, the ship was travelling from Triangle Island to Cape St. James, on the southern tip of the Queen Charlotte Islands, when it was lost at sea with 36 people on board. Vessels raced to the point where the last signal was reported, but there was no sign of the vessel. Only one body was recovered. The loss of the *Galiano* affected four Nanaimo families and one from South Wellington. The men who died were Frank Greenshields, John Young, Peter Aitken, and Douglas Bate; and from South Wellington, Matthew Dobbyn.[16] Douglas's name is on the honour roll at St. Paul's Church.

By this time, Bate and Hannah had spent as much time in England as they did in Nanaimo since their marriage. Hannah, who had suffered from stomach cancer for some time, died on February 26, 1919, at their family home on Hecate Street.[17] Once more Bate's musical friends in the Silver Cornet Band led the cortège from his residence to St. Paul's Church and then to the cemetery, as they had done for his first wife, Sarah. Two of Hannah's children survived her, John H. Harrison, in Nanaimo, and her daughter, Mrs. G.F. Farron, in Birmingham, England.

BATE THE WRITER

After Hannah's death, Bate was in a reflective mood and began writing his memoirs of Nanaimo. While no one knows what became of Bate's manuscript, it is mentioned in a letter he received from R. Edward Gosnell, dated October 3, 1922:

I note in a recent edition of the Province that you had completed your memoirs of Nanaimo. I am deeply interested in all such matters and as soon as the book is published, will you please send me a copy with bill for the same. Put me down as a subscriber. You will, of course, remember me as a former librarian, archivist, etc. and private secretary of a half dozen premiers etc. I have pleasant recollections of some of your expressions of appreciation.[18]

Gosnell was a former reporter who supervised the opening of the British Columbia Legislative Library on November 1, 1893, and in 1908 he was charged with overseeing the new provincial archives. In 1906, he published *A History: British Columbia*, in which he wrote a short biography about Mark Bate, listing not just his accomplishments in Nanaimo but those of his children as well. This tome reveals something new about Bate:

On his arrival he worked at engine driving and weighing coal, and then entered the Hudson's Bay Company office as a clerk, continuing thus until the whole Nanaimo estate was sold to the Vancouver Coal Company. In 1863 he became the successor of James Farquahar as accountant of the VCML and in 1869 was promoted to local manager.[19]

Previous articles about Bate say he became clerk on his arrival in Nanaimo.

About the same time Bate received another letter from another prominent journalist, Bruce Alistair McKelvie, who was then editor of the *Daily Province* in Vancouver. McKelvie worked for almost all the major newspapers of the day, the *Vancouver Province, Daily Province, Daily Colonist* and *Vancouver Sun*. Bate had whet his appetite for writing when he co-published Nanaimo's first newspaper, the *Gazette*, then later the *Tribune*. He knew many of the journalists in the early days of the province, including De Cosmos and David William Higgins of the Victoria *Daily Colonist*. McKelvie's letter accompanied some notes he was returning to Bate:

> I was extremely sorry that I could not get over to Nanaimo to add my mite of tribute to the honour done you, and which you so justly deserved. I am enclosing the notes you so kindly loaned me last summer on "Nanaimo." I may say that it is only the further indefinite character of my prospects of getting over to your fair city for some time that makes me consent to mail them now.[20]

McKelvie had tried unsuccessfully to meet Bate and deliver the notes in person.

McKelvie's history of British Columbia was published in 1926, and was entitled *Early History of the Province of British Columbia*. This book, at 116 pages, was much shorter than the Gosnell book, which had over a thousand pages. Bate's contribution is duly noted in the introduction.

FINAL YEARS OF A PIONEER

In 1924 Bate joined 250 "pioneers of British Columbia" being fêted at the Empress Hotel in Victoria by the British Columbia Historical Association. The host for the evening was MLA Dr. J.D. MacLean, honorary chairman of the group. He said, "It was rare to have two hundred and fifty guests who have been here for fifty-three years and upwards gathered under one roof. It is a magnificent tribute to the loyalty of these pioneers."[21] Bate, who could never resist reminiscing about the early days, responded on behalf of the pioneers, saying it was gratifying to be honoured in this way. He then gave a speech about the time following his arrival on Vancouver Island in 1857:

> There are occasions when we may count ourselves happy beings, and this great gathering of Pioneers certainly is one of them. It

was a happy thought, whoever conceived it, to arrange this useful fraternal meeting—to bring together for right royal entertainment hundreds of Pioneers from different parts of the Province—give them an opportunity to come face to face, and renew old, or make new, acquaintances. A noble idea, truly, to my mind, and I think all present will agree with me.

Audiences appreciated his perspective, given his long and accomplished life. He recalled how the "Black Diamond City," as the town was sometimes called, looked when the *Princess Royal* pioneers arrived. He remembered the abundance of food, and the ready supply of coal and wood, when forests were alive with game and the waters teemed with fish. Despite the primitive living conditions and lack of communication with the outside world, "they had food in plenty—fresh fat salmon and venison always."[22]

The next month, June 18, 1924, he travelled again to England, from Quebec to Liverpool on the *Caronia*. His destination was Manchester. He returned to Canada in September that year.

The year 1925 was a busy one for Bate. At age 88, he could be forgiven for not being as active in the public life of the community as previously, but that was not his style. He was present when Lieutenant Governor W.C. Nicholson laid the cornerstone for a new Nanaimo hospital, on August 20, 1925. Another former mayor, John Hilbert, joined Bate at the ceremony. The two men had been members of the first hospital board, so this would have been an important milestone for them. A 54-man guard of honour attended from the HMS *Capetown*, which happened to be in port at the same time, and as with most important community events, the Silver Cornet Band entertained.[23] Bate remembered the first hospital on Chapel Street—a few log cabins connected together for the care of injured miners. The second hospital, on Franklyn Street, had opened in 1883, but it needed to be replaced. The new hospital on Machleary Street opened in 1928.

On December 24, 1925, Bate's friend and associate Samuel Gough died at the age of 76. Bate had first appointed him city clerk in 1880; he served the city in that position and others until his retirement 45 years later. He and Bate had much in common. Both played musical instruments and loved music, and they were interested in the city's early history. In 1924, the *Nanaimo Free Press* wrote that it was indebted to Gough "for much of the interesting data" contained in the Jubilee Edition of the newspaper. Gough was awarded the city's appreciation medal shortly before his death.

Bate was in a reflective mood when he addressed a meeting of the Native Sons and Daughters of British Columbia on December 11, 1925:

> To me it is inspiring to recall—to relate—pleasing impressions formed in many passing years. Voices and faces long silent and gone seem to come in to one's very presence. To think of them is like living a part of your life over again. I feel like exclaiming,
>
> Oh, that youth would leave us never!
> Oh, that summer would last for ever!
> O, that the joys we have in the spring
> For ever their happy song would sing,
> And music and friendship never take wing,
> But stay with us for ever!
> Then, ah then, if such joys were given,
> Most of us mortals would feel near Heaven.
> To the Pioneers, in the sunset of their days, let me say,
> What if the summer life is past
> And autumn out of hand,
> The clouds of winter as they go
> Reveal "The Better Land."

FINAL DAYS

In August 1927, Bate, at 90 years old, decided to take another trip to England. His daughter Lizzie accompanied him, at the advice of his doctor. This was clearly intended to be the final journey home to visit family and friends. Even on this trip he never stopped writing. He left behind a diary of his last few days. It is a very small diary, about two by four inches, allowing only enough space for brief comments, and it is written in pencil so not all his words are legible. It shows he was active until the day he died.

For most of his last week the weather was rainy, as it sometimes is in Britain in August, but this did not stop him visiting his niece Hannah Bate and her daughter. He wrote, "We enjoyed music, singing, and had tea." He also visited Clara, the sister of his second wife, Hannah.

Vancouver Island was never far from his thoughts, as he noted in the diary the death of British Columbia Premier John Oliver on August 17. The rain may have kept him indoors but he was happy reading and listening to music. He listened to the radio on August 21, he wrote, and heard "quite distinctly a service from St. Martin-in-the-Fields." This is an Anglican church located in Trafalgar Square, London, known as a musical venue. In the evening he enjoyed some "fine music on the gramophone."

The next day he went to the Netherton Cemetery and to Holly Hall and Woodside. He does not say whose grave he visited, but his family had close ties to the area. The former is located over a mile south of Dudley by the Stourbridge Canal. When he visited his cousin Mary and niece Hannah, he gave them a "picture."

Bate's last entry was on August 24, when he travelled to Evesham with his cousin George Bate and his family. The small market town is on the River Avon in an area known for its fruit and vegetables. He described the day as "the most wretched outing I have ever had; it was blowing and raining hard nearly the whole trip." If it had been a nice sunny day he could have listened to live music from the Victorian bandstand in Abbey Park. Not on this day, however; he wrote that the weather was "very violent at Evesham." He spent the evening talking with George. This was the last entry in his diary.

Bate died three days later, on August 27, 1927. His death certificate gave the cause of death as "apoplexy," or a stroke.[24] His nephew H. Simmons, Clara's son, signed the certificate. Bate had been staying with the family in Erdington, a suburb of Birmingham.

The *Western Daily Press*, the paper for southwestern England, reported his death on August 30, 1927:

> Canadian Pioneer dies on re-visiting native place. Mr. Mark Bate, age 90, a prominent figure in Canadian Freemasonry, has died at Birmingham, his native place, which he was revisiting. Seventy years ago he joined his uncle in what is now the City of Nanaimo, where the Hudson's Bay Company, was conducting a coal mining enterprise, of which his uncle had charge. The little community grew, and Mr. Bate had a large share in its progress, being its first Mayor. He also became a newspaper proprietor.

The *Nanaimo Free Press* reported his death the same day:

> Mr. M. Bate Jr., Victoria Road, received a cable today informing him of the death in Birmingham, England, this morning of his father, Mark Bate, probably Nanaimo's best known and most respected citizen, who passed away suddenly while on a visit to relatives and friends in Birmingham, England.

The newspaper recounted Bate's many attributes and his long history of service to Nanaimo. Civic honours, it said, would be paid to the memory of the man who so closely identified with the development of the city.

On September 3, 1927, the newspaper published this tribute

to the "First Mayor of Nanaimo," a poem that captures how the community regarded their distinguished citizen:

FAREWELL MARK BATE
by Chas. Meek

Nanaimo city truly mourns today
Her oldest citizen has passed away.
He was a man of dignity and worth
And he knew this city from its birth.
His sprightly walk we will not soon forget
Nor glad his smile for everyone he met.

. . .

Mark inherited the genius of his sires,
Which always labours upward and aspires.
At last he reached this hamlet in the wood,
He looked upon it and pronounced it good.
Was many year our mayor and magistrate
Now he is gone—farewell to you Mark Bate.

HOME TO NANAIMO

Flags flew at half mast in the city Bate loved, served, and called home for 70 years. The body of Nanaimo's first mayor had arrived from England.

After lying in repose at the Masonic Hall on Saturday and Sunday, Bate's body was moved to his Hecate Street home. On Monday, September 19, 1927, the six pallbearers—aldermen Edward George Cavalsky, John Barsby, James Renney, Charles Ironside, Tom Smith, and William Hart—gathered there, along with Reverend David Stephenson and members of Nanaimo City Council. The six men carried the casket from the home to the hearse.

Nanaimo residents gathered along the hearse's route to pay tribute to the city's most prominent and valued citizen. The

Silver Cornet Band, which Bate had formed many years ago, led the solemn cortège through the residential area, along Prideaux Street to Victoria Road, and down to Victoria Crescent, then down Commercial Street, where the shops and businesses had closed out of respect, and along Comox Road to the cemetery. The *Daily Herald* of September 18, 1927, gave the order of the procession: "Marshall, Silver Cornet Band, police, members of Nanaimo Fire Department, civic workmen, members of Masonic Order, ex mayors and aldermen, hearse, mourners and general public." The honorary pallbearers were the current Mayor Frederick Busby and five former mayors—Victor B. Harrison, Senator Albert E. Planta, Thomas Hodgson, John Shaw, and William Manson.

21

BATE'S
LEGACY

MARK BATE CAME TO VANCOUVER Island as a young man seeking adventure, following the dream of a new life in the new world. With the enthusiasm of youth he tackled each task with diligence and perseverance, even if at times daunted by all the demands placed on him.

As a mine manager, he struggled with uncertainty; making decisions was difficult and frustrating because of having to wait for directives from London or San Francisco. His relationships with Robert Dunsmuir and John Bryden were troubling. He worked very well with Dunsmuir on committees that benefited the community, but he watched warily as Dunsmuir grew in stature and took advantage of every business opportunity that presented itself. Dunsmuir's Wellington mines were stiff competition for Bate's company in the coal market, competition he could only helplessly observe as it outpaced Bate's own world. With Bryden, he often disagreed on how to handle the workforce; Bate preferred to make concessions and play the peacemaker, instead of being the forceful manager Bryden believed was necessary when employees complained about wages or working conditions.

As the city's first mayor he set the tone and priority for development of the city's first roads, streets, and bridges, and created the climate for businesses to grow. There was no precedent set on how to establish a municipality, other than that learned in Victoria or New Westminster, so he relied on the Municipal Act to guide the way forward. Under his leadership, the mining village became a town and then a city with a future. As mayor, he welcomed Canada's first prime minister, Governor Generals, and politicians of all stripes, reminding every visitor of the importance of Nanaimo and its seaport in the future of the province.

Bate's impact on the city he called home for 70 years is evident throughout Nanaimo. Bates Square at Victoria Crescent and Albert Street was named in his honour. Ashlar Lodge, which Bate initiated in 1873, the first Freemason's lodge in the province, still holds pride of place on Commercial Street. Mark Bay and Bate Point on Newcastle Island are named after him, and a small lane in front of city hall is aptly named Mark Bate Lane. The Nanaimo Concert Band continues to entertain Nanaimo audiences. The band can trace its beginning to the small group of musicians formed by Bate all those years ago.

Bate's last residence on Hecate Street still stands, but his previous homes are gone. He did not live to see the Nanaimo Hospital open on Machleary Street, though he did witness the cornerstone being laid in 1925. He had served on the very first hospital board, established after the death of his ten-year-old son. The second Fire Hall on Nicol Street still stands as a reminder of the earlier fires that destroyed the first fire hall in 1894 and many businesses on Commercial Street. Fire prevention was one of the causes Bate strived for when he was left homeless following a fire in what was known as "the boarding house."

Family life was important to Bate. He diligently kept in touch with his friends and family back in England, while raising ten children with wife Sarah, and ensured all his children had a good education. He loved listening to and performing music and enjoyed writing. Perhaps his greatest legacy was his writing; he witnessed and wrote about the people and the growth of the community, leaving a written historical record for future generations.

RECENT MEMORIALS

On Easter Sunday, April 1992, about 50 relatives of Mark Bate gathered at St. Paul's Anglican Church on Chapel Street, to dedicate a stained-glass window in his honour. Cyril Mardon Bate, a great-grandson, came from New York; he had purchased the window in his great-grandfather's memory on his behalf and that of his sister Lucie Bate Sunde. Others came from California and Arizona, heeding the call for the family to get together once more.

As this book shows, the Bate family had a long history with St. Paul's Anglican Church, through baptisms, marriages, and funerals. The church has gone through several transformations since first built in 1860, three years after Bate arrived on the island. The first building was demolished in 1907 and the second destroyed by fire in 1930. Today the church continues to serve and has a valued place in the community.

In June 2002, bronze busts of Mark Bate and Snuneymuxw Chief Che-wich-i-kan, historically referred to as "Coal Tyee," were unveiled together at the Mark Bate Memorial Tree Plaza on the waterfront. It was Coal Tyee's delivery of "black diamonds" to the blacksmith in Victoria that led to the founding of Nanaimo. These sculptures, by Dorothea E. Kennedy, are displayed in a public space so that everyone can learn more about these important figures in Nanaimo's history.

APPENDIX 1

Thomas Bate (bap. Feb. 24, 1805), m. Elizabeth Robinson, Nov. 1, 1824
Thomas died May 6, 1845; Elizabeth m. William Thomas in 1853

Ann (bap. May 15, 1825), m. William Sharratt
  Children: Ann Marie, William Henry, Emma, Sophia, Elizabeth

Ezra (bap. Apr. 8, 1827, buried Feb. 8, 1829)

Joseph (bap. July 5, 1829), m. Sarah Ann Beesley, Oct. 13, 1851
  Children: Caroline (1850), Thomas (1852), Mary (1855), Mark (1856),
    Elizabeth (1858), Joseph (1861)

Ezra (bap. Dec. 25, 1831, buried Oct. 24, 1832)

Sarah (bap. Dec. 22, 1833, d. May 25, 1853)

Mark (bap. Feb. 12, 1837), m. Sarah Ann Cartwright, 1859
  Children: Emily (1857), Mark Jr. (1860), Sarah Ann (1861), Thomas Ezra (1863),
    George Arthur (1865), Lucy Alicia (1866), Mary Beatrice (1869),
    William Charles (1871), Elizabeth Ada (1873), John Augustus (1876)

Elizabeth (b. Jan. 4, 1840), m. Adam Grant Horne, Feb. 22, 1859
  Children: Adam Henry (1859), Ann Elizabeth (1862), Lucy Amelia (1865),
    Sarah Maria (1867), Herbert Lewis (1871), Thomas Charles (1869),
    Emily Maude (1874), Lucy (1875), David William (1878), George Grant (1881),
    Lindley Dallas (1885)

Lucy (b. Jan. 13, 1843), m. Peter Sabiston, Apr. 19, 1863
  Children: Adopted daughter Aggie Pawley

DESCENDANTS OF MARK AND SARAH BATE

Mark Bate m. Sarah Ann Cartwright in 1859, exact date unknown

Emily Bate (b. Feb. 8, 1857), m. Charles Alport, July 10, 1873
Children: Blanch Emily (1874), Charles Percy (1877), Maud Lucy (1875),
Percy John (1884), Harry Battiscombe (1882), Alexander McDonald (1888),
Phyllis Eleanor (1890), Frederic Augustus (1892), Mildred Mary (1895),
Queenie Rose Marie (1897), Constance Cherry (1900)

Mark Bate Jr. (b. May 17, 1860), m. Amelia Agnes Planta, Aug. 16, 1883
Children: Cyril Alport (1884), Gertrude Beatrice (1885), Katharine Emily (1887),
Arnold Arthur Stacy (1892)

Sarah Ann (Sally) (b. July 16, 1861), m. William J. Goepel, Feb. 24, 1881
Children: Percival (1882), Clarence (1884)

Thomas Ezra (b. Mar. 31, 1863), m. Anabella Beatrice Dixon (?)
Anabella died 1906; Thomas m. Jean Muir Liddle Apr. 7, 1909
Children: Evelyn Beatrice (1891), Vivian Mary (1893), Mildred Hastings (1886),
Dayrell (?), Anabella Beatrice (?), Reginald Francis (1903), Muriel Lucy (?)

George Arthur (b. Apr. 18, 1865, d. Jan. 3, 1876)

Lucy Alicia (b. Nov. 18, 1866), m. Montague Stanley Davys, Apr. 18, 1891
Children: Guise Stanley (1894), Lilias (1893)

Mary Beatrice (Mar. 18, 1869), m. G.W.B. Heathcote, June 15, 1895

William Charles (b. Feb. 12, 1871), m. Bridget (Edna) Jones, May 20, 1891
Children: Blanche Emily (1892), William Herbert (1893),
George Douglas Stanley (1895), Sarah Ann Alicia (1897), Elsie Viva (1899),
Clarence Clifton (1901)

Elizabeth Ada (Lizzie) (b. Feb. 18, 1873), m.
James Hurst Hawthornthwaite, June 7, 1890
Children: Alan (1891), Victor (1892), William Esmond (1893),
Gilbert Shafto (1895), Leonore Kinghurst (Nora) (1897),
Cecilia Eros (Star) (1899), twins Joan and Gwen (1902), James (1908)

John Augustus (Gussie) (b. Sept. 10, 1876), m. Edith Perchet, Oct. 5, 1900

APPENDIX 2

Mark Bate held office for 16 terms, 12 by acclamation.[1]

1875	Mark Bate (defeated James Harvey by 17 votes)
1876	Mark Bate (acclaimed)
1877	Mark Bate (acclaimed)
1878	Mark Bate (acclaimed)
1879	Mark Bate (acclaimed)
1880	John Pawson (Bate declined to run)
1881	Mark Bate (acclaimed)
1882	Mark Bate (acclaimed)
1883	Mark Bate (acclaimed)
1884	Mark Bate (acclaimed)
1885	Mark Bate (acclaimed)
1886	Mark Bate (defeated Richard Gibson by 33 votes)
1887	Richard Gibson (Bate declined to run)
1888	Mark Bate (defeated Richard Gibson by 16 votes)
1889	Mark Bate (defeated John Hilbert by 8 votes)
1890	John Hilbert (Bate declined to run)
1891	John Hilbert
1892	Andrew Haslam
1893	Andrew Haslam
1894	Edward Quennell
1895	Edward Quennell
1896	Joseph Henderson Davison
1897	Joseph Henderson Davison
1898	Mark Bate (acclaimed)
1899	Mark Bate (acclaimed)
1900	Mark Bate (acclaimed)

ENDNOTES

ABBREVIATIONS
BCA   British Columbia Archives, Victoria, BC
DALHS   Dudley Archives and Local History Service
HBCA   Hudson's Bay Company Archives
NCA   Nanaimo Community Archives, Nanaimo, BC
NM   Nanaimo Museum
VCMLC   Vancouver Coal Mining and Land Company

CHAPTER 1: A LIFE OF PUBLIC SERVICE
1   Speeches, Mark Bate fonds, NCA.

CHAPTER 2: A HUMBLE BEGINNING
1   W. Lee, *Report to the General Board of Health into the Sewage, Drainage, and Supply of Water, and the Sanitary Conditions of the Inhabitants of the Parish of Dudley, in the County of Worcester* (London: Eyre and Spottiswoode, 1852).
2   England Census 1831, DALHS.
3   Charles Dickens, *The Posthumous Papers of the Pickwick Papers* (London: 1837, Chapman & Hall), from Chapter 50.
4   J. Bentley, *Bentley's Directory of Worcestershire, 1840–1842*, vol. 1, *Bentley's Directory of Dudley, 1840* (London).
5   England Census 1841, DALHS.
6   St. Thomas Parish Records and Wesleyan Chapel records, DALHS.
7   Woodside Methodist Church records, DALHS.
8   Midland Mining (South Staffordshire), Reports from Commissioners. 13 of 18 vols. 1843, p. 101.
9   St. Thomas Parish Register, DALHS.
10 *The Towns Messenger* (Dudley), May 9, 1845.
11 Death certificate of Thomas Bate, Wolverhampton East, County of Stafford.
12 J. Mitchell, *Report to the Children's Employment Commission 1842*, British Parliamentary Papers, vols. 15–17 (London, 1842).
13 Lee, *Report to the General Board of Health.*
14 Val Worwood, Woodside Memory and History Group, Woodside, England.
15 Lee, *Report to the General Board of Health.*
16 England Census 1851, DALHS.
17 Marriage certificate of Joseph Bate and Sarah Ann Beesley, Tipton Parish Church, Dudley, Staffordshire.
18 England Census 1861, DALHS.
19 A.T.C. and E.M. Lavender, "The Woodside Ironworks," *The Blackcountryman* 17, no. 2 (1984): n.p.
20 F.W. Howay and E.O.S. Scholefield, *British Columbia from its Earliest Times to the Present*, vol. 4 of 4 vols. (Vancouver: S.J. Clarke Publishing Company, 1914).
21 Dudley Grammar School Collection, DAHLS.
22 Thomas Bryant to Rev. W.L. Hall, 1929, Thomas Bryant Letters, BCA.

23 Letter dated March 9, 1874, VCMLC fonds, NCA.

24 Death certificate of Sarah Robinson Bate, Dudley, County of Worcester.

25 England Census 1841 DALHS.

26 Bate family fonds, file #2, NCA.

27 P. Nicholls, *From the Black Country to Nanaimo 1854*, 5 vols. (Nanaimo: Nanaimo Historical Society and Peggy Nicholls, 1991–1995), vol. 1, section called "From Brierley Hill to Vancouver's Island."

28 Ibid.

29 George Robinson letters, Hudson's Bay Company Archives, A/10/35 Fo 305d.

30 Nicholls, *From the Black Country*, vol. 1, section called "From Brierley Hill to Vancouver's Island."

CHAPTER 3: JOURNEY TO THE NEW WORLD

1 E. Blanche Norcross, ed., *Nanaimo Retrospective: The First Century* (Nanaimo Historical Society, 1979), 29.

2 Nicholls, *From the Black Country*, vol. 2, section on the Thompson family.

3 Ibid., section on Samuel Gough.

4 "Edward Stuart, Charles, biographical sketch," B.239/k/3/fo.243, HBCA.

5 Land transfer: Crown to Hudson's Bay Company, File AC 90 H86, NCA.

6 D.T. Gallacher, "Men, Money, Machines: Studies Comparing Colliery Operations and Factors of Production in British Columbia's Coal Industry to 1891" (Ph.D. diss., University of British Columbia, 1979), p. 72.

7 Gallacher, "Men, Money, Machines," p. 72.

8 Hudson's Bay Company daybook (Stuart), September 1, 1855, NCA.

9 R.S. Vickers, "A Time of Trouble and Sorrow," *Vancouver Island Pioneer George Robinson*, November 27, 1983, http://crunchers.bc.ca/robinson/trouble.html.

10 Ibid.

11 Bryant, October 10, 1929, Thomas Bryant Letters, William Lashley Hall fonds, BCA.

12 J. Barman, *The West Beyond The West: A History of British Columbia* (Toronto: University of Toronto Press, 1991), p. 85.

CHAPTER 4: BATE BEGINS A NEW LIFE

1 Cornelius Bryant diary, Cornelius Bryant fonds, BCA.

2 M. Bate, "Speech to Native Sons and Daughters," Mark Bate fonds, NCA.

3 Ibid.

4 Cornelius Bryant diary, January 30, 1857, Cornelius Bryant fonds, BCA.

5 M. Bate "Reminiscences of Early Nanaimo," *Nanaimo Free Press*, February 9, 1907.

6 Ibid.

7 Bate, "Speech to Native Sons and Daughters."

8 M. Bate, "Speech in Response to the Toast of the Pioneers," Mark Bate fonds, NCA.

9 *Nanaimo Free Press*, February 16, 1907.

10 M. Bate, "A Story of Olden Days," *Daily Herald* (Nanaimo), 1907.

11 Nicholls, *From the Black Country*, vol. 5, section on the Meakin family.

12 Vickers, "Nanaimo's Bryant Family," *Vancouver Island Pioneer George Robinson*, http://crunchers.bc.ca/robinson/bryant_family.html.

13 S.A. Brown, "Progress of Education in Nanaimo 1849–1869: History of

Education #423," (thesis, Dr. C.F. Goulsoil, March 8, 1969), NCA.
14   Cornelius Bryant diary, Cornelius Bryant fonds, BCA.
15   Patricia M. Johnson, "Teacher and Preacher: Cornelius Bryant," article in Cornelius Bryant file, NCA.
16   M. Bate, "Speech in Response to the Toast of the Pioneers," Mark Bate fonds, NCA.
17   Bate to Thomas Hughes, November 29, 1873, Letter Book: March 14, 1873–July 14, 1879, Series 1, Administrative records, VCMLC fonds, NCA.
18   J.D. Belshaw, "The Standard of Living of British Miners on Vancouver Island, 1848–1900," *BC Studies* 84 (Winter 1989-90), p. 58, n86.
19   M. Bate, "A Story of Olden Days," *Daily Herald*, 1907.
20   Ship log: *Princess Royal*, C.1/979, HBCA.
21   Ibid.
22   Diary of A.G. Horne 1859, Horne family file, NCA.
23   R.S. Vickers, "The Second Wife," *Vancouver Island Pioneer George Robinson*, http://crunchers.bc.ca/robinson/2nd_wife.html.
24   R.S. Vickers, "Sojourn in England," *Vancouver Island Pioneer George Robinson*, http://crunchers.bc.ca/robinson/england.html.

CHAPTER 5: NEW MANAGEMENT

1   M. Bate, "Reminiscences of Early Nanaimo Days," *Nanaimo Free Press*, Feb. 9, 1907, Mark Bate fonds, NCA.
2   Ibid.
3   M. Bate, "Speech in response to the Toast of the Pioneers," Mark Bate fonds, NCA.
4   S. Meen, "Colonial Society and Economy," in H.J.M. Johnston, ed., *The Pacific Province: A History of British Columbia* (Vancouver: Douglas & McIntyre, 1996), p. 103.
5   G.P.V. Akrigg and Helen B. Akrigg, *British Columbia Chronicle 1847–1871: Gold and Colonists* (Vancouver: Discovery Press, 1977), p. 142.
6   M. Bate, "Reminiscences: Sketches of Old Time Nanaimoites," *Nanaimo Free Press*, March 9, 1907.
7   Charles Edward Stuart, Family History file, NCA.
8   D. Blakey-Smith, "The Reminiscences of Doctor John Sebastian Helmcken," (Vancouver: UBC Press, 1975), p. 229.
9   M. Bate, "A Stroll Around Nanaimo in 1874," Mark Bate fonds, NCA
10   W.J.M. Zu Erpen, "Towards an Understanding of the Municipal Archives of Nineteenth Century British Columbia: A Case Study of the Archives of the Corporation of the City of Nanaimo, 1875–1904," MA thesis, University of British Columbia, 1985, p. 34.
11   Gallacher, "Men, Money, Machines," pp. 101–102. See also Dorothy Blakey Smith, ed., "The Journal of Arthur Thomas Bushby, 1957–1959," *British Columbia Historical Quarterly*, 21, nos 1–4 (January 1957–October 1958): 185.
12   Papers relating to Nanaimo Coal Mine, 1852–1862, HBCA.
13   M. Bate, "Reminiscences: Something of the Old Time Nanaimoites," *Nanaimo Free Press*, Feb. 23, 1907.
14   A.W. Currie, "The Vancouver Coal Mining Company: A Source for Galsworthy's Strife." *Queen's Quarterly* 70, no. 1 (1963): 50–63.
15   Gallacher, "Men, Money, Machines," pp. 85–87.

16 M. Bate, "Toast to the Pioneers," Mark Bate fonds, NCA.
17 Gallacher, "Men, Money, Machines," p. 87.
18 Patricia Johnson, "Teacher and Preacher: Cornelius Bryant" (article), Cornelius Bryant file, NCA.
19 Church information file, NCA.
20 T.D. Sale, "St. Paul's Anglican Church Nanaimo 1861–1986," pamphlet, NCA.
21 *Daily British Colonist*, March 16, 1864.
22 Vital Statistics, BCA.
23 M. Bate, "A Stroll Around Nanaimo in 1874," Mark Bate fonds, NCA.
24 *Daily British Colonist and Victoria Chronicle*, June 26, 1870.

CHAPTER 6: MORE FAMILY ARRIVE

1   Ship log: *Princess Royal*, C.1/982, HBCA.
2   Cartwright file 96-015-A, NCA.
3   Letter dated April 12, 1875, VCMLC fonds, NCA.
4   P. Sabiston, BC Metis Mapping Research Project. University of British Columbia, http://document.bcmetiscitizen.ca.
5   Vickers, "The Bate Family of Nanaimo," *Vancouver Island Pioneer George Robinson*, http://crunchers.bc.ca/robinson/bate_family.html.
6   J. Peterson, *Kilts on the Coast: The Scots Who Built BC* (Victoria. Heritage House Publishing, 2012), p. 48.
7   "Spence, John C.: Biographical sketch," RS/AA30.7/2, BCA.
8   Ibid.
9   *Daily British Colonist*, Sept. 30, 1865.
10 J. Peterson, *Black Diamond City: Nanaimo—The Victorian Era* (Victoria: Heritage House Publishing), pp. 84–85.
11 Nicholls, *From the Black Country*, vol. 2, section on the Gough family.
12 Quote from *The Flint Glass Makers Magazine* (Stourbridge, England, 1851), cited in W.B. Stephens, *Education, Literacy, and Society, 1830–70: The Geography of Diversity in Provincial England* (Manchester: Manchester University Press, 1987), p. 130.
13 Bate, "A Stroll Around Nanaimo in 1874," Mark Bate fonds, NCA.
14 Nanaimo Literary Institute Report 1862, Mark Bate fonds, NCA.
15 *Nanaimo Gazette*, May 5, 1866.
16 E.B. Norcross, ed., *Nanaimo Retrospective: The First Century* (Nanaimo: Nanaimo Historical Society, 1979), p. 49.
17 *Daily British Colonist*, February 13, 1864.
18 B.R.D. Smith, "A Social History of Early Nanaimo," BA thesis, University of British Columbia, 1956, p. 24.
19 Nicholls, *From the Black Country*, vol. 5, section on the Meakin family.
20 *Daily British Colonist*, January 31, 1863.
21 Ibid.
22 *Daily British Colonist*, August 9, 1865.
23 Ibid.

CHAPTER 7: CHANGING TIMES

1   Vital Statistics, BCA.
2   Gallacher, "Men, Money, Machines," p. 102, n34, citing the *Fourth Report* by VCMLC director, London, 29 Nov. 1864; "Request for locomotive and rails," (PAM) F33/1, HBCA.

3 "Coal ships and others," F33/1, HBCA.
4 Gallacher, "Men, Money, Machines," p. 104.
5 Ross Lambertson, "Bryden, John," in *Dictionary of Canadian Biography*, vol. 14, University of Toronto/Université Laval, 2003–, accessed November 17, 2016, http://www.biographi.ca/en/bio/bryden_john_14E.html.
6 Mark Bate to the City Clerk, letter dated December 6, 1915, City Clerk's Office Correspondence 1905–1948, NCA.
7 "Sale of Nanaimo Lots," *Daily British Colonist*, May 17, 1864.
8 In the HBC's accounting, the English pound had been replaced by the dollar, which became legal tender in Canada in the late 1850s.
9 Farm census of Nanaimo District 1865, Nicol family file, NCA.
10 The Fourth Report of the Directors of the VCMLC, extracted from "The Mining News" of Victoria, V.I., May 12, 1864, F33/1, HBCA.
11 Ibid.
12 Franklyn papers, BCA.
13 Howay and Scholefield, *British Columbia from Its Earliest Times to the Present*, vol. 2, pp. 225–226.
14 Alport family file, NCA.
15 M. Bate, "Recollections," Mark Bate fonds, NCA.
16 *Daily British Colonist*, September 23, 1865.
17 J.E. Hendrickson, ed., *Journals of the Colonial Legislatures of the Colonies of Vancouver Island and British Columbia 1851–1871*, vol. 1 of 5 vols. (Victoria: Provincial Archives, 1980).
18 *Daily British Colonist*, April 20, 1866.
19 Hendrickson, *Journals of the Colonial Legislatures*, vol. 2, May 7 and May 28, 1866.
20 A.W. Currie, "The Vancouver Coal Mining Company: A Source for Galsworthy's Strife." *Queen's Quarterly* 70, no. 1 (1963): 50–63.
21 Ibid.; also "VCMLC," *Mining Journal* May 25, 1867, p. 345, cited in Gallacher, "Men, Money, Machines," p. 114, n63.
22 *Mining Journal*, November 6, 1869, p. 828, cited in Gallacher, "Men, Money, Machines," p. 114, n66.
23 Currie, "The Vancouver Coal Mining Company."

CHAPTER 8: BATE APPOINTED MANAGER
1 Mark Bate fonds, series 3, file 1, NCA.
2 *Daily Colonist*, June 24, 1887.
3 *The San Francisco Call*, Dec. 2, 1911.
4 C. Davidson, *Historic Departure Bay—Looking Back* (Victoria: Rendezvous Historic Press, 2006), pp. 62–63.
5 *Nanaimo Gazette*, Feb. 5, 1866.
6 Letter from Wild to Mark Bate, VCMLC 1869–1888, Mark Bate fonds, NCA.
7 Letter Book, August 24, 1873, Administrative records, VCMLC Series 1, NCA.
8 May 6, 1874, VCMLC fonds, NCA.
9 W. Rayner, *Scandal! 130 Years of Damnable Deeds in Canada's Lotus Land* (Victoria: Heritage House Publishing, 2001).
10 May 5, 1875, VCMLC fonds, NCA.
11 January 21, 1874, VCMLC fonds, NCA.
12 Ibid.

13   May 20, 1874, VCMLC fonds, NCA.
14   December 10, 1874, VCMLC fonds, NCA.
15   June 24, 1875, VCMLC fonds, NCA.
16   July 27, 1878, VCMLC fonds, NCA.

CHAPTER 9: A RENAISSANCE MAN

1   *British Columbian*, May 18, 1887.
2   September 4, 1873, VCMLC fonds, NCA.
3   Bate, "A Stroll around Nanaimo in 1874," Mark Bate fonds, NCA.
4   Ebenezer Robson, diary entry for August 28, 1885, Ebenezer Robson fonds, BCA.
5   J.D. Belshaw, *From Colonization and Community, The Vancouver Island Coalfield and the Making of the British Columbian Working Class* (Montreal and Kingston: McGill-Queen's University Press, 2002), p. 177.
6   J.D. Belshaw, "The Standard of Living of British Miners on Vancouver Island, 1848–1900," *BC Studies*, 84 (Winter 1989–90): 40. Belshaw's source for this information on wages for miners is John Bryden's diary.
7   Ibid., 44.
8   *Daily British Colonist*, May 8, 1867.
9   Kathleen M. Savory, for Dr. C.Y. Lai, "Nanaimo's Chinese Community," Box 1, Code 13, Ethnic groups, Chinese #2, NCA.
10   Wikipedia talk: "WikiProject Shipwrecks/Archive 2," #11, Coal barque Panther, https://en.wikipedia.org/w/index.php?title=Wikipedia_talk:WikiProject_Shipwrecks/Arc.hive_2&oldid=642149001.
11   February 25, 1874, VCMLC fonds, NCA.
12   November 18, 1874, VCMLC fonds, NCA.
13   SS *Prince Alfred* (+1874), *WreckSite*, www.Wrecksite.eu.
14   June 20, 1874, VCMLC fonds, NCA.
15   November 13, 1873, VCMLC fonds, NCA.
16   February 25, 1974, VCMLC fonds, NCA.
17   Folder 6, Masonic Records 1880–1927, NCA.
18   "The formation of the Ashlar Lodge," folder 6, Masonic Records 1880–1927, NCA.
19   April 19, 1875, VCMLC fonds, NCA.
20   June 22, 1875, VCMLC fonds, NCA.
21   June 27, 1885, Aug. 20, 1887, and Feb. 4, 1888, Ancient Order of Foresters, BCA.

CHAPTER 10: TENSIONS RISE

1   E.G. Prior, "Letter to the editor by E.G. Prior on the death of John Bryden on March 27, 1915," March 30, 1915. *Rootsweb*, http://home.rootsweb.ancestry.com.
2   Bate, letters dated December 1, 1873; December 3 1873; January 7 1874; September 17, 1874, VCMLC fonds, NCA.
3   Gallacher, "Men, Money, Machines," p. 121.
4   Marriage certificate of John Bryden and Elizabeth Dunsmuir, 1866, BCA.
5   Census 1881.
6   A. Leynard, *The Coal Mines of Nanaimo*, Research paper (1982), p. 6, NCA.
7   Bermingham obituary, *San Francisco Call*, Dec. 2, 1911.
8   San Francisco directory 1899, National Archives at San Francisco.
9   Peterson, *Black Diamond City*, p. 133.

10 *Daily British Colonist and Victoria Chronicle*, Oct. 7, 1870.
11 C.M. Tate, "Autosketch," Box 22, #13, United Church Archives, Toronto.
12 H.L. Langevin, Report on British Columbia, Ottawa, 1872.
13 British Columbia Parliament, *Sessional Papers: Third Session, Second Parliament, and First Session, Third Parliament* (Victoria, BC: Government Printing Office, 1878), p. 595.
14 "Robert Wallace (Canadian politician)," Wikipedia, last modified March 2, 2016.

CHAPTER 11: FAMILY LETTERS

1 Bate to mother, April 4, 1873, VCMLC fonds, NCA.
2 Bate to mother, May 3, 1873, VCMLC fonds, NCA.
3 Bate to mother, May 3, 1873, VCMLC fonds, NCA.
4 Bate to mother, August 15, 1873, VCMLC fonds, NCA.
5 Bate to Dear Cousin, March 17, 1874, VCMLC fonds, NCA.
6 Bate to Aunt Sarah Bryant, March 18, 1874, VCMLC fonds, NCA.
7 Bate to son Victor Ernest, January 3, 1875, letter cited in Vickers, "The Bate Family of Nanaimo," *Vancouver Island Pioneer George Robinson*, http://crunchers.bc.ca/robinson/bate_family.html.
8 Bate to Aunt Sarah Bryant, March 18, 1874, VCMLC fonds, NCA.
9 Bate to mother, May 9, 1874, VCMLC fonds, NCA.
10 Bate to Wild, October 2, 1873, VCMLC fonds, NCA.
11 Ibid.
12 Alport family file, NCA. Also marriage certificate of Emily Bate and Charles Alport, 1872, BCA.
13 Bate to John Wild, October 2, 1873, VCMLC fonds, NCA.
14 Ibid.
15 Bate to C. Loat, July 31, 1873, VCMLC fonds, NCA.
16 Bate to Wild, August 1, 1874, VCMLC fonds, NCA.
17 Bate to Wild, October 2, 1873, VCMLC fonds, NCA.
18 Bate to mother, October 3, 1873, VCMLC fonds, NCA.
19 Bate to cousin David, October 4, 1873, VCMLC fonds, NCA.
20 Bate to Wild, December 1, 1873, VCMLC fonds, NCA.
21 Ibid.
22 Bate to David Pearce, November 13, 1873, VCMLC fonds, NCA.
23 Bate to Thomas Hughes, November 29, 1873, VCMLC fonds, NCA.
24 Bate to brother and sister, Feb. 24, 1874, VCMLC fonds, NCA.
25 Bate to Wild, December 2, 1874, VCMLC fonds, NCA.
26 Bate to Wild, March 3, 1875, VCMLC fonds, NCA.
27 Bate to Wild, June 24, 1875, VCMLC fonds, NCA.
28 Alport family file, NCA.

CHAPTER 12: LABOUR ISSUES AND LAND TRANSACTIONS

1 Bate, "Nanaimo Reminiscences," *Nanaimo Free Press*, February 16, 1907.
2 Bate to Wild, August 1, 1874, VCMLC fonds, NCA.
3 P. Johnson, *Quarantined: Life and Death at William Head Station, 1872–1959* (Victoria: Heritage House Publishing Company, 2013), p. 53.
4 Obituary of Dr. William Macnaughton-Jones, *Daily Colonist*, May 5, 1896.
5 *Nanaimo Free Press*, June 18, 1879.

6   Bryden diary, Sept. 26, 1879, p. 498, John Bryden fonds, BCA.
7   Belshaw, *Colonization and Community*, p. 178.
8   William McGregor, B16/11, Industry file, NCA.
9   Bryden diary, Letters to Samuel M. Robins, p. 432, John Bryden fonds, BCA.
10   Bate to Nicholas and Francis, Oct. 12, 1874, VCMLC fonds, NCA.
11   L. Bowen, *Three Dollar Dreams* (Lantzville: Oolichan Books, 1987), pp. 216–217.
12   July 27, 1978, VCMLC fonds, NCA.
13   Bate to Wild, December 22, 1979, VCMLC fonds, NCA.
14   Bate to Rosenfeld, April 24, 1880, VCMLC fonds, NCA.
15   Jamie Morton, "Shakespeare, Noah," in *Dictionary of Canadian Biography* vol. 15, University of Toronto/Université Laval, 2003–, accessed November 17, 2016, http://www.biographi.ca/en/bio/shakespeare_noah_15E.html.
16   Nicholls, *From the Black Country*, vol. 3, section on the Webb family.
17   July 11, 1874, VCMLC fonds, NCA.
18   July 22, 1874, VCMLC fonds, NCA.
19   June 24, 1875, VCMLC fonds, NCA.
20   Morton, "Shakespeare, Noah," in *Dictionary of Canadian Biography*.
21   March 4, 1876, VCMLC fonds, NCA.
22   October 10, 1874, VCMLC fonds, NCA.

CHAPTER 13: FIRST MAYOR OF NANAIMO
1   January 6, 1875, VCMLC fonds, NCA.
2   Bate, "A Stroll Around Nanaimo in 1874," Speeches, Mark Bate fonds, NCA.
3   October 10, 1874, VCMLC fonds, NCA.
4   Smith, "A Social History of Early Nanaimo," p. 80.
5   *The Comet* (Nanaimo), January 18, 1875.
6   Nicholls, *From the Black Country*, vol. 2, section on the Gough family.
7   *Daily British Colonist*, December 18, 1874, p. 3.
8   Zu Erpen, "Towards an Understanding of the Municipal Archives," p. 48.
9   Ibid., p. 18.
10   Ibid., p. 56
11   Ibid., pp. 73–74.
12   Bate's inaugural address, Nanaimo History, Box 1, Code 5, NCA.
13   Zu Erpen, "Towards an Understanding of the Municipal Archives," p. 226.
14   M. Bate, "Reminiscences: Sketches of Old Time Nanaimoites," *Nanaimo Free Press*, March 9, 1907.
15   December 30, 1874, VCMLC fonds, NCA.
16   Smith, "A Social History of Early Nanaimo," p. 89.
17   *Nanaimo Free Press*, February 20, 1878.
18   *Nanaimo Free Press*, April 19, 1909.
19   March 30, 1875, VCMLC fonds, NCA.
20   March 3, 1875, VCMLC fonds, NCA.
21   April 6, 1875, VCMLC fonds, NCA.
22   April 20, 1875, VCMLC fonds, NCA.
23   February 23, 1876, VCMLC fonds, NCA.
24   May 5, 1875, VCMLC fonds, NCA.
25   Zu Erpen, "Towards an Understanding of the Municipal Archives," p. 166.
26   Ibid., p. 169.
27   April 12, 1875, VCMLC fonds, NCA.

28 Headstone of Arthur Bate, from CanadianHeadstones.com.
29 February 21, 1876, VCMLC fonds, NCA.
30 November 29, 1876, VCMLC fonds, NCA.
31 Zu Erpen, "Towards an Understanding of the Municipal Archives," pp. 175–76.
32 August 21, 1877, VCMLC fonds, NCA.
33 July 27, 1878, VCMLC fonds, NCA.
34 Nanaimo Regional General Hospital fonds, NCA.
35 R. Gwyn, *Nation Maker: Sir John A. Macdonald: His Life, Our Times* 2 vols. (Toronto: Random House, 2011), vol. 2, p. 256.
36 October 12, 1875, VCMLC fonds, NCA.
37 Mayor's office correspondence, July 8, 1876, NCA.
38 M. Bate, "Speech to Lord Dufferin," Mark Bate fonds, NCA.
39 Ibid.
40 Letter from Lord Dufferin to Bate, Mark Bate fonds, NCA.
41 M.A. Ormsby, *British Columbia: A History* (Toronto: Macmillan, 1958), p. 275.
42 Ibid., p. 276.
43 Bate, "Reminiscences."
44 October 12, 1875, VCMLC fonds, NCA.
45 Mark Bate fonds, NCA, and *Nanaimo Free Press*, May 25, 1878.
46 September 30, 1878, VCMLC fonds, NCA.
47 Ibid.
48 February 26, 1879, VCMLC fonds, NCA.

CHAPTER 14: BUSINESS OPPORTUNITIES
1 September 17, 1881 and October 4, 1881, VCMLC fonds, NCA.
2 Olga Blanche Owen, "Adam Grant Horne," unpublished biography, February 1980.
3 April 12, 1879, VCMLC fonds, NCA.
4 B. Merilees, *Newcastle Island: A Place of Discovery* (Victoria: Heritage House Publishing, 1998), p. 49.
5 *Guide to the Province of BC for 1877–8* (Victoria: Hibben & Co., 1877), pp. 336–337. Accessed November 21, 2016. URL: http://www.vpl.ca/bccd/index.php/browse/title/1877-1878/Guide_to_the_Province_of_BC.
6 Census 1881, *ViHistory*, http://vihistory.ca/content/census/1881/census1881.php.
7 *Nanaimo Free Press*, March 24, 1881.
8 Mine Manson family file, NCA.
9 E.G. Prior, BC Mining Report 1879, p. 250.
10 September 20, 1879, VCMLC fonds, NCA.
11 January 7, 1878, VCMLC fonds, NCA.
12 T. Reksten, *The Dunsmuir Saga* (Vancouver: Douglas & McIntyre, 1991), p. 48.
13 Prior, BC Mining Report 1878.
14 Ibid., p. 48.
15 November 16, 1877, VCMLC fonds, NCA.

CHAPTER 15: BRYDEN RESIGNS
1 Dec. 22, 1879, VCMLC fonds, NCA.
2 July 14, 1879, VCMLC fonds, NCA.
3 Bryden diary, March 18, 1880, p. 514, NCA.

4   Ibid., p. 515.
5   Gallacher, "Men, Money, Machines," p. 123.
6   April 7, 1880, VCMLC fonds, NCA.
7   Bryden diary, Letter to Samuel M. Robins. April 9, 1880, NCA.
8   Bryden diary, April 9, 1880, NCA.
9   April 15, 1880, VCMLC fonds, NCA.
10   Gallacher, "Men, Money, Machines," p. 123.
11   April 13, 1880, VCMLC fonds, NCA.
12   June 28, 1880, VCMLC fonds, NCA.
13   September 1, 1880, VCMLC fonds, NCA.
14   July 24, 1880, VCMLC fonds, NCA.
15   R. Slater, *Telegraphic Code, to Ensure Secrecy in the Transmission of Telegrams* (London: W.R. Grey, 1870).
16   June 9, 1880, VCMLC fonds, NCA.
17   September 8, 1880, VCMLC fonds, NCA.
18   Reksten, *Dunsmuir Saga*, p. 122.
19   April 12, 1879, VCMLC fonds, NCA.
20   October 15, 1880, VCMLC fonds, NCA.
21   November 20, 1880, VCMLC fonds, NCA.
22   December 7, 1880, VCMLC fonds, NCA.
23   *Nanaimo Free Press*, March 10, 1881.
24   January 6, 1882, VCMLC fonds, NCA.
25   September 17, 1881, VCMLC fonds, NCA.
26   October 4, 1881, VCMLC fonds, NCA.
27   October 21, 1881, VCMLC fonds, NCA.
28   December 6, 1881, VCMLC fonds, NCA.
29   January 6, 1882, VCMLC fonds, NCA.

CHAPTER 16: CITY IMPROVEMENTS
1   Davidson, *Historic Departure Bay*, p. 125.
2   John Dunham on Nanaimo Harbour, 1967, tape no. 33 93-006-M, NCA.
3   Norcross, *Nanaimo Retrospective*, p. 80.
4   Student research 2003–2005, History 358, Malaspina College/Vancouver Island University.
5   *Nanaimo Free Press*, February 9, 1907; Bate, "Reminiscences of Early Nanaimo Days."
6   Terry Simpson research on Bate family history.
7   *Nanaimo Free Press*, January 10, 1880.
8   December 28, 1880, VCMLC fonds, NCA.
9   Sally's wedding invitation, Mark Bate fonds, NCA.
10   *Guide to the Province of BC for 1877–8*, p. 340.
11   "Memoirs: The Year 1877," Music file, NCA.
12   March 28, 1881, VCMLC fonds, NCA.
13   Bate to Wild, February 26, 1879; *British Columbia City Directories: Nanaimo*, 1883.
14   "Music in Nanaimo Long Ago," Mark Bate fonds, NCA.
15   January 28, 1881, VCMLC fonds, NCA.
16   April 21, 1882, VCMLC fonds, NCA.
17   Reksten, *Dunsmuir Saga*, p. 54.

18   S.W. Jackman. *Portraits of the Premiers: An Informal History of British Columbia.* (Sidney, BC: Gray's Publishing, 1969), p. 57.
19   Prior, BC Mining Report, p. 864.
20   W.A. Taylor, *Crown Land Grants: A History of the Esquimalt and Nanaimo Railway Land Grants, the Railway Belt and the Peace River Block* (Victoria: Crown Land Registry Service, Ministry of Environment, Lands and Parks, 1975), p. 5.
21   *Nanaimo Free Press*, April 28, 1884.
22   Reksten, *Dunsmuir Saga*, p. 64.
23   Elections British Columbia. *Electoral History of British Columbia, 1871–1986.* Victoria: Elections British Columbia and the Legislative Library, 1988: 5th General Election 1886.
24   *Daily British Colonist*, August 14, 15, 1886.
25   Political Papers, Mark Bate fonds, NCA.
26   Early buildings, Martha Kenny file, NCA.

CHAPTER 17: CHANGE OF JOB AND HOMELESS
1   J.W. Trutch, Report on Public Works in British Columbia, for Year Ending 30th June, 1883, Annual Report of the Department of Public Works for the Fiscal Year 1882–83, *General Report of Canada* (Ottawa: Macdean, Roger & Co.), p. 176.
2   Prior, BC Mining Report 1883, p. 417.
3   Sam Robins family file, NCA.
4   *Nanaimo Free Press*, August 30, 1882.
5   *Nanaimo Free Press*, April 20, 1884.
6   *BC Directories: Nanaimo 1884-5.*
7   Land records, Mark Bate fonds, NCA.
8   *Nanaimo Free Press*, May 7, 1884.
9   *BC Directories: Nanaimo 1884-5.*
10   Ibid.
11   J. Gray and J.A. Chapleau, Report on the Royal Commission on Chinese Immigration, No. 2, 1885, pp. 118–119.
12   Ibid., pp. 110, 127.
13   *BC Directories: Nanaimo 1886.*
14   Zu Erpen, "Towards an Understanding of the Municipal Archives," p. 311.
15   Dick, BC Mining Report 1886, p. 243.
16   *Nanaimo Times*, July 15, 1975.
17   Ibid.

CHAPTER 18: OUR GREAT DISASTER
1   *Nanaimo Free Press*, August 4, 1886.
2   Ibid., based on an article Bate found by M. Vital, Ingenieur des Mines.
3   *Nanaimo Free Press*, May 4, 1887. (Gibson was at work that day; this was incorrectly recorded in Peterson, *Hub City*, p. 14.)
4   Dick, BC Mining Report 1887, p. 289.
5   *Nanaimo Free Press*, January 14, 1888.
6   Ibid.
7   *Nanaimo Free Press*, January 18, 1888.
8   *Nanaimo Free Press*, February 8, 1888.

9   H. Keith Ralston and Gregory S. Kealey, "Myers, Samuel H.," in *Dictionary of Canadian Biography*, vol. 11, University of Toronto/Université Laval, 2003–, accessed November 17, 2016, http://www.biographi.ca/en/bio/myers_samuel_h_11E.html.
10 *Nanaimo Free Press*, April 13, 1889.
11 *Nanaimo Free Press*, April 18, 1889.
12 Bate, "Something of the Old Time Nanaimoites," *Nanaimo Free Press*, February 23, 1907.

CHAPTER 19: DEATH OF LOVED ONES

1   *Nanaimo Free Press*, January 11, 1890.
2   Paper on the early history of Nanaimo, Mark Bate fonds, NCA.
3   Mark Bate fonds, NCA.
4   "Mark Bate," Native Daughters' Scrapbook Collection, p. 196, Scrapbook ART-71, NCA.
5   See J. Peterson, *Hub City, Nanaimo: 1886–1920* (Victoria: Heritage House Publishing, 2003), pp. 17–18.
6   Currie, "The Vancouver Coal Mining Company."
7   Dick, BC Mining Report 1891.
8   Allen Seager, "Hawthornthwaite, James Hurst," *Dictionary of Canadian Biography* vol. 15, University of Toronto/Université Laval, 2003–, accessed November 17, 2016, http://www.biographi.ca/en/bio/hawthornthwaite_james_hurst_15E.html.
9   *Daily Colonist*, June 11, 1890.
10 Census 1891.
11 *BC Directories: Nelson, 1895*.
12 R. Welwood, "Nelson Club," *B.C. Historical News*, 26, no. 1 (Winter 1992–93): p. 3.
13 *Nanaimo Free Press*, May 21, 1891; also Gayle Jesperson research.
14 *BC Directories: Cumberland, 1909*.
15 Bryant to Bate, written from Mt. Tolmie, July 1, 1895, Peck and Snow Estate Records, Mark Bate fonds, NCA.
16 *Doug Gent's History Pages*, http://www.gent-family.com/Terrace/kalumlake.html. Permission granted.
17 Peck and Snow Estate Records, Mark Bate fonds, NCA.
18 Ibid.
19 "Mark Bate," Native Daughters' Scrapbook Collection, p. 196, Scrapbook ART-71, NCA.
20 *Nanaimo Free Press*, May 11, 1897.
21 Correspondence, 1897, Mark Bate fonds, NCA.
22 Bate to Bryant, November 15, 1897, Correspondence, 1897, Mark Bate fonds, NCA.
23 Bryant to Bate, November 22, 1897, Mark Bate fonds, NCA.
24 *Nanaimo Free Press*, January 11, 1898.
25 Zu Erpen, "Towards an Understanding of the Municipal Archives," pp. 124–129.
26 City council to Victoria, November 26, 1897, Correspondence, Mark Bate fonds, NCA.
27 November 9, 1898, Correspondence, Mark Bate fonds, NCA.
28 *Nanaimo Free Press*, January 16, 1903.

29   BC Mining Report 1898.
30   John Shaw, "The Clan Survives," *Daily Colonist*, May 12, 1957.
31   Bowen, *Three Dollar Dreams*, p. 379.
32   John (Jack) Charles McGregor, "The Klondyke Gold Rush" (manuscript), John Charles McGregor Pamphlet file, NCA.

CHAPTER 20: BEGINNINGS AND ENDINGS

1   "Darryl Bate to the Nanaimo Historical Society," November 8, 1966, Sound Recordings, Series 2, Nanaimo Historical Society fonds, NCA.
2   *Nanaimo Free Press*, January 1901.
3   Marriage certificate of Mark Bate and Hannah Harrison, No. 5813743-1General Register Office, County of Lancaster.
4   Marriage certificate of Edith Perchet and Augustus Bate, October 5, 1900, BCPA B11380.
5   Census 1911.
6   Marriage certificate of Annie Sarah McKenzie and John Harvey Harrison, June 27, 1911, BCPA B11381.
7   Interview by author with Mildred Simpson, May 21, 2013.
8   *Nanaimo Free Press*, August 10, 1901.
9   *Nanaimo Free Press*, December 14, 1903.
10   *Nanaimo Free Press*, Evening Edition, February 9, 1907.
11   Canadian Collieries fonds, NCA.
12   Currie, "The Vancouver Coal Mining Company."
13   *Nanaimo Free Press*, February 28, 1903.
14   Bate to City Council Clerk, December 6, 1915, Correspondence 1905–1948 City Clerk's Office, NCA.
15   Ibid.
16   *Nanaimo Free Press*, October 30, 31, November 1, 1918.
17   File 2, Bate family fonds, NCA.
18   Correspondence, Mark Bate fonds, NCA.
19   R.E. Gosnell, *A History: British Columbia* ([Victoria]: Lewis Publishing Company, 1906), p. 335.
20   Correspondence, Mark Bate fonds, NCA.
21   Jane Watt, "When Nanaimo Was Colville," *Ormsby Review* 3 (2014), online at *BCBookLook*, http://bcbooklook.com/2014/01/27/article-3-when-nanaimo-was-colville.
22   Speeches, Mark Bate fonds, NCA.
23   P. Mar, *The Light of Many Candles: One Hundred Years of Caring Service* (Nanaimo: Nanaimo Auxiliary to NRGH, 2000) NCA, p. 22.
24   Death certificate of Mark Bate, No. 4473867-3, General Register office, Birmingham North.

APPENDIX 2

1   "Mayor & Council of Nanaimo from 1875–1979," Nanaimo Archives, http://www.nanaimoarchives.ca/online-resources/mayor-and-council-1875-1979/; *Nanaimo Free Press*; Zu Erpen, "Towards an Understanding of the Municipal Archives," p. 301.

BIBLIOGRAPHY

ARCHIVES AND RECORDS
BC Archives, Victoria, BC
  Ancient Order of Foresters
  Cornelius Bryant fonds
  Ebenezer Robson fonds
  Thomas Bryant letters
  William Lashley Hall fonds
  Vital Statistics
British Columbia City Directories 1860–1955
Dudley Archives and Local History Service, Dudley, Staffordshire, UK
  England Census 1831, 1841, 1851
  Mechanics' Institute, Dudley
  St. Thomas Parish Register, Dudley Grammar School Collection
  Wesleyan Chapel Records, Dudley
  Woodside Methodist Church
  Woodside History Group
Hudson's Bay Company Archives, Winnipeg
Nanaimo Community Archives, Nanaimo, BC
  Bate family file
  Canadian Colleries
  City Clerk correspondence
  John Charles McGregor file
  Mark Bate fonds; includes the letter book of the Vancouver Coal Mining and
    Land Company
  Martha Kenny file
  Masonic records
  Nanaimo Historical Society fonds
  Nanaimo Regional General Hospital fonds
  Native Daughters' Scrapbook Collection
National Archives, San Francisco
United Church Archives, Toronto

NEWSPAPERS
British Colonist (Victoria)
British Columbian (Victoria)
Daily British Colonist (Victoria)
Daily Colonist (Victoria)
Daily Herald (Nanaimo)
Manchester Courier
Nanaimo Free Press
Nanaimo Gazette / Tribune
Nanaimo Times
Queen's Quarterly (Kingston, ON)
The Colonist (Victoria)

The Comet (Nanaimo)
The San Francisco Call
The Towns Messenger (Dudley, England)
Western Daily Press (Southwest England)
Wolverhampton Chronicle

GENERAL

Akrigg, G.P.V., and H.B. Akrigg. *British Columbia Chronicle 1847–1871: Gold and Colonists*. Vancouver: Discovery Press, 1977.

Barman, J. *The West Beyond The West: A History of British Columbia*. Toronto: University of Toronto Press, 1991.

Belshaw, J.D. "The Standard of Living of British Miners on Vancouver Island, 1848–1900." *BC Studies* 84 (Winter 1989-90): 37–64.

Belshaw, J.D. *Colonization and Community: The Vancouver Island Coalfield and the Making of the British Columbian Working Class*. Montreal and Kingston: McGill-Queen's University Press, 2002.

Bentley, J. *Bentley's Directory of Dudley, 1840*, vol. 1, *Bentley's Directory of Worcestershire, 1840–1842*. London: n.p.

Blakey-Smith, D., ed. *The Reminiscences of Doctor John Sebastian Helmcken*. Vancouver: UBC Press, 1975.

Bowen, L. *Three Dollar Dreams*, Lantzville: Oolichan Books, 1987.

British Columbia Parliament, *Sessional Papers: Third Session, Second Parliament, and First Session, Third Parliament*. Victoria: Government Printing Office, 1878.

Brown, Sandra. "Progress of Education in Nanaimo 1849–1869: History of Education #423." (Thesis, Dr. C.F. Goulsoil, March 8, 1969), NCA.

Bushby, Arthur Thomas. "The Journal of Arthur Thomas Bushby, 1957–1959," ed. Dorothy Blakey Smith. *British Columbia Historical Quarterly*, 21, nos. 1–4 (January 1957–October 1958): 185; *British Columbia Historical Quarterly*, 21, nos. 1–4 (January 1957–October 1958): 83–198.

Currie, A.W. "The Vancouver Coal Mining Company: A Source for Galsworthy's Strife." *Queen's Quarterly* 70, no. 1 (1963): 50–63.

Davidson, C. *Historic Departure Bay—Looking Back*. Victoria: Rendezvous Historic Press, 2006.

Dick, A., BC Mining Report 1886, in Fourth Annual Report of the Minister of Mines for the Year Ending 31 December 1886, Being an Account of Mining Operations for Gold, Coal, etc., in the Province of British Columbia, BC *Sessional Papers*, 1887.

Elections British Columbia. *Electoral History of British Columbia, 1871–1986*. Victoria: Elections British Columbia and the Legislative Library, 1988.

Gallacher, D.T. "Men, Money, Machines: Studies Comparing Colliery Operations and Factors of Production in British Columbia's Coal Industry to 1891." Ph.D. diss., University of British Columbia, 1979.

Gosnell, R.E. *A History: British Columbia*. [Victoria]: Lewis Publishing Company, 1906.

Gray, J., and Chapleau, J.A. Report on the Royal Commission on Chinese Immigration, No. 2, 1885.

Guide to the Province of British Columbia for 1877-8. Victoria: T.N. Hibben & Company.

Gwyn, R. *Nation Maker: Sir John A. Macdonald: His Life, Our Times.* 2 vols. Toronto: Random House, 2011.

Hendrickson, J.E., ed. *Journals of the Colonial Legislatures of the Colonies of Vancouver Island and British Columbia 1851–1871.* 5 vols. Victoria: Provincial Archives of British Columbia, 1980.

Howay, F.W., and E.O.S. Scholefield. *British Columbia from Its Earliest Times to the Present.* 4 vols. Vancouver: S.J. Clarke Publishing Company, 1914.

Jackman, S.W. *Portraits of the Premiers: An Informal History of British Columbia.* Sidney, BC: Gray's Publishing, 1969.

Johnson, P. *Quarantined: Life and Death at William Head Station, 1872–1959.* Victoria: Heritage House Publishing Company, 2013.

Johnson, P.M. "Teacher and Preacher: Cornelius Bryant." *The Beaver* 292 (1961): 34–39.

Johnston, H.J.M., ed. *The Pacific Province: A History of British Columbia.* Vancouver: Douglas & McIntyre, 1996.

Langevin, H.L. Report on British Columbia. Ottawa, 1872.

Lavender, A.T.C., and E.M. Lavender. "The Woodside Ironworks," *The Blackcountryman* 17, no. 2 (1984): n.p.

Lee, W. *Report to the General Board of Health into the Sewage, Drainage, and Supply of Water, and the Sanitary Conditions of the Inhabitants of the Parish of Dudley, in the County of Worcester.* London: Eyre and Spottiswoode, 1852.

Leynard, A. *The Coal Mines of Nanaimo.* Nanaimo: n.p., 1982.

Mar, P. *The Light of Many Candles: One Hundred Years of Caring Service.* Nanaimo: Nanaimo Auxiliary to NRGH, 2000.

McGregor, J.C. "The Klondyke Gold Rush." Unpublished manuscript, n.d., NCA.

Merilees, B. *Newcastle Island: A Place of Discovery.* Victoria: Heritage House Publishing, 1998.

Midland Mining Commission (South Staffordshire), Reports from Commissioners, vol. 13, 1843.

Mitchell, J. *Report to the Children's Employment Commission.* British Parliamentary Papers, vols. 15, 16, 17. London: William Strange, 1842.

Nicholls, P. *From the Black Country to Nanaimo, 1854.* 5 vols. Nanaimo: Nanaimo Historical Society, 1991–95.

Norcross, E.B., ed. *Nanaimo Retrospective: The First Century.* Nanaimo: Nanaimo Historical Society, 1979.

Ormsby, M.A. *British Columbia: A History.* Toronto: Macmillan, 1958.

Owen, Olga Blanche. "Biography of Adam Grant Horne." Unpublished manuscript, dated February 1980.

Peterson, J. *Black Diamond City: Nanaimo—The Victorian Era.* Victoria: Heritage House Publishing, 2002.

Peterson, J. *Hub City, Nanaimo: 1886–1920.* Victoria: Heritage House Publishing, 2003.

Peterson, J. *Kilts on the Coast: The Scots Who Built BC.* Victoria. Heritage House Publishing, 2012.

Prior, E.G., BC Mining Report 1879, in Sixth Annual Report of the Minister of Mines for the Year Ending 31st December, 1879, Being an Account of Mining Operations for Gold, Coal, etc., in the Province of British Columbia, BC *Sessional Papers*, 1880.

Rayner, W. *Scandal! 130 Years of Damnable Deeds in Canada's Lotus Land*. Victoria: Heritage House Publishing, 2001.

Reksten, T. *The Dunsmuir Saga*. Vancouver: Douglas & McIntyre, 1991.

Savory, Kathleen M, for Dr. C.Y. Lai "Nanaimo's Chinese Community." Unpublished manuscript, NCA, Box 1, Code 13, Ethnic groups, Chinese #2.

Slater, R. *Telegraphic Code, to Ensure Secrecy in the Transmission of Telegrams*. London: W.R. Grey, 1870.

Smith, B.R.D. "A Social History of Early Nanaimo." BA thesis, University of British Columbia, 1956.

Stephens, W.B. *Education, Literacy, and Society, 1830–70: The Geography of Diversity in Provincial England*. Manchester: Manchester University Press, 1987.

St. John, M. *The Sea of Mountains: An Account of Lord Dufferin's Tour through British Columbia in 1876*, vol. 1. London: Hurst and Blackett, 1877.

Taylor, W.A. *Crown Land Grants: A History of the Esquimalt and Nanaimo Railway Land Grants, the Railway Belt and the Peace River Block*. Victoria: Crown Land Registry Service, Ministry of Environment, Lands and Parks, 1975.

Trutch, J.W., Report on Public Works in British Columbia, for Year Ending 30th June, 1883, Annual Report of the Department of Public Works for the Fiscal Year 1882–83, *General Report of Canada*. Ottawa: Macdean, Roger & Co.

Watt, Jane. "When Nanaimo Was Colville." *Ormsby Review* 3. Online at *BCBookLook*, http://bcbooklook.com/2014/01/27/article-3-when-nanaimo-was-colville/.

Welwood, R. "Nelson Club." *B.C. Historical News*, 26, no. 1 (Winter 1992–93).

Zu Erpen, W.J.M. "Towards an Understanding of the Municipal Archives of Nineteenth Century British Columbia: A Case Study of the Archives of the Corporation of the City of Nanaimo, 1875–1904." MA thesis, University of British Columbia, 1985.

WEBSITES

BC Metis Mapping Research Project, University of British Columbia, http://document.bcmetiscitizen.ca.

Canadian Headstone Photo Project, CanadianHeadstones.com.

Dictionary of Canadian Biography, University of Toronto/Université Laval, 2003, http://www.biographi.ca/.

Gent, Doug. *Doug Gent's History Pages*, http://www.gent-family.com/Terrace/kalumlake.html.

Guide to the Province of BC for 1877–8 (Victoria: Hibben & Co., 1877), online at http://www.vpl.ca/bccd/index.php/browse/title/1877-1878/Guide_to_the_Province_of_BC.

History Department, Vancouver Island University. "Nanaimo in the 1890s." (student project), 2003. https://www2.viu.ca/history/devnanaimo/. Last accessed 2016.

Rootsweb, http://home.rootsweb.ancestry.com.

Vickers, R.S. *An Account of the Life and times of Vancouver Island Pioneer George Robinson*, http://crunchers.bc.ca/robinson/index.html.

INDEX

Abrams, James Atkinson, MPP, 157
aerial tramway, 91–92, 93, 135, 203
Albion Iron Works (Victoria), 191
Alport, Charles Augustus ("Charlie"; wife Emily Bate), 80, 90, 118–21, 124, 187, 233–34
Ashlar Lodge, 12, 102–3, 224, 252

Bastion, 11, 31, 40, 41, 43, 112, 154, 167, 184, 192
Bate, Ann (sister of MB), 20, 114
Bate, Elizabeth (sister of MB), 20, 23, 114
Bate, Elizabeth Ada ("Lizzie"; daughter of MB), 202, 221
Bate, Emily (daughter of MB), 52, 64, 114, 118–21, 123, 124, 148, 187, 233–34
Bate, George Arthur (son of MB), 96, 114, 148–50
Bate, Hannah (née Harrison; MB's second wife), 234–36, 237, 239, 242
Bate, John Augustus ("Gussie"; son of MB), 235–36
Bate, Joseph (brother of MB), 20, 23–24, 65
Bate, Lucy (sister of MB), 20, 64, 65, 66, 161
Bate, Lucy Elicia (daughter of MB), 66–67, 96, 114, 202, 221, 222, 233
Bate, Mark Jr. (son of MB), 64, 101, 114, 123, 188, 201, 202, 248
Bate, Mark: accountant, 61; appointed mine manager, 96; copying clerk, 48, 58, 61, 122; death, 248–49; death of father, 23; death of son George, 148–50, 252; death of wife Sarah, 224–25; first mayoral election, 137–40; magistrate, 57, 156, 165–66; music, 22, 49, 69, 72, 101–2, 122, 188, 225, 246–47, 252–53; relationship with Bryden, Dunsmuir, & management, 248, 60, 78, 107, 168, 178, 215, 251; position on incorporation, 80–2, 85, 136–37; salary, 58, 243; view of alcohol abuse, 128
Bate, Mary Beatrice (daughter of MB), 202, 222
Bate, Sarah (née Cartwright; MB's first wife), 12, 25–26, 50–51, 52, 64, 108, 114, 117, 118 124, 133, 121, 148, 150, 152, 187, 188, 202, 224–25, 226
Bate, Sarah (sister of MB), 20, 23, 25
Bate, Sarah Ann ("Sally"; daughter of MB), 64, 114, 148, 150, 187, 221, 222, 234
Bate, Thomas and Elizabeth (parents of MB), 18, 20, 23, 115, 252
Bate, Thomas Ezra (son of MB), 64, 101, 114
Bate, William Charles (son of MB), 202, 221
Bate, William Thomas (stepfather of MB), 25, 116
Bayley, Charles, 32, 36, 47.
Beaumont, James, 161–62, 179, 180, 181, 193, 200
Bermingham, John, 86, 92, 100, 103, 104, 109, 131
Berryman, Henry, 110, 168
Benson, Dr. Alfred (wife Ellen Phillips), 52, 58, 87
Black Diamond Fire Company, 159, 160, 252. *See also* fires
Black Country, England, 16, 17, 22, 27, 31, 37; Brierley Hill, 16, 25, 27, 49, 101, 122; Dudley, 15, 23–24, 27; Holly Hall, 16, 20, 23, 26, 114, 247; Kingswinford, 18, 25, 27; Woodside, 16, 18, 20, 23, 24, 247, 257, 270, 272

Blessing, Jacob, 71, 161
Bryant, Cornelius (cousin of MB, wife Elizabeth), 10, 11, 25, 36, 37–39, 38,
    40, 46, 52, 68, 70, 115, 188, 222, 224
Bryant, Thomas (cousin of MB), 18, 115–16
Bryant, Thomas and Sarah (uncle and aunt of MB), 18, 116–17
Bryden, John (wife Elizabeth Dunsmuir), 12, 78, 82, 106; alderman, 140;
    Chinese workers, 99, 204; marriage, 107; mine accident, 209–12, 213,
    230; mine manager, 87, 110, 126, 127, 129, 144, 165, 167, 168, 194; MPP,
    140, 215; relationship with Bate; 25, 252; resignation from VCML, 170–81;
    Wellington mine manager, 194
Bulkley, Captain Thomas, 89, 91–93, 163

Cameron, David, Judge, 41, 48
Cameron Island, 33, 59, 77, 93, 181, 183, 135, 203
Cape Horn, 30, 31, 65, 93, 188
Carpenter, Chauncey, 159, 160, 188
Cartwright, William, 64, 65
Cedar, BC, 57, 108, 185, 203, 221, 237
cemetery (Nanaimo), 35, 57, 133, 146–47, 149, 210–11, 214, 219, 225,
    242, 250
Chandler, Robert, 129–30, 161, 213
Chase River, 87, 109, 128, 135, 141, 154, 165, 179, 193, 205; mine fire 180
Chinese, 99, 108, 164–66, 184, 211, 267, 271; Chinatown joined the city, 204;
    coal miners, 110, 128, 208, 228; opposition to, 213, 214, 164
Coal Mines Regulation Act, 164, 167, 211, 214
"Coal Tyee" (Chief Che-wich-i-kan), 41, 253
Colvilletown, 29. See also Nanaimo
Cooper, Rev. C.E., 236, 237
Copperman, William, 73, 79, 238
Cornishmen, 128, 129, 264
Cridge, Rev. Edward, 40–42, 47, 48

Dallas, Alexander Grant, 48, 56, 59, 61, 156
Dallas Square (Nanaimo), 62, 101, 218
Davidson, John, 225, 226
De Cosmos, Amor, 74, 75, 90, 244
Departure Bay, 45, 50, 78, 87, 88, 92, 110, 136, 149, 163, 174, 192, 215
Deverill, George Charles (Deverill Square), 240, 241
Dick, Archibald (Inspector of Mines), 179, 185, 200, 206, 207, 209
Dick, John, 141, 161
Diggle, Wadham N., 109, 168, 174, 191
Dominion Post Office, 154, 198, 218
Douglas Island. See Newcastle Island
Douglas, James, 28, 31, 32, 41, 42, 47, 48, 56, 58, 60, 61, 74, 77; mines,
    128, 205
Dunsmuir, James (son of Robert), 94, 110, 167, 174, 189, 215, 220, 230

Dunsmuir, Robert (wife Joan White), 11–12, 45, 60, 73, 189, 191, 195, 197; attempt to purchase VCMLC, 174; death of, 214–16; Harewood mine manager, 87–88; John A. Macdonald's visit, 196–97; mayoral races, 144, 185; relationship with MB, 139, 170, 175, 180–81, 251; politics, 191, 192–93, 195, 213; discovery of Wellington coal seam, 108–9, 110; mines, 44, 45, 160–63, 167–68, 174–175, 180–81, 193, 204, 209, 212–13, 214. *See also* Esquimalt and Nanaimo Railway

Earl, William, 184, 189
education, 24, 69, 253, Board of Education, 185; first teachers, 36, 46–48, 63, 65, 72, 142–43, 185; importance of, 63, 142–43; schools, 184–85
Esquimalt and Nanaimo Railway, 147, 189–196, 197, 199, 204, 215, 273; Carnarvon Terms, 153–54; Land Grant, 267; Nanaimo Railway Bill, 151; Railway Reserve Land, 146–47

Fawcett, Thomas Lea, 139, 143
Finlay, Christopher, 6
fires, 160, 172, 201–2, 227, 252
Franklyn, Captain William Hales, 57, 58, 73, 79, 102, House, 202, 221
"friendly societies," 104; Court Nanaimo Foresters, 12, 104, 189, 224, 270; Knights of Labour, 214; Odd Fellows (IOOF); 12, 104, 105

Gabriola Island, 183, 185
Ganner, Joseph, 47, 136
Gibson, Richard, 205, 209, 210, 211, 212, 220, 225, 256, 267
Gilmour, Boyd, 26, 94
Goepel, William J. (wife Sally Bate), 187, 221, 234
Good, Rev. John Booth, 69, 70
Gordon, David William, 70, 71, 151, 157; wharf, 135
Gough, Amanda Theresa, 68, 137
Gough family, 27, 47
Gough, Samuel, 27, 31, 137, 138, 70, 76, 246; city clerk, 186, 226
Governor Generals of Canada: Dufferin, 151–54, 199; Lorne, 191–93

Harewood Estate, 87, 93, 203, 220; aerial tramway, 92–93, 135, 203; coal mine, 60, 89, 91, 92, 93, 109, 154, 163, 205; railway, 88
Harrison, John Harvey (wife Annie Sarah McKenzie), 235
Harrison, Victor B., 13, 250
Harvey, James (wife Agnes Dunsmuir), 12, 129, 139–40, 184; militia, 136
Hawthornthwaite, James Hurst (wife Elizabeth Bate), 220, 221, 232, 268
Hilbert, John, 205, 217, 245, 256
Higgins, David William, 50, 74, 244
Hirst, John, 44, 135, 141, 156, 160
Hotels, 62, 66, 133, 136, 138, 140, 162, 183, 193, 196, 218, 227, 236, 244
Horne, Adam Grant (wife Elizabeth Bate), 51, 114; death, 236; Horne & Son business, 161–62, 165; mine, 162, 51; wedding, 51–52
hospitals, 22, 151, 207, 245, 252

Houghton, Col. Charles Frederick (wife Marion Houghton Dunsmuir), 177·
Hudson's Bay Company (HBC), 11, 26, 33 46, 56, 243, 248; Nanaimo Coal
    Company, 10, 26, 30, 33–34
HBC forts: Comox, 97, 161; Rupert, 29, 45, 51, 65, 67, 109; Simpson, 32, 41,
    66, 97; Victoria, 54

Jingle Pot Mine, 161–62
Jones, Nicholas J., 70, 145, 152

Klondike, 225, 230
Knights of Labour, 214

literary (or mechanics) institutes, 69–70
Lorne, Marquess of (John Douglas Sutherland Campbell, Governor General
    of Canada), 191–94

Macdonald, Prime Minister John A. (wife Agnes), 95, 112, 152, 190, 193, 194;
    opening of E and N Railway, 195–97
McGregor family: Jack, (son of William) 225; John (father), 29, 31, 35–36,
    179; William (son of John), 179, 209–13, 220, 229, 230
McKay, Joseph William, 32, 41
McKelvie, Bruce Alistair, 243–44
McNaughton-Jones, Dr. William, 101, 126, 127
Manson, Mike, 165–66
Manson, William, 227, 239, 250
McVitty, Thomas family, 234–35
Meakin, family, 27; Amanda, 46, 210; John William (brother of Amanda), 72,
    184, 79, 80, 210
Methodist church, 18, 22 25, 39, 48, 62, 63, 64, 67, 184, 188, 210
Morgan brothers (Thomas and John), 101, 102, 184, 185, 188
Muir, Archibald (Archie), 175, 210
Muir, John, 29, 31
music, 22, 101, 102, 122, 193, 225, 242, 246, 247, 252. *See also* Silver Cornet
    Band; Wellington Brass Band
Myers, Samuel Henry, 214

Nanaimo, City of: bridges, 136, 137–38, 145–46; bylaws, 141, 142, 143, 145,
    150, 185–86, 205, 219, 228; city hall, 205; lot sale, 78–79; incorporation,
    82–84, 136–39; street improvements, 146, 160, 185–86; letter by MB
    about parks and squares, 240–41; origins as Nanaimo Estate, 78–79, 203;
    town design, 79, 240; ward system, 183–85; water supply, 227–28
Nanaimo Coal Company. *See* Hudson's Bay Company
Nanaimo Fire Department, 202, 250; Bate house ("boarding house") fire,
    201–2; Black Diamond Fire Company, 160; fire engine and bell, 160; fire
    halls, 252, 227; fire of 1878, 159, 227; fire of 1894, 227. *See also* fires
Nanaimo jail, 165, 167, 220, 236

Nanaimo Literary Institute, 12, 69–70, 134, 145, 184, 187, 208; building bought by city, 205; membership, 70–71

Native Sons of British Columbia (also Native Sons and Daughters of British Columbia), 13, 237, 246

Nebb, David, 101, 188

Newcastle Island, 45, 49, 135, 163; Fitzwilliam Mine, 100, 129, 163; Newcastle Mine, 100, 129, 163–64; Newcastle quarry, 111, 141, 199, 203, 218, 252

newspapers (Nanaimo), 81, 83, 96, 243, 250

Nicol, Charles Samuel (wife Maria Aspinwall), 56, 70, 76, 79, 80, 85, 135; HBC general manager, 58–59, 60, 61, 62, 69, 77, 78, 90, 98, 241; position on incorporation, 84

Nightingale, Richard, 141, 151, 184

Norris, George (wife Amanda Gough), 68, 137–38, 141, 199, 208, 214

Pacific Mail Steamship Company, 109, 110, 168

Pawson, John, 141, 151, 186

Peck, Thomas E., 76, 133, 140, 165, 182, 183

Planta, Albert Edward (son of Joseph), 237

Planta, Joseph P., 185, 212, 232, 250

population of Nanaimo (1854) 32, (1857) 44, (1861) 16, (1863) 72, (1866) 135, (1871) 112, (1882) 183

Praeger, Dr. Emil Arnold, 210

Princess Royal (pioneers' ship), 14, 27, 30, 37, 47, 51, 53, 55, 64, 65, 67, 151, 164, 184, 245

Protection Island (formerly Douglas), 31, 33, 59, 139, 149, 203, 229, 230

Prior, Edward Gawlor, 106, 107, 179, 209; Inspector of Mines, 167, 168, 169

Quennell, Edward, 150, 22

Randle, Joseph, 101, 104, 188

Raybould, William (wife Elizabeth), 131, 141, 190; MPP, 195

Richardson, Richard, 27, 47, 55, 96

Ring, David Babington, 75, 137

Rippon Estate, 131–32

Robins, Samuel, 86, 124, 127, 209–10; arrival in Nanaimo, 198; mine superintendent, 199–201, 203–4, 206, 212, 214, 239; Robin's Garden, 206; secretary of VCMLC, 60, 86–87, 121, 130, 137, 172–73

Robinson, George, (uncle of MB), 21, 26, 27, 30, 31; HBC mine manager, 32, 33, 34, 35, 36, 42, 44, 52, 53, 179, 229; tragedy, 34; in Victoria, 67, 68, 131

Robinson, Maria (aunt of MB), 23, 36, 44, 65, 123, 222; first marriage, 67; second marriage and death, 223–24

Rosenfeld, John, 100, 109, 126, 130, 149, 168, 171, 173–76, 178, 180, 181, 187, 210, 220; Nanaimo visit, 162–63

Royal Commission on Chinese Immigration, 204

Sabiston, James, 133

Sabiston, John, 67, 70, 182, 184

Sabiston, Peter (wife Lucy Bate), 66–67, 161, 162

Saint Mondays, 97, 127

Shakespeare, Noah, 131, 141, 264

Ships: *Alexander*, 192; *Amethyst*, 152; *Arkwright*, 99, 102; *Beaver*, 31, 39, 42, 48, 67; *Cadboro*, 30, 67; *City of Topeka*, 230; *Colinda*, 40; *Emma*, 99; *Forward*, 87; *Galiano*, 242; *Leviathan*, 183; *Maude*, 99, 183; *Norman Morrison*, 30; *Otter*, 49, 99; *Panther*, 99, 100; *Prince Alfred*, 99, 100; *Prince Constantine*, 77; *Prince Rupert*, 67; *Princess Louise*, 203; *Recovery*, 31, 32, 42; *Robert Dunsmuir (Dirty Bob)*, 196; *Sparrowhawk*, 111; *Vancouver*, 67; *Wilson G. Hunt*, 183; *Boxer*, 111. *See also* Princess Royal

Silver Cornet Band, 102, 192, 225, 242, 245, 250

Slater's Telegraphic Code, 176

Snuneymuxw First Nation, 30, 33, 46, 63, 72, 135, 222; "Coal Tyee," 41, 253; traditions, 43 193; treaty with HBC, 33; villages, 44, 45; workforce, 46, 128, 204, 228

Spalding, Magistrate Warner Reeve, 135, 140, 143, 145, 181

sports, 97, 184

Sproat, Gilbert Malcolm, 90–91

St. Andrew's Presbyterian Church, 66, 230, 236

St. Ann's Convent, 185

Stephenson, Rev. David, 249

Stewart, William, 103, 137, 143, 192

Stirtan, Josiah Walter, 160

Stone House, 43, 141, 142, 155

St. Paul's Anglican Church, 32, 62, 70, 72, 184, 210, 222, 253

strikes, 110–11, 126, 171–74, 177, 179–81, 193, 240, 241

Stuart, Charles Edward, 32, 33, 34, 35, 52, 56, 57, 156

Texada Island scandal, 90–91

Thompson, Adam (city clerk), 226

Thompson, John, 27, 31

tramway. *See* aerial tramway

Vancouver Coal Mining and Land Company (VCML, Vancouver Coal Company in text), 73, 79, 86, 87, 92, 109, 138, 161, 198, 200, 203, 205, 219, 239; "boarding house" office, 96; Dunsmuir's attempted takeover, 175–78, 186; employees, 128; expansion, 179; founding, 59–61, 73, 243; railway and harbour, 76–78; board, 59, 84, 177; mines, 135, 239; mine explosion (1887), 214; name change, 219–20, 237; Robins management, 205–6; sale of lots, 78–80; shipping, 98, 207; wages, 19, 29, 46, 61, 98, 105, 110, 111, 117, 128, 171–74, 178, 180–81, 204, 229

Walkem, Premier George H., 90, 91, 145, 146, 157, 158

Wellington (town), 11, 108, 136 163, 193, 213, 230

Wellington Brass Band, 194

Westwood Estate, East Wellington mine, 130

Wild, John, 84, 86, 90–92, 98, 120–21, 124, 126, 133, 143–44, 157, 170, 175; relationship with Bate, 60, 89–90

Young, Charles Newton, 142–43

JAN PETERSON has spent the last twenty years researching and writing the history of Port Alberni and Nanaimo, BC. A former journalist, Peterson retired to Nanaimo in 1996, where she continues to research and write. She has published eleven non-fiction books, including *Port Alberni: More Than Just a Mill Town*; *Kilts on the Coast: The Scots Who Built BC*; *Hub City: Nanaimo, 1886–1920*; and a personal memoir of her life in Scotland, *Listen tae Yer Granny*. She has a lifelong interest in painting, writing, and history, and is recognized for her many years of involvement in the arts and in community service.